Titanic and the Making of James Cameron

Titanic and the Making of James Cameron

The Inside Story of the Three-Year Adventure That Rewrote Motion Picture History

PAULA PARISI

NEWMARKET PRESS • NEW YORK

This book is published in the United States of America and in Canada.

ISBN 1-55704-364-7

Manufactured in the United States of America

For Flora Parisi,
who taught me the world is my oyster,
and an abiding fondness for pearls.

Prologue

> There are more valid facts and details in works of art than there are in history books.
>
> —Charlie Chaplin

THOUGH THE trailer was not imposingly large, its door was decisively shut. Twentieth Century-Fox president Bill Mechanic was determined to get a word in anyway, even if it meant interrupting James Cameron's lunch—if that's what you could call a 2 A.M. meal. He knew the director would not be happy about the intrusion and, quite frankly, neither was he, but it had to be done.

Less than halfway through a long production schedule, *Titanic*'s meter was already ticking at $75 million. It would easily be the most expensive film ever produced by Fox, and appeared well on its way to surpassing *Waterworld* as the most expensive film ever made. While Mechanic had little to do with the circumstances that had gotten the project to this point, it was his job to contain what had become a crisis of international proportions.

Fox had literally altered the topography of a nation to accommodate the vision of its prize filmmaker, blasting a 17-million gallon hole in the Baja coast to create the world's largest open-air tank and building a state-of-the-art, forty-acre movie studio around it. Poised in the beachfront pool was Cameron's 775-foot-long likeness of the grand ship. It was a surreal experience to wind along the Autopista, clear a rise, and have the ten-story *Titanic* re-creation come into view, a majestic thing lording over miles of shabby shoreline. By day it exuded gray grandeur. By night, it blazed outrageously. "It's insane—the biggest bathtub toy in the world," thought Mechanic the first time he'd seen it. On the other hand, he admired its authenticity and the obsessive force that got it there—a force he was about to take on.

He rapped on the door, and within seconds was admitted. Cameron barely had to get up to open it, that's how small the trailer was. Say what you would about his profligate spending, it certainly wasn't on personal luxury. The director turned his attention back to a plate of pasta and what appeared to some sort of cold meat. He was touchy about studio executives showing up on his sets. If they were there to harass him, he didn't hesitate to give it right back. *Suits,* he called them, even though this one was dressed in jeans and a sweater. Cameron actually liked Mechanic but was not happy he chose this night for what the director had been warned would be a strongly worded conversation about budget and schedule overruns.

Tonight they were shooting one of *Titanic*'s toughest sequences—the grand finale, where the back of the ship upends at a ninety-degree angle, pointing like a finger to the sky. Known as "the tilting poop deck," it involved tumbling a hundred stunt people off a ninety-foot recreation of the ship's stern, hydraulically rigged to tip up. In an intricate feat of photographic choreography, five cameras rolled for each take—and Cameron was operating one of them himself. Strapped into a harness, the director would slide down the deck with a hand-held, getting some great point-of-view shots as he tangled with the performers. Needless to say, he'd taken his share of knocks that evening.

Mechanic could see Cameron was not in the mood to talk, but motivated by the pressure of millions in red ink, he forged ahead, trying to keep things as congenial as possible. "Looked really great out there tonight," he remarked about the elaborate sequence, which ends with the film's stars, Kate Winslet and Leonardo DiCaprio, clinging to the very top of the stern railing as the ship sleds into the sea. "And we want to do everything we can to keep it looking great, but you've got to appreciate our position. From a financial standpoint this film is wildly out of control. Nothing is going to change that. All we can do now is contain it. So here are some scenes we'd like you to cut from the shooting schedule." With that he slid a two-page typed list across the booth-style table.

Cameron's eyes—the pupils already dilated from lack of sleep—widened appreciably. He scanned the list of suggestions, dismissing each as impossible. He'd already cut about thirty scenes, or pieces of scenes, and felt that was enough. "You want me to hack apart the film I've already put four years of my life into? If you want to cut my film you'll have to fire me, and to fire me you'll have to *kill* me!" he shouted. "If you're such a fucking expert, then you can finish the movie yourself!" He stormed off into the night.

Mechanic sat there stewing. Driving down, he'd thought of little else but firing Cameron. It was a last resort, a desperate measure, but Fox was in a desperate situation. Still, chances were that letting Cameron go would just make matters worse. Forgetting the stench of failure that would hang over such a messy split, there was the question of replacing him. This was an extremely complicated production with many disparate elements. As writer, director, and editor, Cameron was probably the only one who could make sense of all the pieces. Mechanic couldn't replace Cameron. His options were either to give up, close down the show and take a sizable write-off, or grin and bear it.

Fox had seen enough of the early footage to know they had something special, maybe even a chance at something great. Fire Cameron now and the studio could be stuck with millions of dollars worth of nothing. Better to gamble the millions on something. He'd give Cameron time to cool off and talk to him again later. Mechanic gathered his things and headed for his BMW and the three-hour drive back to Los Angeles. With a little luck he'd have about two hours to relax before sliding behind his sprawling oak desk at his office on the Twentieth Century-Fox lot in Century City.

As Cameron stalked off he was fuming, but even in that agitated state he was concocting a plan. He'd stay away just long enough for Mechanic to get the message and leave. It was the first time in seven films that Cameron had left the set during a shoot, theoretically shutting down what averaged out to be a $300,000-a-day operation. But there was still some lunch time to burn. He'd only wind up losing a half-hour. As he walked past the big tank he saw the superstructure of *Titanic* outlined against the night sky. In the heat of production, every project seemed a matter of life or death to him, but for reasons even he couldn't quite explain, this one meant much more.

The real *Titanic* lay two-and-a-half miles beneath the ocean's surface, at a depth 416 atmospheres greater than that of the earth's surface—millions of pounds of pressure. Cameron was beginning to think he knew what that type of lethal pressure felt like. In time, the pressure would build to the tune of $200 million. "It's easy for us mere mortals to bandy a figure like $200 million around," says Lewis Abernathy, a close friend of the director. "Next time you're in downtown Los Angeles, take a look at the tallest skyscraper. That's what $200 million buys. Now imagine you can invert it and wear the point like a hat, the entire weight of that building on your head and shoulders. That'll give you a fair idea of where Cameron is at. It's a lot of pressure, particularly if you're trying to do well."

Why would he want to do it any other way? At this point in his career, Cameron had the clout and inclination to realize his wildest dreams. Besides, he had *been* to the *Titanic.* He'd visited death and found it both dangerous and beautiful. But even there, in all that blackness, the forces of creation were at work. The metal of the *Titanic*'s hull had succumbed to rusticles, a consortium of single-cell bacteria that linked to function as a single organism. Gradually, the rusticles were absorbing the iron of the ship. At the present rate of decay, she'd disintegrate into nothingness toward the middle of the next century. Dissolve.

Chapter One

> There will always be twenty bean-counters and twenty logicians standing around waiting to tell you why you can't do something. It doesn't mean you can't do it.
>
> —James Cameron

It is August 1992 and thirty-seven-year-old Hollywood director James Cameron is cruising down a Russian freeway in a battered nine-year-old Volga owned and driven by the scientist and submarine pilot Dr. Anatoly Sagalevitch. Cameron and his fifty-four-year-old friend Al Giddings exchange amused glances when the car breaks down. Automotive misadventure is something of a novelty to the rich Americans—Cameron owns a collection of high performance Corvettes and Giddings four-wheels it over the open roads of Montana. They've flown to Moscow to discuss with Sagalevitch the possibility of chartering his ship, the *Akademik Mstislav Keldysh.* There are only five submersibles in the world capable of diving below 12,000 feet and the *Keldysh* is home to two of them. Cameron needed the research vessel to make his film.

Clearance to use the ship is a problem. Careful to keep his enthusiasm in check, Cameron has flown 14,000 miles to do a little wooing. Even in these post-Cold War climes, some higher-ups at *Keldysh* central, the P. P. Shirshov Scientific Institute of Oceanology, still harbor a residual Communist snobbery about letting a premiere scientific asset be put to crass commercial use. The Soviet deep sea program had been developed in conjunction with its cosmonaut initiative. In fact, the submersibles share their name with the country's space station, *Mir,* which in Russian means *peace.* The Russians revere their sub pilots with the awe Americans reserve for astronauts. The *Keldysh* is nothing to be trifled with.

Sagalevitch, however, is a pragmatist. As head of the Shirshov's Deep Manned Submersibles Laboratory, he is commander-in-chief of the *Keldysh* and fiercely protective of the ship, its crew, and the future of *Mir 1* and *Mir 2.* He has an almost paternal pride in the twin subs, which he helped design. They were built at a cost of $100 million in 1987. As far as Sagalevitch is concerned, keeping his 445-foot floating marine lab solvent means collecting paydays like the one represented by Mr. Hollywood here. He is determined to do the project if there is any way to put even the thinnest veneer of research on it. In any event, the exposure offered by a major motion picture would be a perfect advertisement for the capabilities of his state-of-the-art ship.

Embarrassed about the vehicular mishap, Sagalevitch steps outside for a look under the hood, leaving his wife, Natalia, a microbiologist, to make small talk with their exotic passengers. She regales them with descriptions of the beauty of their destination, Zagorsk, a quaint cathedral village in the countryside, but the men find it hard to concentrate with traffic whizzing by only inches away from the hunched figure of her husband, clearly visible through the windshield. One truck actually seems to brush his pants. Ministering to the wounded motor, Sagalevitch curses the timing of this pitiable display. Brushing off, he slides back into the car, apologizing that his teenage son had been riding the thing roughshod. For his part, Cameron is impressed that the Russian has remedied the motor with string. Relieved at their smiles, Sagalevitch adds reassuringly, "The *Mirs* are beautiful machines. We have the problems with them practically never!"

The next day the foursome hop an Aeroflot commuter shuttle north to Kaliningrad, the rundown port city that is home to the ship Giddings calls "the Starship *Enterprise* of the marine world." The *Keldysh* cuts a pretty picture, sleek of line in a way that defies chunky Russian design, yet humble in the way only practical objects can be. It is hard to believe this utilitarian vessel can be integral to bringing the director's lavish vision of *Titanic* to the screen.

Cameron conceived of the film as a kind of living history. "I wanted to give audiences an experience of the event that was subjective, to make them feel like they were a part of it and that people were doing things they understood because they might have reacted the same way. A lot of period films focus on the differences between then and now. But people were the same. Human nature was the same. Their loves, their hates, their fears were the same. When you connect to a big event in that way it has a lot more resonance."

The director's goal was to put viewers on the deck of *Titanic* as it sank, and to do it he would ultimately wind up recreating a life-sized version of the liner. The bulk of his story would be set in period, 1912, but to help modern audiences connect with the drama of the tragedy he added a contemporary plot line involving fortune hunters searching for a lost diamond necklace. This would be the set-up for showing present-day footage of *Titanic*. A legitimate plot device, it was also a great excuse for Cameron, an ardent diver, to explore the world's most famous undersea wreck.

With its twin submersibles, the *Keldysh* offered the only practical possibility for actually photographing a sub at *Titanic*. Cameron actually needed two subs—one to carry the camera, the other to appear on screen. In addition to being the support system for his deep water shoot, the *Keldysh* itself would also have an on-screen role. Cameron would shoot some of the modern day scenes on its decks. The ship would need a fresh coat of paint, he thought, as he stood examining the vessel with Giddings and Sagalevitch. The outline of the once-familiar hammer-and-sickle emblem was still faintly visible beneath the brown enamel of the smokestack.

In addition to his love of diving, Cameron had always been something of a history buff, particularly ancient history and archaeology. His fascination with *Titanic* began in 1985 with Dr. Robert Ballard's discovery of the wreck. Ballard had spent years at the Woods Hole, Massachusetts-based Deep Submergence Laboratory developing an instrument to undertake the search. The fruit of his labor was *Argo,* an unmanned camera vehicle that could be towed through the ocean, sending images topside via a fiber-optic umbilical. Revolutionary at the time, it has since come to be referred to as "the dope on a rope" by the more elitist members of the clubby deep-diving community. Working aboard the American ship *Knorr* with a Franco-American expedition team, Ballard trolled for three months before getting lucky on September 1, 1985. He subsequently went back with the manned submersible *Alvin* and the remotely operated camera vehicle *Jason Jr.* The visual testament of that expedition was showcased in a 1987 National Geographic Explorer documentary that caught Cameron's eye. He thought the images looked cosmic, and was inspired to do a film that would treat underwater like outer space, utilizing state-of-the-art technology like deep water subs and remote vehicles. That film was *The Abyss.* "I didn't even know they were called ROVs [remotely operated vehicles] at the time," he laughs. "I just saw this cool little robot doing all this stuff, and I just got it. It had little propellers on it and I thought, it's a robot camera. It just made sense to me."

Dated 1987, Cameron's initial *Titanic* notes read: "Do story with bookends of present day scene of wreck using submersibles intercut with memory of a survivor and re-created scenes of the night of the sinking. A crucible of human values under stress. A certainty of slowly impending doom (metaphor). Division of men doomed and women and children saved by custom of the times. Many dramatic moments of separation, heroism and cowardice, civility versus animal aggression. Needs a mystery or driving plot element woven through with all this as background." The title *Titanic* was added to his development slate, the lineup of projects being groomed for future production.

Giddings also had an interest in *Titanic.* He had spent the summer of 1991 on the *Keldysh,* diving the wreck for the CBS documentary *Treasures of the Deep,* which he directed and produced. When Cameron attended the 1992 premiere of *Treasures,* he was actively seeking a follow-up to *Terminator 2: Judgment Day.* Coincidentally, Cameron had recently screened the 1958 British film *A Night to Remember,* which he vaguely recalled having seen on TV as a kid. Two days later the mail brought a black card covered with rivets and the big red letters TITANIC. "Wow," he thought of Giddings's invite, "a message from the ether." Something was bubbling in the *Titanic* zone.

At the *Treasures* screening, Giddings's images of decaying, underwater opulence moved him deeply, while the footage of the men working the high seas aboard the *Keldysh* appealed to his sense of adventure. He was impressed with the technology of the *Mirs.* The cinematic possibilities with two subs were immediate and irresistible.

After the show, Giddings lingered in the aisle, ignoring the other guests, talking to Cameron until the janitorial staff evicted them. Arguably the world's finest underwater cinematographer, Giddings was familiar with Cameron's fluid creativity and fiery temperament. Giddings had been director of underwater photography on *The Abyss.* On that film, the two had been working together at the extreme, spending five months of ten- to twelve-hour days under forty feet of water. Given the stressful circumstances it was no wonder that tempers had flared, and, in fact, after his work was completed, Giddings left the shoot with hurt feelings. Cameron had proven to be a brutal taskmaster and, adding insult to injury, had picked off some of the underwater veteran's best crew members to help finish the film. Like many Cameron initiates, Giddings felt at the time that if he never had to work with the director again, it would be too soon.

Though the men parted without acrimony, they hadn't spoken much since. Now here they were, three years later, discussing the possibility of working together. Giddings had every reason to expect that Cameron—who was only thirty-four when he ventured into *The Abyss*—had toned down his kick-start temper. Judging by the fervor with which he spoke about diving *Titanic,* he apparently had not lost his taste for headlong thrills. "He said, 'Al, I'd really like to dive *Titanic.*' And I said, 'You're kidding! You can do models. You can do miniatures.' And he said, 'Think about it. If we can go to *Titanic,* I'll be able to say if you see this movie you'll be seeing the real thing." Cameron's overriding reaction to the screening was, "Al, let's go to Moscow!" Within days the duo had their visas and were on an eighteen-hour flight to Sheremetyevo Aeroport. Maintaining a shroud of secrecy, they code-named the project "Big Boat."

As he stood scoping out the *Keldysh,* Cameron's entire working knowledge of the ship was derived from the information contained in Giddings's *Treasures* film. He knew that when not crawling along the belly of the sea, the twin submersibles reposed in antiseptic white docking bays along the right rib of the ship. The *Keldysh* had bragging rights to 40 percent of the world's deep diving assets. The others were France's *Nautile,* Japan's *Shinkai,* and the U.S. Navy's *Seacliff,* the only one not available for commercial charter. The elder statesman of the lot, *Alvin,* the Woods Hole submersible used by Ballard, had recently been downgraded to 12,500 feet, making it ineligible to return to *Titanic.* (This is a common precautionary step with subs and other deep-water equipment, an attempt to compensate for the strain of repeated dives on structural integrity.)

During expeditions, life on the *Keldysh* revolved around the twin bays and the endless cycle of diving and recharging the *Mirs.* The subs dove untethered, run by high-powered, energy-efficient French batteries that cost roughly $1 million each. The batteries drove all sub functions, including main propulsion, on dives that typically lasted eighteen hours but had gone as long as twenty-eight. In a pinch they could sustain emergency life support for up to five days.

Not the newest kids on the block—that would be *Shinkai*—the *Mirs* are considered by many to be the most elegant of design.

Among their assets is that they're speedy, capable of five knots. And they were designed for full mission capability, which means that while most deep-water submersibles are geared toward operation on the bottom of the sea, the *Mirs* can function optimally anywhere in the water column as a result of their unique hydraulic ballast system—they draw in water to sink and displace water to rise. While the other deep-water submersibles pump some water to "trim," or fine-tune their positioning, they rely mainly on lead weights, which are discarded on the bottom of the sea at the end of each mission.

The *Mirs* are rated to withstand 30,000 feet of water pressure—their 20,000-foot working depth plus a 50 percent safety margin—or the equivalent of 9,000 pounds per square inch. In typical configuration, the front of each twenty-five-foot sub is equipped with high-intensity lights, a collection basket, and two six-foot hydraulic manipulator arms used to move heavy objects or gather biological and geological specimens. Their advanced array of peripherals also includes water samplers and radiation sensors, and a video and photographic system rated top in its class. The *Mirs* are accessorized for each mission—loaded up or stripped down, depending on the task.

As Sagalevitch delivered a running commentary, Cameron stood gazing silently at the subs, taking in the technology, undressing them with his eyes. It was apparent to him that undertaking this particular mission would require an ambitious degree of re-outfitting. Cameron envisioned the *Titanic* in wide-angle shots that would capture large portions of the superstructure in sweeping, graceful movements. He was adamant about designing some sort of housing for a 35mm film camera that would mount outside of *Mir 1,* with *Mir 2* carrying the lights. The design challenges were extraordinary. No one had ever built a motion picture camera that could operate at such crushing depths. The task would fall to his brother Mike, a former aerospace engineer who'd be expected to accomplish the feat in well under a year, an extraordinary achievement even for a guy who'd routinely come to clear the formidable design hurdles big brother threw his way.

Picking up a plastic bucket lying nearby, Cameron used it to approximate the camera, briefly discussing with the *Keldysh* engineers the possibility of using the manipulator arms as a pan-and-tilt mechanism. He really clicked with the Russian crew. "These were like sleeves-rolled-up, greasy-hands kind of guys who worked with these subs, and I was fascinated. I wanted them to show me how the arms worked, how the systems worked. They let me get inside and powered up." His only disappointment was that he didn't get to actually dive, even in the polluted Baltic Sea, where visibility on a good day was maybe three feet.

As interested as he was in the technology of the *Mirs,* for Cameron the most interesting aspect of the trip was sociological. On the Sunday night before the Americans departed, one of the crewmen threw a party. Gena Khlevnov was a huge, barrel-chested Slav whose job was to pilot the Zodiac boat that did runs off the *Keldysh.* Known affectionately as Captain Zodiac, he was much admired for his ability to make the little craft dance on the water. For the party, about fifty people were crammed into his apartment for a feast that probably cost him a month's pay, or about $160.

Seating was segregated, with the men at a long narrow table in the middle of the room and the women in chairs along the wall—all but Natalia who, as a scientist, got privileged positioning. The food, including roast chicken, khachapouri cakes with cheese, pelmeni, and pirogis, was piled high on the tables and sideboards, and needless to say, so was the vodka. In front of every place setting was a fifth. The room teemed with good scents and high spirits and Cameron was taken by the group's exuberance. "They were tons of fun. They really loved their work. They loved advancing the cause of science, even though most of them were working crew."

No sooner were they in their seats than the vodka started flowing and the toasting began—Russian, translated to English. As the ranking official, Sagalevitch got up first, raising his glass, as he normally would, to commemorate the specific occasion, in this case Hollywood and Russian science trying to work together. Everyone poured. Next, the host, who saluted his American guests. Another round served. The third toast was always to the women. The fourth, to your comrades who were not there—if you were on land, to the ones at sea; if you were at sea, to your friends on land. Next, it was Cameron's turn. Then Giddings's. And on and on. "You eat, you talk, you have a toast. The bottle is empty. They bring another one. Phew!! That's how they have a big, celebratory dinner," Cameron recalls. It wasn't long before Sagalevitch got out his guitar and started singing sad Russian songs, and several of the saturated guests began weeping. Nobody threw up or got unruly, and a handful of women—designated drivers—sat in the corner with their arms folded and touched no alcohol at all. For most of the Russians, the vodka went down like water. For the Americans, it was another story. Cameron, who is a light drinker, lost track of the sizable shots after midnight. "Then I thought I was gonna die..." But before his brain tuned to static, he heard Sagalevitch's excited toast: "We do it! We make Hollywood movie!"

He thought happily to himself, "We got the deal! We got the ship!"

Chapter Two

> If there is no struggle, there is no progress. Those who depreciate agitation are men who want rain without thunder and lightning, the ocean without the awful roar of its many waters.
>
> —Frederick Douglass

ON THE FLIGHT back to Los Angeles, Cameron hammered Giddings with questions about the logistics of shooting the wreck. The newly designed camera configuration would be the linchpin of the plan, but an underwater lighting system was another key component. Cameron wanted to light up *Titanic* like a Christmas tree, making it the most elaborate prop in movie history. Art-directing the film in his imagination, he raised the possibility of building a huge grid-array of lights that could be lowered and hung over the top of the wreck. Wouldn't it be cool, he thought, to make it look like an archeological dig? He was buzzing with the possibilities.

"We talked a lot about capacity," says Giddings, "how much lighting could run for how long, how many dives we might make during what period, Jim saying all the while that besides shooting some of the present-day adventure and action on *Keldysh,* using the submersibles, he wanted to dive *Titanic.*" On one hand, it sounded like a multi-million-dollar thrill ride to the bottom of the sea. It was certainly that, but also much more to Cameron. Like any artist, his projects sprang from personal passions and interests. His way of transcending self-indulgence was by raising the bar of achievement so high that it actually hit the pain threshold. Like a thoroughbred, which can only run *fast,* it was natural as breathing for Cameron to push the envelope. In a town that boasts its share of overachievers, his intense inner drive kept him ahead of the pack. If the dive was motivated largely by the selfishness of his own curiosity, it also served his filmmaker's need to open his imagination to those looking for diversion in the flickering light of darkened theaters, an experience he once described as "consensual dreaming."

Though there were a few loose ends to tie up, the two men left Russia with an agreement in principle to rent the *Keldysh.* From where Cameron sat—Lufthansa, first class, cruising altitude—the outlook was good. A little luck with the numbers and some carefully applied science and he'd be off to the races: a filmmaker of fortune on a deep ocean diving expedition with a Russian research vessel and a few of his closest friends. No sweat.

Like any A-list director, he had no shortage of studios competing for his services. Cameron happened to have a first-look deal with Twentieth Century-Fox, which meant the studio had first rights of refusal on any project he decided to make. If they took a flier, he was free to shop it elsewhere. That would be a given. Cameron was not the type of director to allow executives to choose a project from column A or column B. A man on a mission at all times, his single-minded pursuit of his cinematic goals was, by his own admission, "relentless."

His track record allowed him that luxury. His six previous films had collectively grossed more than 1.2 billion dollars at the world box office—*Terminator 2* alone made nearly $500 million, *True Lies* another $375 million. For him, it was a seller's market. A nice feeling, but it wasn't always that way. When Cameron and producer Gale Anne Hurd were peddling their first project, *The Terminator,* all the best doors in town were slammed in their faces.

Cameron met Hurd, whom he would later marry, during his two-year apprenticeship at Roger Corman's New World Studios, a B-movie factory-cum-boot camp for aspiring actors and auteurs.

Corman staffers were hired primarily for speed. New World graduates included Martin Scorsese, Francis Coppola, John Sayles, and Ron Howard. Unlike those alumni, Cameron had no fancy film school degree. A physics major who later switched to English at Fullerton College, Cameron put himself through school with odd jobs that included driving a truck for the board of education. He leveraged his way into Corman's domain in 1979, impressing him with a short science-fiction film he had made called *Xenogenesis* ("of alien origin"). The project was funded with $25,000 from a consortium of local dentists who hoped to leverage themselves into the business. In addition to handling writing, directing, and cinematography chores, the twenty-three-year-old Cameron also built the models and—long before computers found their way into film—pulled off some impressive in-camera special effects. He was hired as a model-maker and went immediately to work on the cut-rate *Star Wars* clone *Battle Beyond the Stars.* At $2 million it was New World's costliest project, and when the art director quit, Cameron got promoted. "He really did go from model-builder to art director overnight, and that can only happen in the world of low-budget, independent filmmaking," says Hurd, who was an assistant production manager with primary responsibility for the art department. Though certainly not "the most exciting mission in the universe," as its marketing materials proclaimed it to be, *Battle Beyond the Stars* was a project in which Cameron, with his experience as an illustrator and strong taste for science fiction, could excel.

Roger Corman recalls Cameron's tireless enthusiasm, even when he was just a gofer. "When things were being moved around a set or on the location I would look to see who was running, and I would always make a note of that guy, because almost invariably that would turn out to be your best man. Some guys will run to get something for the shot, and others will walk. Jim ran."

The veteran producer recalls one instance dressing a spaceship set. "I always like to have what I call kluge, all kinds of dials and things on the walls, to make it seem more efficient and more technical, and I could see from the camera angle that there was one spot on the wall—and they were getting ready to shoot the first shot of the picture—that was blank. And I said, 'Jim, quick! Run and get something, anything, and put it on that wall right away. Don't bother anybody on the crew, just stick it up there.' And he went and got some dial thing, with stuff connected to it, he grabbed it and glued it and put in one nail and put some wires around here and dragged it down there. And I said, 'It looks great, Jim! You know, a spaceship really wouldn't fly without one of those things.' And he laughed and said, 'I knew that, I was just testing your knowledge of physics.'"

Cameron's next assignment was as co-visual effects supervisor on *Escape from New York,* a non-New World film that Cameron secured as an outside client for Corman's effects department. In an ironic twist, the future director of *Aliens* next found himself working on *Galaxy of*

Terror, a copycat attempt to cash in on the success of Ridley Scott's *Alien.* In typical low-budget film fashion, Cameron multi-tasked, designing sets, miniatures, and costumes in addition to handling second unit direction. But he always viewed art direction as an entry level job. Even back then his sights were set higher. Actor Bill Paxton, another New World veteran, remembers how the gang would hang out behind the hangar-like shed of the Corman studio, Cameron diverting them with the adventures he was dreaming up for this character called the Terminator. "We'd look forward to those breaks so we could find out what happened next," Paxton laughs.

Though Cameron was on the fast track to direct for Corman, that opportunity actually arose serendipitously. Two Italian producers who'd acquired the sequel rights to New World's 1978 film *Piranha* were strolling through the New World facility and happened upon the aspiring auteur directing a scene of a maggoty, dismembered arm. Mealworms were the stars of the shot. Cameron cleverly wired their container with electricity so he could shock a performance out of the sluggish creatures. As he called "Action!" a technician offstage threw the juice. "The worms started moving like crazy. Then I said, 'Okay, that's good. Cut.' He pulls the plug and the worms stop. I turn around and these two producers are just gaping. I guess they figured if I could get a performance out of maggots I should be okay with actors, so they offered me their film."

Though the original *Piranha* was a respectable enough little horror movie directed by Joe Dante, *Piranha 2: The Spawning* turned out to be a mess. Cameron had little control over the film, which the producers commandeered. He later discovered he'd been hired simply to fulfill a contractual obligation to Warner Brothers for a U.S. director and cast. Tellingly, the most interesting part of this awful film are the drop-frame underwater shots of the title villains. It was a painful experience, but Cameron came away wiser for the experience and with a firm plan for his future. He would write a great script and attach himself as director.

While at New World he and Hurd made a pact to work together after they independently honed their crafts. While he'd been directing *Piranha 2,* Hurd had produced Corman's *Smokey Bites the Dust.* In 1982 they decided it was time to team up. Cameron set to work on a script about that Terminator character he'd been kicking around, giving Hurd co-writing credit and selling her the rights for $1 so she could be the producer. Though the script itself was well received, the newcomers were not. "There were a lot of people who were hoping we'd take the money and run, but the more we heard 'This is a great project, but we want to get real producers and a real director to do it,' the more convinced we were that we had something good," says Hurd. Their persistence finally paid off when a scrappy little company called Hemdale agreed to finance the film, with some help from HBO and Orion Pictures.

And in an unexpected turn of events, the buzz on Cameron's well-circulated script turned him into a hot writer, securing two additional assignments. *Rambo: First Blood, Part 2* marked the first and last time he would pen a script for someone else to direct (such was his unhappiness at star Sylvester Stallone's rewrite, including the flag-waving speech at the end). He considered the sequel *Aliens* the more interesting assignment, since he much admired the 1979 original. Cameron penned both scripts while waiting for his *Terminator* star Arnold Schwarzenegger's schedule to clear so he could begin directing that film.

In the industry as well as the pop culture, *The Terminator* was a sensation upon its release, opening in the number-one box office position with $4 million in ticket sales for the weekend of October 26, 1984. The film made a bona-fide box-office star out of Schwarzenegger and put newcomer Linda Hamilton on the map. An unexpected success, it garnered the designation of "sleeper" hit, capturing the industry's attention in a big way by outperforming two of the year's most hyped sci-fi efforts: *Dune,* from then high-flyer David Lynch, and *2010,* the sequel to *2001: A Space Odyssey. Terminator* grossed nearly $40 million at the North American box office, a veritable gusher, particularly for a film that only cost $6.4 million to make. Cameron had crashed the Hollywood A-list and it would never be the same. So when Twentieth Century-Fox president Larry Gordon had trouble finding a helmsman for *Aliens,* it was not an overreach to offer the job to the film's screenwriter. Cameron brought Hurd on as producer and the two were wed prior to leaving for England, where the film would be made in order to take advantage of the favorable exchange rate and cheaper labor. *Aliens* also marked the beginning of what would be a long-term alliance with Fox, which immediately signed him to a three-picture deal.

Producing *Aliens* for a thrifty $18 million, the duo managed to make their budget go far. The 1986 film went on to score $157 million worldwide—a resounding success.

It was at the premiere of *Aliens* that Cameron met John Bruno, the man who would have major impact on the look of his future films. At the time, Bruno was already an established special effects supervisor, having worked on *Poltergeist* and *Ghostbusters*. Bespectacled and bearded, the soft-spoken cine-magician was a stark contrast to the lanky, hyperkinetic Cameron. "I was a huge fan of *Terminator*, so I introduced myself, and he said, 'Oh yeah, I know your work. I don't do any fancy effects like that. I just do cheap stuff.' It was very funny." The effects in *Aliens*, supervised by Stan Winston, were in fact largely pieced together with bubble gum and garbage bags. That didn't stop it from winning an Academy Award, breaking a six-year winning streak by George Lucas's Industrial Light & Magic and earning Cameron immediate respect from Hollywood's techie elite.

Fox was eager to get its rising star back behind a camera, and he and Hurd were just as eager to get back to work. She urged him to write a script from a story he once told her, conceived of in a high school essay. Boldly titled *The Abyss*, it provided an early glimpse of Cameron's probing nature. He got the inspiration from an honors science course he attended at nearby Buffalo University while still in high school. "They wanted to offer a taste of higher education, and I was one of the kids that got tapped," says the erstwhile president of the science club and self-described teenage geek. "It was like, 'Do you want to go do this? You do it on your own time, you don't get any credit, and you do it because you're interested.' And I said, 'Sure! That makes sense to me!'" The first seminar he attended was on childbirth. "My first response was, 'Oh my god!' But then I realized, 'Wow! There's all kinds of stuff I don't know anything about!'" The second one featured an audio-visual presentation by a burly commercial diver named Frank Falejczyk, the first person to breathe oxygenated liquid. Cameron was fascinated by the images of Falejczyk on the operating table, intubated with tubes that filled his lungs with a saline solution. Falejczyk panicked and thought he was dying. "The problem," says Cameron of the experiment, mounted by resident Duke University scientist Dr. Johannes Kylstra, "was oxygenated saline wasn't the answer. The answer was this fluorocarbon emulsion that they eventually wound up using." And which he himself used to dramatic effect in *The Abyss*, first in a scene involving a white rat, and then with actor Ed Harris. "Though we didn't really make Ed breathe the fluid," he recalls, "the rat did."

Cameron's original adolescent tale was set in an underwater science lab on an abyssal shelf. "It was really about scientific curiosity," he says, explaining how "one by one, the crew descend the precipice using fluid breathing suits, and are lost. At the end there's only one guy left, the lab's all wrecked, and he goes out to see what happened to the others, knowing he's not going to come back. The story ends with him being drawn deeper and deeper by his curiosity. I think I described it, in this bullshit high school way, as being like 'The Tell-Tale Heart'—a pulse at the bottom of the ocean."

He and Fox were about to be sucked into a vortex of logistical complications that, when it was all over, would make them feel as if they'd been to hell and—surprise! It was wet! Among the problems from the studio's standpoint, the film was behind schedule and over budget. "Fox was clearly caught off guard by the enormity of that project," says Hurd. "They had no idea just how ambitious it really was," she maintains. Released in 1989, *The Abyss* was originally budgeted at $37 million and wound up costing $41 million. "Everyone was running around screaming and pulling their hair out about how it was the most expensive movie in history, which of course it was not," Cameron says, recalling it as the third most expensive film of that year. Still, it was at the high end of the spectrum at a time when the average film cost $18 million.

The story of an underwater oil drilling crew recruited to salvage a wrecked nuclear submarine, the action plays out against a love story between a rough-hewn rigman (Ed Harris) and his engineer wife (Mary Elizabeth Mastrantonio). Things take a fantastic twist midway through as the group discover aliens living undersea, a plot device that inspired Cameron to push the envelope with a new type of special effect—computer generated images. The digitally designed water tentacle created by ILM set Hollywood on a new trajectory and garnered a second Academy Award for a Cameron film, though it was the effects team that received the actual award. (It also landed Bruno, despite all his other fancy filmwork, his first award.)

Computer imaging was just one area in which the project pushed the technological limits. Another complicated "mission" of a film, *The Abyss* required significant research and development in the areas of lighting, propulsion vehicles, and underwater camera gear to take Cameron where no Hollywood director had gone before—namely to the bottom of a nuclear reactor. The containment vessel was refitted, at his request, as a tank. Cameron's goal was to film underwater with the same facility with which he worked topside. To do that, he commissioned the creation of a submersible videotap system that allowed him to see what he was filming as he directed the actors in the drink. Up until this point, directors whose films required underwater work were content to run a tap to the surface, watching from a comfortable vantage point and effectively letting the underwater cameraman direct the scenes. Cameron insisted all his actors—and the producer and most of the crew too—get scuba certified so they could do their own wet work. To interact underwater, he ordered up a subsurface acoustic communications system that allowed helmet-to-helmet contact with the cast and crew. Cameron could talk to the cast and crew but they couldn't respond, a system of one-way communication that was the source of many jokes and much consternation.

"These were all firsts," says Charlie Arneson, a square-jawed marine biologist and undersea photographer who got his first taste of feature filmmaking on *The Abyss.* Working at Scripps Institute, he was recruited by Giddings to serve on the photographic team. Having maintained a relationship with Cameron over the years, he went on to board *Titanic,* serving in a variety of capacities and ultimately becoming manager of the Fox Baja studios. "Nobody had asked for this stuff before. This is typical of Jim. He has the idea, and he just keeps probing until he finds the people that will come up with the technology that allows him to execute it." The litany of new equipment included modified helmets that allowed for underwater dialogue recording and had their own interior light source so the actors could be photographed more effectively.

"Sometimes the great thing about filmmaking is you sweep people up in this passion to create," says Cameron contemplatively. "You sort of will into existence something that wasn't there before. Propose problems that there aren't existing solutions to, and the smart people will say that just because a solution doesn't exist doesn't mean we can't make it exist."

While the gearheads were working on their hardware assignments, a former nuclear plant—built and abandoned by the Duke Power Company in the seventies—was refurbished by a local entrepreneur, who would then rent it to Fox. The giant containment tank and a smaller turbine pit were turned into underwater sound stages holding 7.5 million and 2.6 million gallons of water respectively. The larger stage, known as A tank, would house Deepcore, Cameron's fantasy of a deep-sea oil-drilling station. The biggest submerged set ever built, it required hundreds of lights and a complicated electrical set-up to operate safely underwater. Despite their best efforts, Deepcore was not completed in time for the film's August 8, 1988 start date. On August 20, with the set still under construction, they began filling the tank from a nearby lake. Production started on that note and went downhill from there. Crises of film-stopping proportions were beaten back with alarming frequency and the film slogged through production.

The tanks were topped with a layer of black polyproylene beads to break the mirror-like reflection at the surface. On top of that, tarps were hung to keep out the sunlight, but early on a freak hurricane shredded the 200-foot lid on A tank, forcing a switch to a night schedule in order to simulate the blackness of the deep ocean. Arneson recalls the director's equanimity in the face of this new fiendishness visited by fate. "Classic Cameron, he turned and said laconically, 'Well, I guess we're on nights.'" So went the switch to 7 P.M. to 7 A.M. workdays. Some of the maritimers found it difficult to make the change. Arneson himself had a fairly intractable biological time clock and ended up falling asleep underwater in his scuba suit.

Though the actors had less demanding schedules, the crew was spending six and sometimes seven *long* days a week submerged. Giddings was concerned about their safety, particularly as it related to the bends, a divers' affliction caused when the pressures of depth force potentially lethal doses of nitrogen into the bloodstream. "If you look at a scuba chart there is no decompression until you go beyond forty feet. We weren't quite that deep, but then again, the chart didn't deal with the frequency we were contending with, so our dive profile really was unprecedented." Giddings had Duke University professor Peter Bennett visit the set to advise them on health and safety precautions. Bennett recommended that to avoid decompression they supplement their breathing with occasional doses of pure oxygen. So three days a week the hardcores would emerge from the tank, go back to their room, flip on "Good Morning America" and relax for thirty minutes breathing oxygen through an oral-nasal mask.

Exhausted after a night of intense work, Cameron would often fall asleep on the sofa watching television with his mask on. On one occasion the oxygen ran out. Mike, who was sleeping nearby, heard scuffling and ran in to find his gasping brother clawing off the mask. He was suffocating. "He has an amazing mix of commitment and pain threshold," marvels Giddings nine years later. "I don't think there's anybody who works the water harder than me, and for Jim to stay with me, shoulder to shoulder, really *shocked* me on *The Abyss,*" says the guy Cameron calls "a sea mammal."

"This is my number one discipline. I've been doing it for thirty years. Jim is not physically as big a guy as I am, yet he took the same blistering physical abuse. We both came out staggering around and sort of blinking in the light. But to give you a clue, the rest of my guys, all pro scuba divers, were at the end of their rope. And these guys are rugged. Jim dazzled them all. This was *not* our idea of a Los Angeles filmmaker—a guy so passionate about what he's doing that he's going to fly the F-15 himself."

Even Cameron found it a challenge to keep his passions fired up when fortune seemed so intent on dousing them. It was midway through production that a major arterial pipe sprung a leak, jeopardizing the integrity of A tank. Only then did the filmmakers discover that in an apparent effort to save money, the contractor used pipe of such cheap plastic it couldn't accommodate a valve. There was no simple way to stop the hemorrhage. "If the pipe broke, all the water would drain out of the tank, ruining the set, which meant that the whole film was lost," says Arneson. "We literally had water blasting out of a pipe at a pressure that would kill someone, and there's Jim Cameron, the director, right in the line of fire, stuffing rags into the cracks with the rest of us crew guys. And once we got that under control there's Jim, right there beside us, patching up all the other little leaks."

It was into this tsunami that the studio brass, panicked over the stories that were trickling back to Los Angeles, began sending emissaries to try and exert some control. Needless to say, Cameron received them with all the warmth of Patton welcoming etiquette instructors to the front. Arneson remembers one incident that left an indelible impression on the crew. "We're down there, scrambling to make everything work. The production executive on the picture, Gene Levy, has just been fired and we were constantly dealing with some new disaster. Into this picture walks, or should I say *drives,* this studio guy, Harold Schneider. He pulls up in this white stretch limousine. I mean, Jim at that point was driving a Jeep and everyone else was driving a piece of shit and it was like 'This Is Hollywood! Hollywood Has Arrived!' Out steps Harold Schneider, in a suit! It was hot, and he's got an entourage with him."

Arneson recalls Schneider, a producer for Fox, going through greeting rituals with some crew members before heading off to skulk the set. They subsequently crossed tracks at two meal breaks, Schneider holding court over his coterie of pals while waiting to talk with the guy in charge. When shooting broke six hours later and the crew was climbing out of the tank, he was still waiting, but Cameron rushed off to look at dailies. Schneider cooled his heels for another forty-five minutes, talking to some crew members he knew. "He was asking 'em, 'Well, what's going on here? Tell me what the problems are. I want to get inside Jim's head.' And I was like, who is this guy? But people he'd worked with a bunch were sort of talking to him, going, 'Well, if we could do this different and that different and—" he pauses and laughs heartily at the memory, "in walks Jim."

"Harold's back is to the door, and Jim stood there behind him and listened for like thirty seconds, then he goes, 'What the fuck are *you* doing on my set?' And Harold Schneider turns around and he puts his arms out and he goes, 'Jim! Jim! Don't worry, I'm just here trying to mix in with the group.' And Jim, without actually *touching* him, starts jabbing his finger at the guy, going 'I never want to *see* you on my fucking set! I want you *off* this fucking set right now! If you want to direct this fucking movie, *you* can direct it. If you're not off this set in five seconds I'm leaving!' And Harold Schneider's going, 'Jimmy, Jimmy, just...' and Jim goes, 'If there's *one* thing that I hate more than some jerk showing up on my set, it's somebody calling me Jimmy! Don't you *ever* fucking call me Jimmy again!' And the next thing is Harold trying to take Jim by the arm, going, 'Just calm down!' and Jim goes, 'If there's one thing I hate more than somebody calling me Jimmy it's someone touching me. You *never* fucking touch me. If you touch me again I'll *kill* you!' It was just escalating to the point where the next thing Jim was going to do was drop a nuclear bomb, you know?"

At one point Cameron grabbed Schneider by the collar and backed him up to the edge of the dive platform, leaning him over the forty-foot precipice and threatening to let go. Harold Schneider and friends beat a hasty retreat from A tank, making their way shakily down the ramp to the white limousine and riding off into the sunrise, at which point Cameron turned to Arneson and deadpanned, "Sometimes you just have to make a statement."

Though Schneider was never to be seen on the set again, he wasn't the last official visitor. Roger Birnbaum, newly installed executive vice president of production, decided he needed to pay a courtesy call. Cameron, who didn't know him from Adam, climbed out of the tank after a particularly arduous night of shooting to find Birnbaum standing on the sidelines, bubbling with new-guy enthusiasm and eager to prove his chops by returning home with the news that he'd talked the mercurial director into cutting twenty minutes from the film.

It was not a great moment to approach the director. Three hours earlier Cameron had run out of air and almost drowned as a result of a technical problem with his diving equipment. The situation required a full bailout, free ascent from thirty-five feet underwater, heavily weighted, and with no fins. "I almost croaked!" Cameron remembers with no little emotion. "So Roger shows up, and he's going to solve all our problems. He's standing there in a suit and tie, and all I saw was a guy with a big bull's eye on him. So I smiled, and said, 'Hey Roger! I hear you're the new guy,' all friendly. I take off the neck dam of my helmet, the thing that seals the helmet on, and I said, 'Here, try this on!' And before he could say anything I pulled the neck dam down over his head. Then I said, 'Okay, here, try this on,' and I put the helmet down over the neck dam and I latched it in the back and front and sealed it shut. There was no air supply to the helmet, so he immediately starts thrashing around. I let him choke for about twenty, twenty-five seconds, then I pulled the helmet off and said, 'That's what it feels like when you're running out of air in a diving helmet and you think you're gonna die, which happened to me a few hours ago. So if you think you know more about this shit than we do, then feel free to tell me what's on your mind. Otherwise, just shut the fuck up and go home.'" Another studio executive disappeared in a trail of dust.

"At that particular moment it was not a good time to try to tell me how to do my thing," Cameron recalls, adding with mock sincerity, "I've since learned to be much more polite with my studio superiors." From his perspective, the interference was unproductive. "The fact is, we're always trying to do something new. So when people come around trying to tell you how to do it, it's like, well, you show me where you've done this before. And if you can't do that, don't try to know more about it than us, because at least we've sort of half done it. We've thought about it enough to try it."

The arduous production put a strain on Cameron's marriage, and by the time *The Abyss* entered post production, he and Hurd were in the process of divorcing, and he had taken up with a fledgling New York-based director named Kathryn Bigelow. They married in 1989, and the union lasted roughly three years.

The Abyss was the first film on which Cameron contractually enjoyed final cut, though he says it's something he's always had "in practice." Among directors, final cut—the last word on the form in which the film is released—separates the men from the boys. Reflecting on the significance of the privilege, he sums it up as "a complicated thing" a filmmaker "earns commercially and retains by behaving responsibly. I also think you get it through a kind of force of personality. [Hemdale president] John Daly tried to recut *Terminator* and I just threatened to kill him," he says, pausing before adding with a conspiratorial smile, "He didn't know I wasn't *serious.*"

The Abyss put that privilege to the test. There were some disagreements over the final version of the film. At 140 minutes Fox felt it was running too long. Cameron complied, removing, at his own discretion, a subplot involving a giant tidal wave—one of the film's costliest effects. Who knows whether *The Abyss* would've done better had Cameron stuck with his original vision? It certainly suffered from having to follow two undersea imitators released earlier that year: *Leviathan* and *Deep Star Six.* Though *The Abyss* outperformed both, it was still no hit. For his part, Cameron is circumspect. "I wouldn't say it failed, but we came out the same weekend as *Uncle Buck* and made *less* money"—$54 million as opposed to $64 million. "But who remembers *Uncle Buck* today? People are still watching *The Abyss.*"

In July 1990 Cameron formed his own production company, naming it for the crackling electrical effect that opens *The Terminator.* The goal of Lightstorm Entertainment was to give the auteur even more control over future projects. He also hoped it would afford him the opportunity to work with up-and-coming filmmakers hired to direct properties Cameron had written or acquired. Lightstorm first hung its shingle in large but utilitarian offices in Burbank, an industrial media center on the outer fringe of Los Angeles. Cameron brought in a former video executive named Larry Kasanoff to oversee operations. Lightstorm's first order of business was the sequel *Terminator 2: Judgment Day,* which the company was producing for a high-flying independent called Carolco. Run rather flamboyantly by a Lebanese national named Mario Kassar, Carolco was famous for high-testosterone action films like the Sylvester Stallone *Rambo* movies. Kassar had his eye on Cameron since the

Rambo II assignment, occasionally chasing him for projects. When it became apparent Hemdale was not long for the world, Cameron advised Kassar that the sequel rights to *Terminator* might be available and indicated his willingness to make the film for Carolco. Hemdale hit the skids and Kassar bought himself into one of the highest stake poker games Hollywood had seen in a while. *T2* rewrote the book from a business standpoint, with a budget that started at $85 million and eventually edged up to about $100 million, a new benchmark in 1991 when most films cost under $30 million.

A tough project, *T2*'s crew of thousands moved in and around Los Angeles through 1990 with the bombast of a major military campaign, their exploits chronicled breathlessly by the press. Its favorite angle: Cameron—again over budget and behind schedule—was wildly out of control. One area where he was most definitely in control was the set, where his autocratic ways prompted embittered gossip: tales of him threatening to fire a crew member who left for the restroom and making the team work through meal breaks. His action sequences were so huge he'd taken to choreographing them with a microphone that amplified his voice to concert pitch. His willingness to hurl insults over the loudspeaker system had crew members in a constant cringe. Those who still had a sense of humor blew off steam with T-shirts that proclaimed "You Can't Scare Me I Work For James Cameron" and "Terminator 3: Not With Me!" There was no denying a little chaos had become a key element in Cameron's filmmaking alchemy. The executive ranks were simultaneously frightened and fascinated. In a business where bragging rights to spending the most money had its own peculiar cachet, the tall cost of Cameron held allure. In the end, *T2* went on to be quite profitable—the last word in Hollywood—earning nearly half a billion dollars worldwide. The blockbuster concept had taken on new meaning.

Ironically, *T2* helped terminate Carolco. Though the film was immensely profitable, the money from international exhibitors trickled in slowly, and Carolco simply did not have the wherewithal to carry a loan of that size. With Carolco shaky, Cameron began scoping out his options. Dazzled by the dollars that rained down on *T2*, Kasanoff felt Lightstorm got shafted when it came time to divvy up profits. He sketched out a plan whereby Lightstorm would produce an incredibly prolific twelve films in five years, financing them through international pre-sales and retaining ownership of all rights. It was essentially the same model Kasanoff used running the low-budget film division of Vestron Video. On a Cameronesque scale, it would be incredibly difficult to pull off. With the exception of George Lucas, no major commercial director had managed to hang onto ownership of his films. The agreement offered precedent-setting freedom for a writer-director, including the ability to greenlight—shorthand for giving the go-ahead to get a picture rolling. "When you work for a studio, no matter how much autonomy you have, you still work for somebody. And I've never wanted to work for anybody," Cameron explains.

After shopping their deal around town, the Lightstorm contingent selected Fox as their U.S. distributor and major financier. Representing Fox was studio chairman Joe Roth. But Roth would be gone within six months, and by the time Cameron initiated his next film, *True Lies,* the deal was scrapped. Lightstorm's patchwork financial plan began splitting at the seams. They couldn't access their bank credit until a completion bond was in place. And since such bonds are typically issued just prior to the start of principal photography, that left them with no preproduction funds. Fox stepped in and provided the necessary funding and Lightstorm's relationship with the studio segued to more traditional distribution terms, whereby the studio owned the negative and the production company got a slice of the profits. Kasanoff was out of the picture. It was in the midst of this transitional turmoil that Cameron embarked on *True Lies.* Meanwhile, Peter Chernin replaced Roth. News Corporation chairman and CEO Rupert Murdoch surprised the industry by selecting the forty-one-year-old Fox Network president to head the studio. If Cameron had any trepidation about dealing with a network nob, his fears were immediately assuaged.

Chernin, realizing Cameron was one of Fox's hottest properties and wanting to come up to speed on the film side of things, invited the director to lunch his first week in office. Cameron was pleased to discover a thoughtful, literarily inclined man who seemed cut from a different cloth than the typical tinseltown mogul. For one thing, Chernin gravitated toward the entertainment industry rather than having clawed his way into it as had most of the ruling class. An English major who launched his career in publishing, Chernin's first job was as a publicist at St. Martin's Press, segueing over to Warner Books, where he started out in marketing and eventually became an editor. He was hired "out of the blue" as a development executive by a successful television producer named David Gerber, riding high on "Police Story." After four years he left to head programming and marketing at cable's Showtime/The Movie Channel, moving on to a brief stint as president of Lorimar Pictures, a start-up feature film division of a very successful television company that was purchased by Warner Brothers shortly after his arrival. The studio stripped it down to the core TV business, shuttering the movie arm. He was then hired by Murdoch to run Fox Network in 1989.

As a director who began every new cinematic adventure with the written word, Cameron thought himself in good hands with the intellectual executive who felt as comfortable discussing Stanley Kubrick as F. Scott Fitzgerald, scripts as the classics. Chernin recalls a similar view of Cameron at that initial meeting, an impression he says has held true even as they've gotten acquainted over the years. "He was the least Hollywood of anyone I'd dealt with in the business. That's something I've felt in all my subsequent dealings with him, and what I like and admire most about him. Jim, who isn't always easy, and God knows has triggered lots of tough, confrontational meetings, has never gotten caught up in the bullshit. It's never about his trailer, or his deal versus somebody else's. For him, it's always about the work. Though he's by no means short of ego, he is almost devoid of pretension, and it's an interesting distinction in my mind."

As Fox transitioned out of the Roth era, Lightstorm was going through its share of changes. Cameron had lured away one of Carolco's best and brightest, a thirty-one-year-old UCLA law graduate named Rae Sanchini, to help him launch his own special-effects firm. Her primary responsibility was to secure backers for the venture. A quick study, she began taking a more active role in Lightstorm's day-to-day business activities, assuming the title of president as the company relocated from Burbank to Santa Monica.

It was amid all this change that Cameron returned from Russia with Giddings in August of 1992. When he came back, he had a big secret. Burned by copycats who hopped on his undersea water wagon with *The Abyss,* he was determined to let no one know he was actively pursuing *Titanic.* But while he was keen on the project, and the Russians seemed willing, there were still a lot of question marks. He didn't even know if it would be possible to build the camera system he felt he needed to shoot the wreck. The R&D alone could take years. *Titanic* was no slam dunk. Cameron's films had become big, complicated productions with long gestation periods. This one, he knew, would certainly be his most ambitious, though even he couldn't have known at the time that it would evolve into what was arguably *the* most ambitious film ever made. Starting down a new road with Fox, there was considerable pressure to get something going, and Cameron opted, for once, to take the path of least resistance. *True Lies* was something he had been developing at the suggestion of his friend and frequent collaborator Arnold Schwarzenegger. A remake of a small French comedy called *La Totale!,* it was the story of an elite intelligence operative who has managed to convince his wife and daughter he's a dreary computer salesman. Broad brushstrokes aside, Cameron's rewrite bears little resemblance to the original script, having been personalized from the smallest dramatic flourishes to the megawatt stunts and special effects.

The film would be the first effort from his own effects company, Digital Domain. Having secured former ILM president Scott Ross as a partner and chief executive there was little trouble drumming up financing for the firm. Sanchini brought aboard IBM as the principal outside backer. Cameron's close friend and effects ally Stan Winston also took a partnership stake. Though famous for creating animatronic and puppet character effects like the Terminator and the Alien Queen, Winston had been interested in branching out into computers. The firm was officially launched in the fall of 1993, with Cameron as chairman, and hit the ground running.

Filming on the Schwarzenegger-starrer commenced in July 1993 in Los Angeles and ran a lengthy six months while the crew hopscotched the country, moving to Washington, D.C., Miami, the Florida Keys, Rhode Island, and Lake Tahoe. Like any Cameron shoot, tales from the set took on mythic proportions: perching a full-sized model of a Harrier jet on top of a Miami high-rise, coordinating fly-bys with a fleet of *real* Navy AV8B Harriers, Cameron hanging leading lady Jamie Lee Curtis out of a helicopter and strapping himself to the skids so he could personally photograph the precariously dangling actress. Though Cameron's first comedy was a hit, it was an expensive film to make and its $375 million worldwide gross made it only marginally profitable for Fox, which only had domestic rights. The film garnered an Academy Award nomination for Digital Domain, impressive for a first showing even though it lost to ILM and *Forrest Gump.*

Juggling this prodigious activity, Cameron still kept a tow rope on *Titanic.* When he chose to embark on *True Lies,* the big question became: Could he keep the Russians interested or would they abandon the project?

Immediately upon his return from Russia, Cameron drafted a proposal for the Shirshov Institute, detailing ways in which his expedition might be of some scientific benefit. Transatlantic negotiations ensued as to how much science a commercial mission could incorporate and who would pick up the tab. Ultimately, he won official approval to charter the *Keldysh.*

Cameron also kept in touch with Sagalevitch, who visited the director's Malibu home during one of the *Keldysh's* stateside stopovers. They played basketball together and further cemented a friendship that continued over the fax and phone lines. Periodically, Sagalevitch would pepper the director with inquiries and gentle urgings about the film they had discussed. With *True Lies* behind him and everyone happy at Fox, the time was right to embark on another wild adventure.

One day, Cameron plucked a fax from the machine in his home office. It was another note from Sagalevitch, but this time the sentiments struck a chord. "There comes a time in one's life when you must do something extraordinary," read the fax. "He was talking about using scientific resources to make a motion picture," Cameron explains, "but it really hit home with me. I thought, yeah, there does come a time to do something extraordinary."

Within minutes he picked up the phone and called Sanchini. "Rae," said Cameron, "we're making *Titanic.*"

Chapter Three

Making a movie is a mathematical operation. It is like sending a missile to the moon.

—Frederico Fellini

JAMES CAMERON was a skinny kid who pooled his lunch money to see weekend matinees. He loved film, everything from *Godzilla* to *Doctor Zhivago*. But he didn't enjoy cinema the way most kids did. Instead, he went home obsessing about how to create the monsters, the robots, the evocative sunsets. He snatched his father's super-8 camera and began experimenting, shooting models he built in the garage.

Growing up in Chippawa, a quaint Canadian town just north of Niagara, Cameron loved to do things that most kids would have considered homework. He was always recruiting his brother Mike for some science project or other. They'd fashion rockets from junk parts lying around in a storeroom. They built a shimmering balloon out of dry-cleaning bags, with multiple candles to fly it. The fire department gave chase, and their "UFO" made the local news. A plastic diving bell carried a mouse to the bottom of the Chippawa Creek, an experiment in pressurized breathing.

The eldest of five children, James was a precocious child who would spend hours at a time reading to his brothers and sisters. His paternal grandmother, Ruth, was a schoolteacher who cultivated his love of books. Science fiction authors such as Clarke, Bradbury, and Heinlein were among his favorites. By age eleven, his room was lined with a wall of paperbacks.

His mother, Shirley, dabbled in landscape painting and instilled in her son a love of art. "He won all the Halloween window-painting contests," says Mike. "Everybody else would do some dumb pumpkin. He would do this wild, high-energy thing that had depth and proportion."

From his father, Philip, an electrical engineer for a paper plant, he inherited technical leanings. Mike recalls his parents doted on Jim, "the smart one." For all that, he was something of a loner—a hyperkinetic, overintellectual kid who would rather play with his pet lizard Iggy than play ball.

Aside from a few anachronisms, Cameron's 1994 description of Peter Parker in his "scriptment" for *Spiderman* seemed applicable to his own youth: "Peter is a bright kid. He doesn't have many friends. He is ostracized for his interest in science. Our MTV culture frowns on people who think too much. Intellectual curiosity is decidedly un-hip. Who cares about where the universe came from or how the Greeks hammered Troy. Did you hear the new Pearl Jam album?"

In July 1994 Mike Cameron received a call from his brother Jim.

Mike and a staff of two had stayed on at the old Lightstorm headquarters in Burbank, developing exotic camera equipment under the Lightstorm Technologies banner. Already feeling overburdened with fourteen "live" projects, Mike was not entirely receptive to the intensity in his brother's voice. He knew that tone meant another big adventure and a lot of really hard work.

"I'm making a movie about the *Titanic,*" Jim said, "and I need to really go to the wreck and film in wide-angle, 35mm. I think we can use the free-swimming Russian *Mir* subs . . ."

"But the *Titanic* is 12,480 feet beneath the cold North Atlantic. How do you plan on directing there and just where do you get Russian subs?" Mike asked.

Despite his skepticism, he paid attention. Jim was not one to blurt out an idea before thinking it through. He hammered away with questions and listened intently for two hours as Jim answered them—after chewing Mike out for doubting the sanity of such a plan. While some exterior video housings had been used to shoot at *Titanic*'s depth, all work involving film cameras had been done through the front port of a submersible. Mike understood why his brother did not want to endure the visual restrictions imposed by six to ten inches of Plexiglas in front of his lens—kind of like snapping a landscape photo through the windshield of your car, only worse. Viewport shooting limited you to long focal length lenses, which produced narrow images. The film he'd seen of the wreck made Cameron feel he was "crawling across a carpet with a magnifying glass and flashlight." *Titanic* loomed large in his imagination. The existing hardware was not suitable for his vision.

The enormity of the challenge was becoming clear to Mike. Jim needed an external 35mm motion picture camera system with pan-and-tilt capability that could be remotely operated from within the submersible but would be physically mounted outside the sub. Specifically, he was asking for a 325-degree pan, 175-degree tilt capability at depths of up to 13,000 feet, where the pressure is roughly 6,000 pounds per square inch in some of the saltiest, coldest seawater on the planet. Mike briefly raised the possibility of using a smaller, high definition video system and later transferring the images to film, but his brother immediately ruled that out.

There was no 35mm film camera in existence small enough to fit into a freestanding housing that could be considered remotely safe. At that depth there is something called "implodable volume" that increases in direct proportion to size. The smallest 35mm housing Mike could imagine would still be twice as big as anything the Russians had ever attached to their subs. Mike knew that at *Titanic*'s depth the implosion of even a fist-sized volume of air would cause a dynamic shock as powerful as a hand grenade—enough to do serious damage to the hull of the sub. A worst case scenario would be a sympathetic implosion of the hull itself. It was immediately clear to Mike that any failure of his design would virtually assure the instant death of his brother and the entire submersible crew.

The director proposed the concept of a computerized housing that would accept a compensating gas introduced in a steady, proportional stream. Keeping the pressure identical inside and out would eliminate the risk of implosion, but it was a concept that would require a lot of testing. With time at a premium, Mike favored the straightforward approach: "Build a big strong can." Another life-or-death link in the research-and-development chain were the "penetrators" that would connect the camera to the controls inside the sub. At six thousand pounds of pressure per square inch (PSI), there is no such thing as a little leak. Even a tiny leak would become a big leak really fast. Water is relentless.

In August, Cameron rang Mike with instructions to begin prepping for an expedition to Truk Lagoon and the Palau Islands in the Federated States of Micronesia. Considered the Mount Everest of wreck-diving, Truk is an underwater graveyard littered with Japanese naval casualties from World War II that are accessible using only scuba gear. Depth varies from 150 to 220 feet. (This is quite deep for recreational diving, as most sport divers stay well above 100 feet.) The brothers had vacationed in Truk in 1991, but this time it was strictly business. The plan was to take an existing 35mm shallow water camera system and use it to test lighting and film stock as well as to get ideas about different angles for photographing the *Titanic.* The exteriors were lensed at night to get a feel for shooting in blackness. The interiors were filmed by day, an exercise to discover what it might look like inside *Titanic.* Cameron planned to re-create certain submerged interiors as sets.

The working photographic group consisted of Cameron, Mike, Charlie Arneson, and Mike's assistant, Vince Catlin. They took along two of the Diver Propulsion Vehicles, or DPVs, that Mike had engineered for *The Abyss.* The underwater scooters were able to create the same fluid moves of a crane or dolly. The DPVs whipped along at 2.5 knots, and because of their speed, Cameron and Arneson were able to use them to "free-dive," without air tanks, to depths below 100 feet, sometimes holding their breath for more than two and a half minutes. "To dive that free among the shipwrecks of Truk is a real high," says Arneson, to which, he added, "We did it on a regular basis."

On the seventeen-hour return flight, Mike made notes about what was needed to manage a deep water camera system remotely for more than twelve hours at a time. How would he get exposure readings? What size could the magazine that held the film really be? How would he temperature-compensate the focus, iris, and shutter-speed control—dynamic parts that required the precision movements of a Swiss watch? The sheer scope and ambition of the problems were daunting.

In March 1995 Cameron and Sanchini had a formal meeting with Chernin and then-president of production Tom Jacobson to officially put forth *Titanic* as his next project for Twentieth Century-Fox. Cameron was winging it; he went in with nothing in writing. His basic pitch was simple. "*Romeo and Juliet* on a boat."

While Cameron wouldn't characterize it as a tough sell, he does remember a touch of skepticism. "They were like, 'Ooohhh-kaaay... a three-hour romantic epic? Sure, that's just what we want. Is there a little bit of a *Terminator* in that? Any Harrier jets? Shootouts or car chases?' And I said, 'No, no, no. It's not like that.'" For all the high-rolling Hollywood action, the community was still essentially risk-averse. Everyone loved to gamble on a sure thing. This concept deviated considerably from Cameron's past successes with robots and aliens. And it didn't sound cheap—his films hadn't been for some time. That part was a given.

As favorably predisposed as they would had to have been about any project their $375 million man presented, a three-hour costume epic was not on top of their wish list. Cameron had actually mentioned the idea to Chernin months earlier, in an offhand way. The executive had been chasing him to do a long-term overall deal with the studio, and in that context he discussed projects under consideration. One of them was *Titanic.* Looking back from the perspective of summer 1997, Chernin recalls nothing but unreserved enthusiasm: "To me, when you say three words—Jim Cameron, *Titanic*—I'm there!" And while on a personal level that's probably true—the drama and scope of the event appealing to Chernin's literary sensibilities—as a businessman he must've been disappointed that it wasn't a box-office slam dunk like *Spiderman* or *Terminator 3* that had caught the fancy of one of Hollywood's most commercial directors. Chernin actually thought the contemporary footage of the real *Titanic* hedged his bet a little "... because it was a way of attaching contemporary Jim Cameron effects-driven, technical filmmaking to a period story."

At the time the director wasn't asking for much, only two million dollars to fund a dive to the wreck. It was an unconventional request but, Cameron argued, it made good business sense. Any big film they chose would require some sort of up-front investment, either to purchase a script or to lock up a big name actor or director in a pay-or-play deal in which the studio essentially "reserves" services for a period of availability, guaranteeing payment whether or not the project gets made. "I'm not asking you to lock me up, I'm just asking you to put out a couple of million dollars to go dive the *Titanic,*" Cameron reasoned. "It happens to be an unusual thing to be plunking down money for, but it's not an unusual amount of money to lock up a slot and to get going on a major piece of production. And when they looked at it that way they said, 'Oh, you're right.'" Chernin agreed to fund the dive, in effect committing Fox to the movie, though he withheld an unequivocal green light contingent on a budget analysis, which was standard procedure.

Cameron began work immediately on the "scriptment," his personal blueprint and bible for each of his stories. Considerably longer than shooting scripts, Cameron's scriptments delve into motivation and back story in a novelistic fashion. Writing them is an exercise that helps him come to grips with his characters, their environment, and the thrust of the action. "They're mini-novels, really amazing little pieces of literature," says Chernin, who received the 169-page *Titanic* scriptment just before Cameron shoved off for the deep sea. Chernin was impressed enough to put aside any reservations he may have had about Hollywood's premiere action director pulling off such a nuanced, sophisticated tale.

With funding to draw on, Cameron jump-started his R&D effort, sending Mike on a building-and-buying spree. "We hit the ground running to make what everybody perceived to be 'the window,' the weather window. It turned out that the weather window and this idea we were going to get there before hurricane season was complete and utter bullshit," the filmmaker remembers. As luck would have it, within that so-called sweet window to be diving *Titanic,* the late-August-through-early-September period, the *Keldysh* encountered two full-blown hurricanes in twenty-one days. But Cameron had no way of knowing that in the spring of 1995, when operating instructions were full steam ahead. Mike had only five and a half months to create a revolutionary new camera system, one that would better the efforts of people who'd spent their whole lives engineering in the deep-water field.

Mike's first step was to designate "critical path items"—important designs that would have to prove out in concept early on for the mission to be viable. On top of the list was the glass dome window for the camera housing, which had to withstand 6,000 PSI without compromising optical quality. Mike found there were only a handful of active investigations underway in "the black art of high pressure glass works." He promptly immersed himself in each, compiling volumes on their individual methods. One thing became immediately clear: the success ratio was very low with attempts to create a glass piece of the size required that would withstand *Titanic*'s depths. Of those that had achieved some measure of success, little was known about the number of cycles, or repeated dives, that the glass could be expected to sustain safely. Microfractures were common and quickly developed into catastrophic failures.

Then there was the size factor. The U.S. Navy had a maximum volume versus distance safety specification that Mike Cameron's design, a cylinder eight inches wide by twenty-four inches long, would exceed by a factor of more than three. This made the Russians very nervous. Based on failure analyses he'd done in the aerospace sector, Mike chose a 2.3 safety factor, which meant he would design the housing to be able to dive 2.3 times deeper than *Titanic,* or 29,000 feet—over one million pounds of force trying to crush that little piece of glass, the equivalent of twenty semitrucks resting on his dome. "At this point in the design phase I was starting to feel some pressure-induced stress of my own," he says, able to chuckle about it in only in retrospect. "Who do I recommend as the glass builder? Chose incorrectly and Jim gets squished!"

To manufacture the dome and housing Mike enlisted Sam Raymond of Benthos, the North Falmouth, Massachusetts-based company. Benthos had done some conceptual work for Woods Hole, and though the facility ultimately lacked the funds to go forward with any of the ideas, "Sam had gotten eighty percent down the road I needed, so I considered his to be the lowest risk engineering," says Mike, who simply did not have time for leisurely exploration. He ordered three units to cover an error margin. Benthos ultimately built four, but only two met Mike Cameron's stringent standards.

Early on in the process Mike decided to work with Panavision optics, largely because he liked their wide-angle Primo lenses, which operated at fast shutter speeds. Panavision had a strong history of innovative engineering, attested to by its seventeen Academy Award acknowledgments for scientific and technical achievement. Beyond that, the company demonstrated a willingness to go the extra mile with filmmakers inventive enough to ask for equipment that pushed the envelope, though no one could quite remember when they'd gone to such lengths for a single film.

For the camera body, Mike was leaning toward the German-made Arriflex brand, which was compact and had a reputation for being rugged. He was intrigued to note that the Arri 3 had only been slightly modified for use on the space shuttle. Ultimately, he settled on an older Arri 2c that had been "Panavised" years earlier (which essentially meant that the lens-coupling devices were changed to accept Panavision optics). Working with Panavision's head of new product development, Nolan Murdoch, he would further modify it to run at what's known as "two-perf" instead of the standard four, allowing them to effectively double the capacity of their film canister.

They did this not by making the area of exposure smaller but by doing away with the wasted "protection" space around the image, which meant that Cameron's framing would have to be dead-on accurate. Conveniently, two-perf also happened to be compatible with the widescreen Super 35 format favored by Cameron, which meant they'd have an easy time cutting his undersea footage into the rest of the movie. But even optimized to this extent, Mike's camera could accept only fifty feet, or roughly ten minutes, of film.

Media Logic of New York was selected to produce the pan and tilt mechanism. The fact they'd never worked on any deep-sea systems didn't discourage Mike from giving them the assignment. In all, twenty-three different companies contributed to *Titanic's* camera setup. But there were a number of technological challenges in addition to the camera system, which was by far the most complicated and crucial. Cameron had designed an ROV that needed to be manufactured. There was the matter of the lights and a freestanding lighting tower that he wanted to use on screen, his concession to the archaeological dig concept. Then there were nuts-and-bolts things like light ballasts and penetrators.

While it was initially intended that Mike oversee all aspects of the engineering effort, by late April it became clear that the camera system was a full-time job, so Cameron decided to hire someone to oversee the subcontractors, which were mainly oil-drilling service companies unfamiliar with the special requirements of servicing a film production. A company called Brantner, out of San Diego, was contracted to manufacture penetrators through their Seacon division. Deep Sea Power & Light would provide the Halogesic Medium Iodine (HMI) lights. Western Space and Marine (WS&M) got the ROV (Remotely Operated Vehicle) contract, primarily on the strength of their articulate hydraulic arms, which were said to be able to open a bottle of champagne underwater.

Ralph White was tapped to coordinate the suppliers and began working on May 2. A former *National Geographic* photographer, an undersea cameraman, and a sometime submersible pilot, White was on the original expedition with Ballard and was famous for having "swiped" the coordinates from under the nose of the scientist-adventurer, who it was said had originally wanted to keep the location of the wreck a secret. (Legend has it that Ballard actually released phony coordinates, though he claimed this was a "typo.") As the only guy who knew where the party was, the energetic, fifty-four-year-old White got himself invited along on three subsequent expeditions and made twenty-three Titanic dives before being hired by Lightstorm. In addition to his formidable techspertise, he also knew the Russians and their ship.

It was a major challenge procuring *Mir* specifications from the Russians, who balked at the idea of letting sensitive technological information out of the country. Mike needed but could not get electrical schematics for the subs. A thirty-point questionnaire faxed to Sagalevitch was returned two days later with the reply, "Mike, *Mir* has big power. No problem."

"I chuckle about it now," Mike recounts, "but at the time it wasn't very funny." It was arranged that White would take a small reconnaissance crew to Hamburg, Germany, where the *Keldysh* was in drydock for service. Included in the week-long jaunt were Terry Thompson of T. Thompson Limited, Vancouver, which was re-outfitting the *Mirs* with the newest technology, Mezotech sector-scanning sonar. On an earlier expedition to *Titanic,* White found the *Mirs'* outdated sonar the weak link in an otherwise impressive system. "I could literally see the *Titanic,* but I couldn't get it on the screen," he remembers of an earlier visit. At his suggestion, Lightstorm made new sonar a condition of their contract. "The *Mirs* are very fast but if you can't see where you're going, you'll run into things." The Mezotech was a high-definition, short-range system, limited to about 450 feet but able to pick up small objects within that range. A sector scanner, it had 60 degrees of visibility.

Among others, Scott Millard, owner of Western Space and Marine, was there to explore how he might attach his ROV to the sub. Eric Schmitz of Media Logic went to check out the electronics on behalf of the camera crew. White had also assigned himself electronics detail, and spent much of his time huddled with ace *Mir* pilot Evegeny "Gena" Chernjaev. Most of the Russians had some form of biology or engineering accreditation, on top of which Sagalevitch strongly encouraged them to pursue advanced degrees in specialty fields. Gena's forte was electronics. Other areas of focus were hydraulics and mechanics.

Meanwhile, Mike was tracking along. Panavision had delivered the camera control system. The housings were being milled. There were only a few places in the country that had the specialized equipment to trepan, or drill, a cylindrical core from large blocks of titanium. Such facilities mainly do military work, since the primary use for shells of that girth would be heavy artillery: missile casings, nuclear housing, or big-time gun barrels (as in tanks). Mike's request brought unusual attention from people representing themselves as agents of some very interesting branches of the federal government. "They demanded to know my background and my plans for the shells. I was told in no uncertain terms that if I did not cooperate, the trepanning company would be instructed not to deal with me." The trepanning needed to be very precise, the wall thickness uniform in every way. Mike was aware that the pressures of depth would incur some sort of shrinkage, and allowed for up to a .003 inch reduction in the overall dimension. It was a significant amount when dealing with optics, and in fact, the camera housing was designed to operate as an extension of the camera itself, the glass dome becoming an element of the lens. The system was essentially inoperative on land; it was designed to reach optimum focus at the depth of *Titanic.*

By June, Mike began receiving some components he could test, but it became clear that the majority of his parts would not be ready until ship date, leaving no time for testing. He approximated the system using an aluminum housing and began experimenting in shallow water. One such exercise, off the coast of Santa Barbara, involved a *Mir* mockup made of a painted water jug and two of the deep-rated HMI lamps built by DSP&L.

Work progressed on "a power curve pace" through the summer, though final products were not delivered until the truck for Halifax arrived, and some of them not even then. "A few of the electronic components came on the airplane with us, and other stuff followed us there," says White.

Well over a hundred shipping crates had already arrived in Halifax by late August 1995, arousing the suspicion of local residents as they were transferred from unmarked trucks to the Russian ship. Though the Cold War was over, guardedness lingered. The *Akademik Keldysh* had been in port five days and a hum of purposeful energy emanated from the crew, which ranged from painters, welders, and machinists to electrical engineers. There was a core technological group of about fifty Russians and Americans who communicated largely through gestures. They were instructed to guard the intent of their mission. To the Americans it became a game to avoid the inevitable grilling they'd receive in town. Are you with that Russian ship? What are you guys doing? An inventive response would run something like looking for thermal vents or exploring the lives of sea urchins. Would you like to see pictures? Invariably the answer was no. From intrigue to disinterest in 3.5 seconds. The general was yet to arrive, but the troops dug in on the mission known as "Planet Ice," a multinational endeavor that combined ambitions in the disciplines of science, art, and commerce, though not necessarily in that order. Twentieth Century-Fox was underwriting against future earnings, the Russians wanted to play with plankton, and James Cameron was interested in making a feature film.

Use of the word "Titanic" was strictly prohibited, punishment enforceable by Lewis Abernathy. A *Titanic* buff who occasionally provided writing services for Cameron, Lewis was said by those who knew him and Cameron to represent the wild side of the disciplined director. The bearish Texan was one of three personal friends Cameron had invited along for all or part of his latest adventure. The others were John Bruno and the actress Linda Hamilton, who'd been involved romantically with Cameron since *Terminator 2.* The couple had a three-year-old daughter named Josephine.

White had assumed the role of expedition leader for the English-speaking contingent. His first hire was longtime associate Valerie Moore, the at-sea production coordinator. Moore was one of the seven deepest diving females in the world. A veteran *Mirs*woman, she'd been down over 17,000 feet off the coast of Africa in 1994, searching for World War II wrecks.

Since the *Keldysh* pulled into port on August 25, the dock had crackled with the nervous excitement of a space launch. The technical challenges of outfitting the *Mirs* combined with the delicate nature of the equipment and the fact that human lives hung in the balance made the analogy particularly apt. There were seven individual projects underway, mainly involving the reconfiguration of the *Mirs. Mir 1* would receive the camera, housing, and a nine-foot lighting boom; *Mir 2* got the ROV and carried the majority of the lights. In all, some $1.5 million worth of equipment had to be made shipshape in just nine days. On September 2 they would set sail for their first stop, a shallow-water test dive in the picturesque Lunenberg Bay, a fishing enclave forty miles southeast.

Cameron arrived on August 26, flying into the tiny Halifax airport with his personal assistant Lisa Dennis and John Bruno. Though the American advance team had set themselves up at the Barrington Hotel, about five miles from the dock, the seafarers decamped directly to the ship. The *Keldysh* loomed above the dock like a seven-story building. On the American team was Steve Quale, a twenty-nine-year-old University of Southern California film school graduate, who joined Lightstorm as a production assistant in 1988. Typical of most of the Americans, Quale had never been on a boat that size, and he remembers encountering the ship with a mixture of awe and confusion. "I fly in, I get to this Russian ship. I don't know the protocol. Do I request permission to board the ship? Or do I just walk on? But the Russians were very friendly." For his part, Bruno was surprised that there was no official greeter to help him aboard with his bags.

At the top of Cameron's list was a look at the camera system, with which he had not previously been able to acquaint himself. Though the director did a formidable share of his own camera operating on land, it was done surreptitiously, skirting the union rules. At sea it was another story. He was the mission's camera operator. Giddings would get to dabble with the film gear, but he was there primarily to document the mission on video. Upon seeing the camera setup, Cameron's reaction was typical: How much further could he push it? Mike had brought an extra camera system along as a backup and was asked to attach the second camera to the other manipulator arm. They only had one pan-and-tilt mechanism, but Jim would be willing to settle for a lockdown position on camera two. Mike actually figured out how to do this, but opted against it for safety reasons. Two cameras would double the chances of banging the housing into something hard enough to cause an implosion.

Beyond the advantages offered by its dual submersible system, the *Keldysh* was large enough to accommodate a film crew and its voluminous gear comfortably. At 422 feet long, it was the largest research vessel in the world. The ship could house a crew of 130, and had eleven single cabins, usually reserved for VIP scientists.

Though Sagalevitch was technically the highest ranking official, the ship's captain had the primo quarters. Both their suites were set up for entertaining, an integral part of Russian life. As key man, Cameron got the third nicest bunk, the Chief Scientist's cabin. While not as large as the other two rooms, it had the luxury of a small sitting area separate from the bedroom. He had it outfitted with a refrigerator, microwave, and fully stocked bar. John Bruno had the old KGB officer's room. Until recently the entire *Keldysh* had been bugged. As a symbolic gesture, the doorway to what used to be the old listening post had been permanently removed from its hinge. Now they used the sound system to broadcast music for their parties.

The Soviets weren't big on creature comforts, but the ship did boast a pool, sauna, and basketball court as well as its own hospital. Often compared to a floating village, it also had numerous stills for producing homemade vodka or, as it was called in Russian, *sheila* ("my friend").

The food, though ample, was considered barely edible by American standards. Lisa Dennis made sure to stock Lean Cuisines in every available refrigerator so that her boss might avoid the unpredictable effect of a prolonged Russian diet. The *Keldysh* kitchen staff was proud of the fact that it managed to feed each crew member for less than $1 per day. This was surely a far cry from Ballard's sumptuous description of mealtimes aboard the *Nautile's* mothership, *Le Suroit,* where an estimated one-third of the expedition budget was spent on food. On *Keldysh,* the fare was usually borscht supplemented by mystery meat. Some members of the crew actually got used to it.

The filmmaker had assembled a small but seaworthy team. Giddings, Bruno, Arneson, and Quale were all Cameron veterans from *The Abyss* days. Giddings would help with sub operations and shoot documentary footage of the trip; Mike would take care of the cameras, in which capacity he'd have the assistance of Catlin and Panavision's Bill Eslick; Arneson was a fine underwater stills photographer with many books to his credit. It was his responsibility to document the mission photographically as well as to fix whatever broke. Bruno was Cameron's first choice for the role of special-effects supervisor on the film, but he was weighing an offer to direct and remained noncommittal. Cameron hoped this adventure would sway him *Titanic's* way. Abernathy, who was invited largely because Jim simply liked having him around, wound up putting together a floating art department, creating dive documentation packets with sketches and room diagrams notable for their accuracy and detail.

An ROV pilot named Jeff Ledda, veteran of the undersea oil drilling field, was hired out of Maryland, and Millard was along to keep the ROV at optimum performance, a task that would ultimately involve many contributors, not the least of them the seventy-eight-year-old Russian machinist known as Anatoly "Golden Hands" Suslyaev. Quale was recruited to run the projection system, do some second unit camera work, and help Cameron preplan his camera moves using an eighteen-foot model of the wreck. White would see to it that the trains ran on time, with the help of Moore, who kept the production logs and liaisoned with the production offices on land, or "the beach," as they called it. It was also her very specific task to accommodate Cameron's creature comforts. "I was the one mooing in the kitchen at one o'clock in the morning if he wanted a glass of milk," she laughs. Cameron liked to work with people who could handle more than one assignment.

The evening of September 1, Sagalevitch threw a sailing party in his suite, where he and Natalia were joined by the director and his girlfriend, Linda Hamilton, who had arrived that day. Also present were Bruno, White, Giddings, and Jon Landau. The head of physical production for Fox, Landau would shortly quit his job to produce *Titanic.* Bruno was excited by the purchase of a new Canon Hi-8 video camera, inaugurated that evening. The guests mingled somewhat shyly. Happy, but a bit nervous. By the end of the evening, when 'Toly regaled them with his acoustic sounds, the vodka had relaxed all of them.

That morning they weighed anchor for Lunenberg, in many ways an appropriately named first stop for James Cameron's *Titanic.* The test went fairly well, all things considered. The so-called shallow dives of 300 to 400 feet were kept short, at three hours. The *Keldysh* had anchored at a distance; two boats and a local diving crew were employed to tow the subs and lighting into the bay and handle the gear in the water. They worked all day and Landau, who had taken a launch out to the *Keldysh,* ordered pizza delivered to the ship. It raised eyebrows among the locals: a giant Russian ship parked in the sleepy bay, and what does it want? Pizza!

The two freestanding light towers worked perfectly. The camera booted up, no problem. HMIs, check. The trouble was the ROV, which was too buoyant—they would need to add weight—and its tether didn't play out properly. It would need to be fixed en route.

That night the civilians, including Landau and Hamilton, headed home. While encamped on the *Keldysh,* Cameron had asked the actress to marry him.

The next day was spent reconnoitering gear and prepping for the launch. There was a big party scheduled for that night. By seven P.M. burgers and steaks were being served in a Russian attempt to stage an American "barbecue." The Yank contingent was amused to note that the food had been precooked and that many of the Russians didn't know what a hamburger was or how to eat one. Bruno observed several of them smearing ketchup and mustard over steaks which they then stuck in hotdog buns. There was, of course, plenty of vodka and lots of music and dancing. Both Sagalevitch and Cameron gave speeches lauding the cooperative efforts of art and science. Sometime after midnight the remaining civilians were ferried back to shore by the boat that dropped the film dailies, and in the early hours of September 4, the *Keldysh* lit out for the high seas.

If James Cameron was trying to outstir the elements in terms of chaos and energy, the crew of the *Keldysh* had the comforts of ritual to fall back on. The Russians were big on ritual: three squares a day and four o'clock tea. When their services weren't in immediate demand, they were big on sneaking naps. There was only one phone on the boat, and it was in the communications room, which the Americans would frequently find locked while the supervisor was off catching a few winks—a source of constant irritation.

Overall, the Russians were an odd mix of inertia and ingenuity, very skilled and highly professional, "but the minute that five o'clock whistle blew, God help you if you got between them and the cork," says Abernathy, who appointed himself U.S. Ambassador to *Keldysh*. "Americans will come up to you and stick their hand out to be friends. The Russians say, 'Let's have a drink.' That met with unmitigated disaster. A drunk Russian will just keep drinking and talking until he falls asleep. Americans drink that much and the next thing you know there's a fight or somebody says, 'Let's play Frisbee.'" The Russians were eager to meet their American co-workers but seemed suspicious of anyone who refused to drink with them—particularly Cameron's mission-oriented brother Mike, whose serious demeanor earned him the designation 'KGB.' "They knew I was involved with the U.S. military and they just didn't know what to make of me," Mike says.

As for Lewis, "They got to trust me implicitly," he says with a sly smile. Abernathy became quite famous for his high seas shenanigans. Early in the trip he got so drunk he barged into Cameron's suite to use the bathroom and passed out on the bed with his pants down. It's evidence of Cameron's abiding fondness for Abernathy that the notoriously hot-tempered director curled up on the couch without protest. Their relationship had had its ups and downs. A self-professed "dive whore," Abernathy was found by Jim and Mike on the curb near the docks during a trip to the Channel Islands.

This was post-*Aliens,* 1986. Abernathy was a graduate of the University of Southern California's Peter Stark Producing Program, working as a detective to underwrite his expensive hobbies, which included screenwriting. The diving was aborted due to weather, and the friendly Texan was tickled to find himself trapped on a boat with the celebrated writer-director. A few years later, Lewis was, as Bruno phrased it, "exiled from the kingdom" after selling his underwater monster saga, *Deepstar Six,* over the objections of Cameron, who didn't want it competing with *The Abyss.* Clearly, that rift had been repaired.

The only Russian Abernathy couldn't drink under the table was Russia's preeminent marine biologist, eighty-year-old Michael E. Vinogradov, who was studying plankton, one of two science projects Cameron had indirectly underwritten. After his initial proposal to the Shirshov Institute was coolly received, Sagalevitch advised Cameron to appeal directly to the Russian Academy of Sciences, whose head academician eventually bestowed his blessing. The expedition was then assigned various experiments. Vinogradov and his team critiqued zooplankton—microscopic animal organisms. The other inquiry was led by then-Academy of Sciences Department of Oceanology chief Vladimir E. Zuev, who studied the interaction of ocean and atmosphere with a blue-green laser. The Tomsk City, Siberia-based researchers also used their homemade laser to communicate with its sister space station as it orbited above earth.

Meanwhile, Cameron's own inquiry was well underway. By 2 P.M. on the first day, the conference room had been converted into a two-perf projection suite, and they were viewing dailies from the shallow shoot. Because the camera was designed to operate at extreme depth, the images were out of focus. Moore faxed daily production notes to the offices on shore. In her September 4 missive she noted visibility in Lunenberg was not good and that they would be stopping for a deep-water test in clearer water en route to the "prime site"—the word "Titanic" was still forbidden in all communications. While a few in the scientific community knew about the project, Los Angeles was still oblivious to Cameron's plans.

Chapter Four

> You can't sit around in a room and write an action picture. You have to get out and get ready to make it.
>
> —Howard Hawks

WHEN CAMERON awoke on September 5, the morning of his first deep ocean dive, the *Keldysh* was 270 nautical miles from Halifax. It was a sunny, clear day, and he was stalking the decks early, excited at the prospect of seeing the ocean floor. At 9:30 he ran into John Bruno at the stern, and they quietly discussed the momentous event. A 10,000-foot-deep ocean dive. This is why he wrote the script, to get to this moment. Ever since he was a kid, Cameron had loved the water. In Los Angeles he lived roughly a mile from the beach, and only when the air was very still could you hear the surf. Chippawa, the tiny Canadian town where he lived from three to seventeen, was three miles north of Niagara Falls, and every night he went to sleep with the falls thundering in his ears.

His passion started with skin-diving in the Chippawa Creek. "I was a strong swimmer. I loved to put on a mask and dive down to explore the bottom of the river. We'd have contests to see who could hold their breath the longest." "Flipper" and "Sea Hunt" were weekly favorites and Jacques Cousteau was his hero. "I was fascinated, watching them take those little scooters inside caves." By sixteen, Cameron had still never seen the ocean, but he was bitten by the scuba bug. There was no place to learn in the city of Niagara, so he had his father drive him twenty-five miles to the YMCA in Buffalo, New York. In the dead of winter they'd drive through blinding blizzards to a heavily chlorinated pool at a local high school. It was 1969, and scuba equipment was in the stone age—klugey two-hose, two-stage regulator systems. It hadn't been reengineered since the late forties, when scuba was invented by Jacques Cousteau.

Back then, scuba diving was not yet a sport, but more of a Naval initiative that was just beginning to catch on with the public. Instruction at the Y was delivered with the earnest discipline of military training. Cameron would stand poolside clutching his gear. At the whistle he'd jump in and sink to the bottom. Holding his breath he'd put on his mask and clear it, get the regulator in his mouth and cinch on the tank, firing it up. Next his weight belt and fins. Two laps and he'd have to take everything off again before his free ascent to the surface.

"They used to do a thing called harassment drill, where you'd go swim around the pool and the instructor would come up to you and rip your mask off and undo your straps and shut your air off. And if you couldn't deal with it, you failed." The training paid off in later years, helping him keep cool in some tough situations. "I got fouled in kelp once and almost drowned, but I knew not to panic because of the training. It was hardcore. They don't teach any of that stuff any more. The equipment has gotten so user friendly and easy."

Once certified, he was determined to make a real dive—in a natural body of water. Problem was, you weren't supposed to dive without a buddy, and the only other scuba-ready citizens were the two firemen who dredged bodies from the water. He wasn't about to go diving with them!

He went down to the river and tied a rope around his waist, his father holding it on the dock. "Of course this rope on me was the dumbest thing in the world, because the current blew it all over the place; twisted it up on a bunch of pier pilings and held me down. I untied it, but my father was panicking because he's pulling it and nothing's happening. He's trying to pull up a pier piling." The next year, the family moved to Southern California and, at seventeen, Cameron finally got his first glimpse of the ocean. After Mike got his scuba certification, the brothers often went shore diving together off the beaches of Orange County.

For Cameron, the ocean had always held the romance and mystery of space. Both represented the adventure of the unknown, but it was a scientific adventure rather than a purely physical one. More typical diversions like mountain climbing or running rapids didn't impress him. "You can fly a plane or a helicopter to the top of a mountain. That's boring. But going into space was fascinating, going to the bottom of the ocean was fascinating. Those were intellectual adventures. For me there was a very, very clear distinction."

All of which had brought him here, to a Russian sub. By 10:30 A.M., the deck crew got word that they were over an abyssal plain which at 13,000 feet was deeper than *Titanic.* The two lighting towers had been dropped overboard. The hatches that covered the *Mirs* were lifted. Launching the subs was the ceremonial act that anchored life on the *Keldysh.* Like a modern dance number, the whirl of motion that accompanied the feat belied its choreographed nature. *Mir 1* was scheduled to drop at 11:30 A.M.

Each launch was preceded by a complicated series of steps, not the least of which involved preparing the A camera. Mike's assistant, Vince Catlin, would carry the loaded camera out from their lab to the *Mir* bay, raja-like, atop the "sled" that docked it into the bullet-shaped titanium shell. To ensure that the housing was free of moisture and contaminants, Mike took a high temperature heat gun to its interior minutes before inserting the Arri. Catlin was still a bit wobbly with the precision load and lock maneuver he'd eventually perfect—teetering under *Mir 1* atop a ladder on the rolling boat. The tiniest slip, the smallest scratch, could render the housing inoperative and potentially lethal at depth.

The three men climbing into the sub wore standard-issue *Mir* attire: nylon suits of robin's-egg blue. Since the tight quarters often result in a tangle of limbs, they remove their shoes before entering the mansphere.

With the deck crew on stand-by and the camera sealed and ready, Cameron made his way up the ladder to the hatchway entrance at the top of the *Mir.* A sizable portion of the *Keldysh* populace turned out to witness the launch, cheering wildly from the crew deck above as Cameron waved and smiled, enjoying his moment in the spotlight. It's probably safe to say that never had so many cameras been turned on a director at a film location. In addition to Giddings's video documentarians, Bruno continued breaking in his Hi-8, Quale was shooting movie B-roll, and Mike, an accomplished lensman who picked up a camera when the urge struck, was rolling too.

Launching the *Mirs* was quite a show. First the little *Koresh* tow boat was craned over the side. It would trawl the subs a half-mile from the *Keldysh* for "blow and go," pilot talk for submergence. The most dangerous moment of launch, nicknamed "feet wet," was the instant when the sub hit the "interface," the surface of the water. "Your electrical is powered up and you're in the water. If something is going to go wrong, this is when it's likely to happen," explains White. Still attached to the crane, the sub is a lethal object—eighteen tons of metal thrashing between the sea and the ship. Lonya Volchek was the tanned Russian sub wrangler with the six-pack stomach whose job it was to uncouple the *Mirs.* Embarking from the *Koresh,* Captain Zodiac would pilot Lonya to the sub in the inflatable rubber Zodiac boat. Once they were close enough, the line man would leap like a bullfrog onto the bobbing orange bull's-eye on the *Mir's* back, riding her like a rodeo bull. Slapped by the sea, Lonya would sometimes disappear under the waves as the metal ball bucked beneath him. If his timing was off by a moment he could lose a finger, a hand, or his life, crushed between the sub and the crane boom.

In one smooth move he unhooked the hawser and snapped on the tow bridle. They were now ready to haul *Mir 1* to launch point. The strategic position was designated by "Little Lev" Simogen, who located it on GPS (Global Positioning Satellite) from the *Koresh.* The *Keldysh* would then motor off, putting a full mile between it and the descending *Mir.* Lonya would then disconnect his charge, freeing it to the elements. The same procedure was repeated a half hour later for *Mir 2.* This inaugural leap into the deep was the first opportunity the Americans had to see the *Keldysh* cowboys in full action and they were impressed. With both subs down, the topside team settled into a waiting mode until their recovery—meals, movies, swapping stories, and learning more about the history of the ship.

Though the *Mirs* themselves were twenty-one feet long, the mansphere occupied by Cameron, Sagalevitch, and the engineer Andrey Andreev was only seven feet wide, allowing each a personal space as wide as a telephone booth—for eighteen hours at a stretch. Cameron settled in for a long, cramped trip. Looking out the viewport he could see some bioluminescent creatures. Visible in the blackness from about 400 to 900 feet, they looked like stars. He then began a more thorough acquaintanceship with his one-of-a-kind camera system. There was a lot to remember. The entire configuration was integrated by computer, and there was a boot-up process of about fifty steps for every outing. It was powered electronically, drawing a low 6 amps from the *Mir* battery. The camera itself was controlled via a small keyboard. Cameron insisted the pan-and-tilt mechanism be modified from the typical joystick configuration used in sea and space missions to a more traditional film mechanism of wheels, which would produce the smoother "ramped" moves afforded by motion picture cameras. After working on the camera, Cameron napped and browsed a book.

At 1,000 feet from the bottom Sagalevitch started to do some basic trim up, slowing their descent speed. At 400 feet the bottom sonar switched on, and they checked its reading against their depth gauge. The last thing a pilot wants is to get surprised and slam into the bottom at high speed. Andreev began the countdown and Sagalevitch pumped a little ballast to lighten up the sub. As they switched on the quartz lights Cameron pressed his face up against the viewport, looking for the bottom. There was nothing. Just blackness and then, all of a sudden, a faint green that resolved itself as the ocean floor. He expected it to be blue, though he later discovered it is really gray and the greenish cast is a reflection of the seawater.

Sagalevitch began pumping the side thrusters to slow the sub down. They soft-landed in a cloud of silt, and waited for the current to blow it away. Looking around, Cameron noticed a couple of rocks and three very large grenadiers, also known as rat-tailed fish. Some brittle stars clung to the mud. In truth, not much to see but Cameron was nonetheless thrilled to arrive. He'd played out that moment many times in his imagination, diving in ten or twenty feet of water as a kid. "The bottom of the ocean looked exactly like the surface of the moon, but more boring, because there are no craters," he recalls with little romance. They set out in search of the light towers.

Meanwhile, on the *Keldysh,* the Americans would occasionally pop into the control room to eavesdrop on intra-sub communications via the Underwater Q-band Communications system, or UQC, an inter-sub sonar system linked to the ship by a transponder hanging fifty feet below deck. The voices were tinny, surreal, beaming in from the Outer Limits. Cameron seemed to be having translation troubles directing the movements of *Mir 2,* where the only English-speaker, ROV pilot Jeff Ledda, was too timid to grab the UQC. Other topsiders gathered in a *Keldysh* conference room where they were screening a Russian-dubbed version of *Judge Dredd.* Ralph White holed up in his room brewing coffee, working the radio, and trying to secure transport to land for the day's film. Cameron insisted on seeing deep water dailies before diving *Titanic.* White thought his best bet was to catch a fishing boat going in, and have a plane air drop it out. He was assisted in the effort by the beach support team based in St. John—Gig Rackauskas, a Hollywood hire, and Duncan Ferguson, a Canadian engineer and local expeditioner who was helping them navigate the local waters. By 10 P.M. it was apparent that *Mir 1* would not be surfacing until about 3 A.M., and people started trickling off to sleep.

At 2 A.M. on September 6, a Russian voice boomed over the loudspeaker: *"Vnimanie! Vnimanie!"* ("Attention! Attention!"). The subs were on the way up. Without the hectic physical activity of the work to keep them warm, Cameron and crew huddled against the creeping cold during the two-and-a-half-hour ascent. On the way up, he and the engineer sang happy birthday to Anatoly, who'd turned fifty-seven the day before.

The last fifty feet were the worst. The sub bobbed like a cork before finally breaking the surface at 3:20 A.M., sixteen hours after launch. "It was amazing," recounts Bruno, "an eerie green glow rising from the depths of an inky black ocean. It looked just like the opening of *20,000 Leagues*."

The recovery at the surface took almost half an hour, during which time they rolled in a sea that had come up quite a bit from what it had been at launch. Cameron climbed out, all smiles, to a hero's welcome, and was blinded by photo strobes and video lights. Almost ceremonially, the entire *Mir* technical crew filed by, shaking his hand and congratulating him. He was now one of them, a member of a very elite club. He generally described the problems and victories of the dive with everyone on the *Mir* deck. The camera and onboard lights worked great. He managed to get a few shots of *Mir 2*. But they couldn't get the freestanding light towers to turn on and the ROV was sluggish, with almost no thrust at depth. The first nine hours went really fast.

Cameron quickly repaired with Sagalevitch to the sauna. At an average submersible temperature of 35 degrees on the bottom, the divers returned chilled to the bone. Alternating stints in the 170 degree Fahrenheit sauna with dips in the 42 degree pool was a post-dive ritual. Going through the social motions, Cameron felt a bit uncomfortable. He thought the dive went much worse than he let on. His filmmaker's reflex for expediency went against years of scientific status quo. Then there was the language issue, and the tendency of the subs to hurl up blinding clouds of sediment whenever they maneuvered at the bottom. The ROV was a complete fiasco. Its thrusters put out a mere fraction of the power they had near the surface and the umbilical stiffened at depth and would not rewind. He pegged it for a pressure or a temperature effect, but knowing what was wrong didn't make him feel any better. And that wasn't even counting the fact that Cameron had tossed his cookies during the bouncy recovery—a not uncommon occurrence among *Mir* travelers, but one heightened by his acute propensity to motion sickness.

At about 4 A.M. *Mir 2* was recovered and everyone gathered in Sagalevitch's cabin for a birthday blowout that was elaborate even by standards of Russian hospitality: smoked salmon, white fish, caviar, Johnny Walker Red, vodka, and champagne. Cameron toasted Sagalevitch as "a great natural leader, and one who leads by example, not from his office, which is rare these days." He gave him a VCR and left at 6 A.M. with the sun rising and the party just revving up. In thirty-two hours they would reach the prime site.

By 1 P.M. the crew had begun tumbling out of bed, spilling onto the drizzly deck. White had failed to raise a shuttle for dailies. At 600 miles from land, a special charter was a costly proposition. He had a line on a nearby fishing boat, but lost it after the ship caught 96 tons of cod and decided to head directly back to port.

The *Titanic* sank on the outskirts of the Grand Banks of Newfoundland, some of the most fertile fishing territory in the world. Also famous for its mercurial weather, the area had earned the designation "Hurricane Alley" from seasoned weather watchers. Many a tropical storm, after blustering its way up the Gulf Stream, went there to die. Seventy-mile-an-hour winds were not uncommon, and speeds of up to 109 had been recorded. Even now, the *Keldysh* was heading into the path of Hurricane Luis. They adjusted their course 50 to 60 miles north to skirt the storm. If they couldn't outrun it, they'd turn around, head into it, and hang on.

The *Keldysh* navigated itself into position over the wreckage of *Titanic* at 2:30 P.M. on September 7, confirming its position on the GPS. The first thing they did was drop four Navac transponders, establishing an electronic grid on the bottom of the ocean that the subs would use to navigate at depth. The swathe of sea at 49D, 56', 38"W by 41D, 44', 01"N did not look unusual. Though icebergs were a common sight in spring—when warm weather caused the polar ice caps to "calve," sending shards of glacial rock floating south—there were none today. Nothing to indicate that some 1,530 people had lost their lives on this very site.

Built of equal parts inspiration and arrogance, the *Titanic* represented every superlative spawned by the so-called "Gilded Age." She cost $7.5 million to build, which would adjust to roughly $600 million in modern currency. A top first-class ticket went for $3,100, or the equivalent of $124,000 today, while a third-class ticket was $32 in 1912, or approximately $1,300 today. The *Titanic* was the biggest, most beautiful, technologically advanced, and luxurious liner built up to that time. An unsinkable ship. Well, not completely unsinkable, but invincible from any threat her builders thought she might reasonably encounter. The oddest thing about the *Titanic* disaster is that there was only one way she could sink—exactly the way she did—and the chances of that happening were infinitesimal.

Everything that could possibly have gone wrong, did. The sea was calm as glass, the worst condition for spotting icebergs, which are identified by the waves breaking at their base. Compounding that problem was the fact that the lookout's binoculars were lost shortly after leaving port and nobody had packed a spare. Repeated iceberg warnings from nearby ships were completely ignored by the otherwise rational captain and crew. The ship was moving fast at the insistence of the owner of the White Star Line, who was interested only in beating the existing transatlantic record of its sister ship, *Olympic.*

The false assurance that *Titanic* was unsinkable stemmed from the sixteen "watertight" compartments traversing her hull. In fact, these compartments were not watertight at all, in the sense that they would only contain water that did not overflow their walls—which of course it would if the ship tilted enough. There were no "lids" on the compartments. She would float upright with any two of them breached, stumble but not sink with the first four flooded. A failure of the first five would send her sinking to the bottom like a brick. It just so happens that at 10:30 on the evening of April 14, 1912, *Titanic* hit a glacier in precisely such a way as to cause that to happen, a long glancing blow along her right, or starboard, side.

The *Titanic* crew spotted the berg about a half-mile off, not enough time to change course on a ship of *Titanic's* proportions. Traveling at a brisk 23 knots, or about 20 miles per hour, it would've taken her at least three-quarters of a mile to comfortably avert the obstacle. The crew responded as best they could, instinctively acting to avoid a head-on collision which, ironically, might've been their best option, since she was in fact designed to take just such a hit. Reflexively, the order was given to turn hard left. The impact was barely felt by the passengers, many of whom had already gone to sleep. Heightening an already impressive level of pathos was the fact that the mortal blow came not with a flourish, but a flutter. The ice beat a delicate tattoo down the flank of the ship, "dit, dit, dit, like Morse code," as Cameron described it in his script. In fact, most passengers were startled not by the dynamics of impact, but by the sudden absence of the engine's hum. The motors were cut moments after the crash. "I felt the engines slow and stop; the dancing motion and the vibration ceased suddenly after being part of our very existence for four days," remembered Lawrence Beesley in his survivor's account.

Most people were simply not prepared to entertain the thought that *Titanic* could sink. The higher up in the ship, the less the impact was felt. If tragedy snuck up on velvet slippers to those in the first class—a point cleverly underscored in Cameron's script, which has Cal, embroiled in a lover's spat with Rose, slamming the door in a cabin boy's face with a brusque, "Can't you see we're busy!"—it was a rude slap to many in less privileged quarters. On impact, the toiling coal chuckers in Boiler Room 6 were hit in the face with jets of freezing water that immediately sent them racing for higher ground. And though it was refuted by certain interested parties at inquiries subsequent to the sinking, the sad fate of steerage passengers—kept below decks behind locked gates as the ship foundered—was documented by others.

These social tensions would constitute a lot of the allure the story held for Cameron, who felt the best way to tell the tale of *Titanic,* with its ironies and injustices, was through characters that represented the two polar extremes of the ship and of the sinking. "A first-class lady stood close to 100 percent chance of survival. A third-class male stood about a one-in-eight chance," he explains, clicking into data-crunch mode. "It laid out in quadrants, basically. If you were a first-class male, you weren't in great shape. It was about 50-50. If you were a first-class female, it was 98 percent in your favor. If you were a third-class female, it was about 50-50, and if you were a third-class male, it was 10 to 15 percent. So it really lays out. You've got two dynamic axes: your X axis is sex and your Y axis is class." Cameron centered his story on a first-class female and a third-class male, diametric opposites in their likelihood of survival, "which is the greatest obstacle to love you can think of," he notes. "The thing it took me a while to express properly, or even quantify, even after I'd written the script, was that when you fall in love, you get up to a certain point, it's a love that's untested by a trial. Here, the trial is life or death. And that's when the story gets interesting."

As it was, the life boats had capacity for 1,178, barely half the 2,235 voyagers (1,320 passengers and 915 crew). Only 705 were rescued. The rest died. Most of them froze to death in the glacially icy North Atlantic waters.

Ever ready with a theory, Cameron thinks the Captain erred by not unloading the passengers onto the iceberg. "They would have been cold, but they would've lived," he offers. As it was, most of the passengers went down with 46,378 tons of metal. Flooding rapidly, *Titanic* split down to her keel, the bow dropping into the water like a slack jaw. Eventually, the weight of the sinking bow would force the stern up vertically in the air, a steel splinter piercing the sea. It bobbed briefly before the last trace of her disappeared at 2:20 A.M., only two hours and forty minutes after the collision.

At the bottom of the ocean, the wreck lies in two pieces, roughly a half-mile apart. The bow parachuted down, planing gracefully into the mud. The stern traveled about three times as fast, plowing into the bottom at roughly 35 miles an hour. Upon impact, it was crushed to the ocean floor and essentially scattered into a junk heap by the huge jetstream of water that swept up behind it, a phenomenon known as "the downblast effect."

It is the roughly 400-foot bow section that captured the imagination of Cameron and previous photographic expeditions (though Ballard scrupulously documented both sections).

The re-creation of the bow, designed to assist Cameron in his shot planning, was loaded aboard the *Keldysh* with much fuss in Halifax. A portion of the ship's stairwell had to be cut away with welding torches to accommodate the model, which was placed on an enclosed weatherdeck near the lifeboats. If Cameron wasn't working in his room, here was where he could usually be found, previsualizing his shots using a videomatic camera system known as the lipstick cam. It was a charge coupled device (CCD) camera only slightly larger than a lipstick that Cameron could use to navigate through his shots.

That afternoon, on the eve of the first *Titanic* dive, Cameron worked on the model with Bruno, Quale, and the Russian pilots from 2:45 P.M. until 7:15 P.M., then reviewed the tape in his room. Bruno remembers these first video workups as looking "pretty damn good," and thought "if we can get these shots, which we all believe is possible, the trip will have been worth it."

At 7:30 P.M. it was time for the expedition's official opening gala.

Festivities centered around a big pig. So big, in fact, at seventy pounds, that the Russians were forced to whip out their welding torches and manufacture a grill big enough to hold it over the 50-gallon drums they'd fired up (not with charcoal, but with coal.) As Sagalevitch remembers it, "Everybody was very happy and a little drunk!" Throughout the festivities, the Russians passed around styrofoam cups, trying to get Cameron and Sagalevitch to sign them. It was part of a time-honored practice—doodling on cups that were then bagged to the outside of the *Mirs.* At 12,000 feet, the cups compressed into dainty miniatures, tough as porcelain, their scrawls shrunken but intact. John Bruno, who began his career as an animator (he worked on *Heavy Metal*) and was still an avid illustrator, was captivated by the custom. "Some of them were pretty elaborate, with illustrations of the *Keldysh* or the *Titanic* drawn in color." By 10 P.M. Bruno was putting the finishing touches on some cups of his own.

At 11:40, the time *Titanic* hit the iceberg, Cameron and Abernathy took a quiet moment to reflect on the tragedy. In an odd way, Cameron had joined the club of those whose lives the event irrevocably altered. He'd already invested more of his strength and spirit into this project than most directors do on any one film. His films consumed him, and this was only the beginning of an effort that would ultimately span more than five years of his life. The last few days alone, with their technical problems, seemed like an eternity. He'd been absorbed by the problems with the lights and the ROV. "It was very much like a space mission, what astronauts must feel like when they're going to the moon. They're dealing with a million technical things. They're not thinking about the big picture. They don't look out the window.

"We got there. We had our little toast at night, which was private, just to sort of tell ourselves we were really there, where the *Titanic* sank, and that was kind of cool. That was emotional." They toasted.

Cameron raised his cup to the people who perished.

His friend countered with an acknowledgment to the survivors.

They dropped their glasses into the sea.

Chapter Five

> The most beautiful thing we can experience is the mysterious—the source of all true art and science.
>
> —Albert Einstein

MIR 1 LAUNCHED at 11:25 A.M. on September 8 and Cameron thought he knew what to expect. The deep test had taken him to the bottom—deeper even than *Titanic.* But for him, every dive held its own allure. "You look out at the water. You don't know what's down there. You're going to find out. You're going to go down there and you're going to explore. You're going to see something that nobody's seen—or that very few people have seen. That's what I like about diving and that's what I like about wreck-diving in particular. For me it was wreck diving, but wreck diving with a sub instead of on scuba." Wreck-diving on the *Titanic* was an elite sport indeed.

Cameron ran his camera through its paces and attempted to keep his own systems in check with the help of anti-nausea drugs. He had little time to marvel that the most famous wreck in marine history lay two-and-a-half miles below his stockinged feet.

By 12:10, *Mir 1* was descending at a rate of ninety feet per minute. One mile an hour. A freight elevator to the ocean floor. Face pressed against the viewport, Cameron saw the color go from blue to deep indigo to black by nine hundred feet. The overriding sensation became one of a slow-motion hurtle through space. With the efficiency of a trained astronaut, Cameron rested on this uneventful portion of the trip, conserving energy for his destination. With about two hours to go, he read *Endurance*, the Antarctic survival story, between naps.

The temperature inside the submarine cooled with the fall, bottoming out at about thirty-five degrees. The cold wouldn't be noticed once work began. With nine hundred feet to go, the pilot began the countdown in Russian. Cameron allowed himself a moment of exhiliration at the thought of seeing the Titanic. For the past eighty-three years she had slept pressed to the ocean floor, wrapped tight in an inky liquid shroud. Few visitors had laid eyes on her.

The director's excitement was tempered by concern about the ROV and light towers, with which the technical crew had been tinkering for the past day. The lights had come on in Lunenberg Bay; he was even able to operate their pan-and-tilt motors, but they were dead in the deep. Still, when he thought about all the technology it took to get him to this moment, he was amazed that somehow all of it managed to converge, pretty much on time and relatively on budget.

Somehow in all the pre-dive turmoil, no one had pressure-tested the ROV, which still had buoyancy problems. And Cameron had been unhappy with the tether management system as far back as Lunenberg. A separate but complementary piece of engineering, it controlled the ROV's eighty-foot umbilical leash. The director didn't like the drum action, which relied on the ROV's forward thrust to unspool.

Cameron thought the drum action "gave it the look of a dog straining at a leash." In fact, in his scriptment he dubbed the ROV "Snoop Dog," as in "walking the dog." Perhaps Millard took him too seriously. Cameron imagined his Snoop descending a staircase trailing an elegant train of tether. To Cameron, the ROV was, in its way, a character in the film, not at all unlike the Terminator in its Stan Winston, exoskeleton incarnation. The performance he was seeking was nothing short of having it dance in thin air, except that it happened to be in water.

The idea was to get the ROV neutrally buoyant—so it would neither sink nor float. Given the severe power restrictions, they didn't want to waste valuable thrust getting Snoop to hold position. It had to be perfect static equilibrium, where the forces of gravity balance the forces of pressure. In the earth's atmosphere of 15 PSI, it would be the equivalent of a helium balloon with paper clips attached to the string just hanging at eye level. The magic zone. This was the way the director wanted it and this was the way it was going to be.

Sagalevitch wanted to see the ROV perform at depth before making any drastic changes. In fact, the problem got worse as the temperature and pressure of the deep ocean increased the viscosity of oil inside the ROV. The aircraft hydraulic fluid Western Space &

Marine (WS&M) used inside the motor and umbilical cable was ten times the viscosity it needed to be to remain fluid, stiffening the tether and interfering with the rewind process.

This was also the cause of the weak thrust, a problem they initially thought was electronic. Cameron's continued displeasure after the deep test had Sagalevitch swinging his machinists into action. The star of the Soviet technical team was the seventy-eight-year-old machinist known as "Golden Hands" because he could build anything. Hand-filing the metal, piece by piece, Golden Hands led the effort to re-engineer Snoop's drum to a pinch-roller system. A "*Keldysh* cocktail" of kerosene was substituted for the oil, and by the third dive the gadget was in good working order. Cameron expected no less from the crew of the man who'd fixed his car engine with string.

After a little more than two hours of descent, Cameron joined the others in the little rituals of readying for touchdown and a long period of work. They pulled on an extra pair of heavy socks, had a cup of tea, and kicked into gear. They switched on the Furuno bottom sonar, a relic from the 1960s, counting down the meters while gently pumping out of the two-hour-and-forty-five minute free fall. Yesterday they had dropped the transponders based on their GPS readings of where *Titanic* was positioned. Even civilian GPS is accurate to within thirty feet, which is plenty close with something the size of *Titanic,* but the transponders drift in the current on the way down, and there's no way to predict where they'll really land. The electronic net would be of no help in locating *Titanic* until they found her and plotted her position on the grid. Sitting on the bottom of the black ocean, they were pretty much on their own.

With the new Mezotech sidescan sonar, theoretically they should have been able to spot the *Titanic* from a third or a quarter of a mile away. The problem was, this was the first dive in which the Russians really tried using the Mezotech. Being unfamiliar with it and under some pressure to locate the wreck, they opted to fall back on the familiar old Furuno, a "fish finder" meant to take readings straight down. Using it to search sideways was kind of like trimming the hedges with a lawnmower. The bow section of *Titanic* is huge, sticking up ninety-five feet from the ocean floor. Even a crude scan ought to be able to pick her up. They did a 360-degree scan and got a trace, went for it, and discovered a rock. They went on like that for two and a half hours, even crossing their own skid trace at one point.

If the walls had been larger, Cameron would have been climbing them. "I was peeved, because it was my equivalent of burning daylight. I was burning bottom time." Meanwhile *Mir 2,* which launched a half-hour behind them, dropped down and got right to *Titanic.* Since the boys in the *Keldysh* control room were able to track the location of the *Mirs* at all times, once *Mir 2* was at *Titanic* it was a simple matter to vector in *Mir 1.* While they waited, *Mir 2* managed to recover the two light towers and get them into position.

Though Cameron wasn't overawed with the navigational skills of his particular team, he was very impressed with the navigational skills of the other team, under ace *Mir* pilot Gena Chernjaev. As Abernathy put it, "A second is an eternity to Mr. James Cameron. He lives in some sort of hyper-reality." Only a few hours into his first *Titanic* dive, he was already looking for more things to do. He decided to take over sonar duties and set out to master the Mezotech. "I started practicing right then, on bottom objects like boulders and things, deciphering what they were on the sonar and then looking out the window."

He limbered up the camera system and lights, all working. There had been problems with the lights. During the tests one bulb had burned out, another had gotten smashed into the bottom and broke. Photography would be greatly impaired by the loss of Cameron's carefully configured lighting plan. Technically, he was in good shape as they drew upon the ship. They knew it was nearby. Then somehow they touched bottom and managed to get into a siltout situation. Sitting on the bottom, Cameron peered out his small viewport, which is canted off slightly to the right. Six feet ahead of him was a steel wall of rivets that he knew wasn't the hull because its edges were jagged. It was just standing there, plunged into the earth like a knife. He didn't have time to react because the current was carrying them sideways and they were about to impact. They weren't going fast enough for him to fear for his life, but Cameron was worried about one of the light booms protruding to the submersible's right. "I'm afraid we're going to break it off, so I'm like 'Anatoly! It's on the right! It's on the right! Just go left!' And he's looking out his window, but his window is aimed straight forward and he can't see it. And I'm like, 'It's there! Trust me! Go left!'" Anatoly didn't trust him. They ran into it.

Sagalevitch overreacted, driving up a blinding cloud of bottom muck. They were still moving and now they had lost track of the wreck. Suddenly, through the particulate haze they glimpsed a mountain of steel about twelve feet ahead. Moving up and at it, there was no time to savor this first glimpse of *Titanic.* Cameron saw a railing and they were traveling straight toward it. "I say, 'Go up! Go up! Go up!' And we do. There's still silt everywhere and we're kind of like going sideways in the current. And Anatoly loses track of where the railing is, so he powers down and he lands us on the deck of the ship. There's a big cloud of mud and silt, and he has no idea where we are."

Cameron had so looked forward to seeing *Titanic,* yet this wasn't like anything he expected. "I went straight from not seeing it, not seeing it, not seeing it, to seeing a wall of rivets, to pure adrenaline, being out of control, being in a big cloud of silt, seeing a glimpse of a railing, slamming down on the deck and my pilot not having a clue where we were. We could have been anywhere on that ship." Wreck-diving is dangerous, and one of the most basic safety requirements is knowing your position in relation to the wreck at all times. Had Sagalevitch downed it just a few yards over, the submersible could easily have become lodged in the gaping number-one hatch, where it would likely have remained to this day.

Cameron panned his camera 180 degrees, viewing the scene behind them on his monitor. He peered out his portal, then out of the one on the left, trying to piece together a picture of where they were. Though this was the first time he'd laid eyes on *Titanic,* he had memorized every detail of her from his model. The deck itself provided the biggest clue. Though the wooden planking had been eaten away by mollusks, he could still see the outline of the deck-plank caulking. There was only one place on the ship where the planking was angled at ninety degrees to a railing: the forecastle deck. He took out a diagram of the ship and drew the *Mir* on it, indicating their location, but Sagalevitch didn't believe him. "Trust me," Cameron instructed, taking a compass bearing. They were pointed south, at about 170 degrees. "Just raise the sub a meter and a half above the bottom. Reverse the heading, so we'll be on zero or ten, then go forward fifteen or sixteen feet, and we'll see hatch number one." The Russian relented. They raised, turned 180 degrees, motored forward, and there it was, hatch number one.

After that, Sagalevitch always believed him and then it started to get fun. Gena had said *Mir 2* was at the bow. Cameron took command. "We're going to go over the forward windlasses, we're going to go around the anchor crane. Now we're heading down the center line of the ship and we're heading toward the anchor crane." No sooner had he said it than they were in another emergency—they were heading right for the anchor crane, a fifteen foot vertical pylon. "If this is how it's going to be, we are never going to get a shot!" he thought woefully as they bounced past it. The lights of *Mir 2* were visible beyond the tip of the bow.

Finally, three hours after touching bottom, Cameron was able to turn his camera on *Titanic.* He would later describe the ensuing six hour period as "a cluster fuck." His first order of business was trying to operate the light towers. After forty-five minutes, Cameron determined that his $160,000 towers would not be a part of the photography. They would later find out that the problem was in the acoustic modem. The manufacturer had imcorrectly rated it for a depth below that at which it could function. Cameron ordered the towers set aside and moved on to get his first shots.

Trying to position the two subs at the wreck in a way that enabled him to photograph one of them and light the scene using his onboard HMIs was "a mess, just a mess." But he did manage occasionally to get the sub and the ship in the shot at the same time. After they shot the entire first roll of film they headed for air. A fifteen- or sixteen-hour round trip to get twelve or fifteen minutes of material.

Mir 1 sighed to the surface at 1:45 A.M. on September 9 in a compromised state. The hydraulic lighting boom had locked in an open position. They tried jettisoning the hydraulic fluid at the bottom, but that didn't work. The ragged edge of sea at the interface was where the outboard equipment was most vulnerable. The arm would have to be secured quickly to avoid getting damaged by the three-to-four-foot swells that heralded the arrival of Hurricane Luis. Charlie Arneson was on scuba duty, swimming out from the Zodiac to make adjustments. The Russians refused to put a man in open water with a submersible after a crewman had died in 1989 on a night dive. He had been trying to fix something on the sub and descended too far, kicking off at 250 feet. Charlie would be the guy in the water. Cameron would phone ahead on the UQC and tell him what the problem was. As Arneson swam up Cameron would talk to him with hand signals through the viewport. The two had spent hundreds of hours underwater together and didn't need words.

Once on deck, Cameron beamed outwardly, exuding the victory of having been to *Titanic.* Inwardly, he was seething. "I actually had this illusion that the Russians knew the wreck, that when you came to it you could see it, which you couldn't. And that driving the submersibles would be a logical, intelligent thing. And it wasn't, in any way. It was a complete and utter circus. It was like flailing at a piñata." Cruising *Titanic* in the *Mirs* was a disorienting experience; an eighteen-ton vehicle the size of a UPS truck sliding over the belly of a leviathan three-fifths the size of a football field. Your natural field of vision was restricted to three tiny portholes, all facing ahead. You couldn't look left or right, just variations of forward. One wrong turn, and you could lose the ship for two hours.

Cameron had briefly discussed the matter with Sagalevitch in the sauna but found himself skirting some of the real issues. Later, he huddled with Giddings and White, sharing his frustration with the T–1 dive. White, who had been to the *Titanic* seventeen times, reassured him that some of his problems were circumstantial. Scientists onboard were investigating the extreme turbidity—1,000 times normal, with a .7 knot bottom current. The conditions were seen as the result of an unusually active Gulf Stream, the whooshing loop of water coursing from the Florida straits to the Grand Banks. The fastest, most energetic current in the North Atlantic gyre, it typically did not reach below 3,000 feet. This seemed to be an exception, triggered by an unusually active hurricane season. The filmmakers had not factored the current in their shot plans. Cameron decided to augment his existing shot list with an alternate plan for poor conditions. Meteorologist Valeria Kozlovitch (whom Cameron dubbed "the Weather Witch" for her uncannily accurate forecasts) was able to offer opinions as to bottom conditions, but it was impossible to predict with any certainty from the surface. He'd just have to take his chances.

There was one problem that did not rest on chance. Both Giddings and White urged Cameron to get Sagalevitch out from behind the steering wheel, suggesting that Gena pilot the camera sub. Sagalevitch, they agreed, was brilliant in his way, a steely amalgamation of scientific and business acumen, but a weekend sub jockey. Still, Cameron knew that this Hollywood movie was important to Sagalevitch. Pride was still a big deal among Russian men, and the hotshot American director trying to unseat the *Keldysh*'s top man would mean nothing short of public humiliation. Cameron was famous for amassing body counts in his relentless pursuit of perfection, but this was a line even he did not care to cross. Anyway, he didn't even know if he could fire Sagalevitch. After all, it was the Russian's ship.

Cameron mulled his dilemma over in his dive diary, writing:

> I can't figure out a way to confront my friend of three years with the idea that he shouldn't pilot his own sub. I will try every other possibility before I ask him to step aside. The lack of visibility and our inability to position the subs and execute even the simplest maneuvers at the wreck have led me to believe that this whole project is a fool's errand and we are wasting our time and money. I'm angry also that Anatoly keeps swapping the crew around, presumably to give all his guys some dive time and keep them current, but at the expense of my project. I spent half the first dive teaching Andrey how to move the long arm lighting boom in conjunction with my camera, and now Anatoly has put a second engineer in his place for the second dive. This makes no sense.

Sagalevitch, who ran the daily Sub Group meetings, rather mildly assessed their "difficulties" during the morning assembly. For Cameron, things had already reached crisis proportions. He pulled the Russian aside afterward and had a frank discussion. "I told Anatoly I want a constant crew. He agreed. I also said I want Giddings in the other sub to help coordinate the lighting, since I know Al will have the balls to take over the UQC, and the balance of power will shift from the Russian to English language between the two subs." A crew list had already been published, and while Sagalevitch refused to issue a new one—a face-saving effort—he assured Cameron the changes would be made.

Dive two was scheduled for 8:30 A.M. the next day. Cameron, Sagalevitch, and Andrey Andreev would be in *Mir 1* and Gena Chernjaev, Jeff Ledda, and Al Giddings in *Mir 2*. Things were improving. Cameron was still stuck with Anatoly's piloting, but decided not to press further on that issue. After all, "Nobody had to know, back on the ship, what happened down in the sub. As long as we came back alive and got the shots." (In fact, Cameron's rages at Sagalevitch would wend their way out of the radio room and through the ranks, where they were recounted with incredulity and amusement.)

Because he was the more skilled pilot, it might actually be more practical to have Gena in *Mir 2*, which he'd be instructing remotely, without the advantage of the gestures and hand signals he relied on with the Russians. Dealing with people in a technical environment, there was a kind of interlanguage that worked when you were working face to face. The UQC was harder. Gena's comprehension of what Cameron wanted was only as good as Anatoly's understanding of what the director had said. Getting the subs into position, beginning the photographic run, the cueing of the other sub to action—it was all a big mess. "I couldn't even get them to turn on their lights," he lamented. Cameron wanted to be able to direct the *Mirs* in the same way he would helicopters, boats, or cars doing an action sequence. With more than a hint of irony he realized, "This was so outside of their realm. These were scientists, and these are scientific vehicles, and I'm trying to treat them like insert cars. But I actually believed we could do it, and we could do it safely."

That night, both dive's worth of film was offloaded onto a sixty-foot fishing boat, the *Michael Mariner*—two rolls from *Mir 1* and three shot topside by the second unit crew. The tiny craft immediately set out in some very rough seas for the thirty-six-hour sail back to St. John. Though John Bruno was supposed to accompany the film to the lab in Toronto, Arneson, White and others urged him not to risk the ride with Luis lurking. He'd be much safer sitting out a hurricane on the sizable *Keldysh*. Bruno stayed put.

A dive briefing at the model was held at 8:00 P.M. Cameron decided he would need to put even more emphasis on planning and previsualization. Abernathy made an overlay of *Titanic* and drew "Arthur Murray dance steps," suggesting them as a visual aid, an idea the director embraced. Cameron also decided to rehearse the pilots by actually having them hold their subs and move them around the model at his direction. "I figured if I couldn't get them to move the models properly, I sure wasn't going to be able to get them to move the subs on the bottom of the ocean."

On September 10 *Mir 1* launched at 8:30 A.M. Cameron was guardedly optimistic, flexing his newfound navigational muscle. During descent, he saw by their plot on the Navac that *Mir 1* was being blown southeast by a hellacious current. They were more than a mile off course by the time they'd fallen 7,000 feet. "I urged Anatoly to make a mid-course correction and we began motoring laterally through the water column. He waited too long to pump us light, and when we saw the bottom he had to use a long sustained burst from the side thrusters to break the fall." They soft-landed in a blinding brown cloud of silt. As it cleared, Cameron saw an incredible sight ten feet ahead: a mound of clay that looked freshly piled by a big bulldozer, the impact point of the bow just below the anchor. On his first try at guiding *Mir 1* down, Cameron practically landed them on the ship, missing it by about thirty feet, which spooked the Russians big time. A hard landing on *Titanic* would be disastrous. Getting wedged into one of the many crevices could potentially make them a permanent part of the wreck. The *Keldysh* was equipped with a 30,000-foot tow line for just such situations, but it was one of those things no one wanted to try. Beginning with dive three, they would land away from the ship, find it on the Mezotech, and drive toward it. They pumped light and lifted off the bottom to explore.

When *Mir 2* showed up, it looked so good hovering over the bow, "like the UFO from *Close Encounters,*" that Cameron shot it before it even got into position. He moved on to a close-up beauty shot of the bow. Anatoly had trouble getting positioned to do a transverse pass but finally got it. Andrey was getting more comfortable with the long-arm light. The Mezotech was at last correctly calibrated, showing a fantastic image of the wreck. It would become their most important tool in positioning the subs. Communications with *Mir 2* were vastly improved with Giddings aboard. Maybe they weren't sunk after all.

Then they were drifting backwards, over the boat deck. Cameron peered out the viewport and saw the forward expansion joint, a large crack that spanned the width of the ship. "I tell Anatoly to take evasive action before we run into the number one boat davit which I know we are about to hit. He rises to clear it and I realize I'm in the ironic position of being the onboard expert on the wreck, based solely on my memorization of the model. The model is so accurate that I'm able to identify our location at any given moment, even when I'm seeing part of it for the very first time. With extensive research and elaborate simulation techniques using models, smoke and fiber optics, I feel like I'm in a familiar place, even though I had never seen any of this before." Dive time was so precious Cameron would often make the split-second decision to shoot the rehearsal move, putting him in the unusual position of shooting film the first time he laid eyes on something—the realm of the documentarian, not the feature filmmaker. The tasks at hand required a concentration that left little room for emotion, though he occasionally allowed himself to consider the drama that played out on these rusting decks eighty-three years earlier.

At 3:30 P.M. they ran out of film and within seconds got word from the *Keldysh* that Luis was arriving ahead of schedule. Ascent would begin immediately. *Mir 1* pumped ballast and shot to the surface like a rocket, bobbing for more than an hour during a tumultuous recovery. With *Mir 2* up, they lit out over twenty-five-foot swells, the wind howling around the ship's superstructure. The storm was upon them and it was time to run. The ship's captain was heading eighty miles southeast toward a high pressure system that promised shelter. Hurricanes like to travel in what's called tropical lows.

The evacuation seemed to set the group off whirling on their own tangents. Cameron, still queasy from being spin-cycled in the *Mir*, decided to pack it in early. After a vodka and sauna with his Russian dive mates, he retired to his room while the others prepared to party into the night. The first few dives had drained him physically and mentally. There was so much to coordinate. He was on, full throttle, around the clock, from the dive planning meetings to the time he stepped into the sub to the moment they ran out of power and surfaced. That night, for the first time, he permitted himself the luxury of contemplation. "I just sat there, and I just started to cry, thinking about the dive and everything I'd seen and experienced. That's the moment my technical guard got let down and I got kind of overwhelmed by it. Then I made myself a promise to always take the time on every dive to be there emotionally. Because otherwise I might as well have been sitting up on the ship driving an ROV. There was no reason for me to be physically down there if I wasn't going to appreciate it."

From that point on, Cameron insisted they land the submersibles on the boat deck to have lunch rather than their usual practice of parking it on the black bottom somewhere. "We'd have some tea and stare out the portholes and think about the all events that had happened. I had already written the scriptment, so I already knew who did what to who and what happened where and what boats were where, what dramas had played out exactly where we were sitting.

"At that point, I realized I was approaching it wrong, and that the important thing, maybe even more important than getting the footage, was capturing the emotional significance of the ship and what happened to it, and what happened to the people on it." In a curious example of life imitating art, Cameron found himself going through the same emotional cycle as Brock, the fortune-hunting character he created for the film. "He goes from being technical and goal-oriented to letting the tragedy actually soak into him. My experience allowed me to really put that spin on his character when I turned the scriptment into a shooting script."

As Cameron soul-searched, his crewmates were equally, if less deeply, diverted. Art cups had become the hot collectible item, and John Bruno had an assembly line going in his room. Lewis Abernathy, riding high on the fact that the storm was named after him, was hosting a "Rock 'n roll, puke-till-you-drop, vodka and Dramamine party." Tentatively, the Americans were reaching across the cultural chasm to explore the Russians' customs.

There were several stills onboard, some of them quite ingenious. The laser scientists made their own cocktails by putting coffee and fruit extract into the 95 percent ethanol usually used for cooling and cleaning their light ware. Occasionally the Americans got embarrassingly drunk. Steve Quale was tucked into bed one night, and his line of questioning the next day ran, "I drank what? Laser coolant! What do you mean?" Abernathy imbibed something he knew was made from hydraulic fluid. "I'm lucky that I didn't go blind on that boat. They'd drink the alcohol right out of the compass," says the Texan, noting the port side needle was inoperative. "Not that they needed it, because we had the GPS and all that electronic stuff."

Since *Titanic* was a tragedy famous the world over, it was a topic they could all talk about, bridging the conversational waters. Only a handful of the Russians knew any English, the Americans no Russian, so most exchanges transpired through interpreter or a casual flutter of hands. Abernathy made it his personal mission to bridge the social gap. His first big accomplishment was Science Day. "I went around to all the different science departments and said what the hell do you do here? They love to talk about themselves and what they're doing." What he found was the Russians have the largest scientific fleet in the world, and the *Keldysh* is the undisputed flagship of their fleet. Since the breakup of the Soviet Union in 1994 the fleet had essentially been in mothballs in Kaliningrad, so Cameron's month-long *Titanic* project was a boon. Still, a bit of the Shirshov hauteur had trickled down to the working men. Many of the scientific crew were less than enthusiastic about renting out their premiere research vessel to an American film company. In a way, Abernathy could see their point. "Invite a film crew into your home some day. As nice as they are, they're going to trash the place. The same thing with the *Keldysh*."

Which, by the way, got a little trashed that night as a result of Abernathy's bash. Some very drunk Americans actually started the sub crane, prompting the Captain to reprimand them over the loudspeaker system, practically causing an international incident. As Luis blew past, they headed back to the prime site, which they reached in time for their midnight rendezvous with the *Ocean Mariner,* which was hauling off the T-2 film.

Cameron still hadn't seen any dailies from the wreck. The first batch was due in by plane that day, September 12. He was a bit uneasy, ready to write off his initial dives from a photographic standpoint, still figuring out what to do and how to do it. They were basically diving every other day. The next trip down was scheduled for the next day, September 13, at 4 A.M., when the turbidity was expected to ebb. They continued to tinker with the ROV, which was still not playing out its tether properly. The lighting configurations on the subs were undergoing adjustment.

By 3 P.M. the crew was readying for the airdrop. Conditions couldn't have been better—sunny skies, glassy seas. The delivery was definitely an "event" by sea standards. Giddings' documentary unit was in the radio room, taping Ralph White as he made voice contact with the pilot, who responded to the query with, "*Titanic* research vessel," prompting White to exclaim, "There goes our cover!" He instructed him to drop the supplies—film, food, spare parts—in three passes and requested an additional "beauty pass" for the cameras. Then they headed out to the deck to await the approaching craft. The *Keldysh* crew hurried to prepare the Zodiac as the captain turned the ship into the wind, providing a sightline for the plane. Word had begun circulating about the drop, and people congregated to see the show. John Bruno recorded the event in his diary:

> The plane hasn't shown up on the radar. Jim spots it. Great radar. The plane makes a slow pass over the ship. It's a Catalina flying boat, World War II variety. Lonya gets the Zodiac into position and Ralph orders the first air drop, asking the pilot to try and hit the Zodiac. The first drop misses it by 150 feet; the second pass by 15 feet. After the third drop, Ralph gives the pilot permission to buzz the *Keldysh* using his own discretion as to altitude. Lining up on the bow, the Catalina passes below us on the star-

board side, brushing the paint. Wagging its wings, the big bird heads back to Halifax. A most excellent exhibition.

There were numerous special requests made of White as supply officer: Snickers bars for the technical team and cigarettes for Abernathy, but all James Cameron wanted was his film. He was viewing dailies by 5:30. The pan-tilt system had the shakes and would have to be adjusted. At f-2, the film looked slightly overexposed. Stopping down to f-4 would give him greater depth of field, compensating a bit, perhaps, for the poor visibility, only about twenty-five feet. Previous expeditions enjoyed visibility of sixty to one hundred feet. Cameron had a theory that the unprecedented string of summer hurricanes that pummeled the eastern seaboard kicked up muck that was being pumped into the North Atlantic by the Gulf Stream. If he was right, he probably wouldn't be getting any great visibility days this outing, a painful prospect, since his intent was to show the *Titanic* in panoramic shots unlike anything that had been seen before. The shot design, selection of camera, lighting, and film were all in service of that objective. He decided then and there to retrench to a more realistic goal of creating closer coverage of the *Mir* subs in proximity to the recognizable sections of the wreck. He would later use those to leverage his wider angles as model shots. It had been worth the trouble and effort to get the dailies flown out. Without them, the whole mission could have been a write-off.

Chapter Six

Chaos is the law of nature. Order the dream of man.
—Henry B. Adams

GIVEN CAMERON'S scaled back expectations, T-3 and T-4 were "textbook operations." The biggest anomaly was a communications breakdown that occurred when ComSAT turned off phone service to the *Keldysh* for nonpayment of their bill by the Shirshov Institute. A film production unit cannot function without a telephone. White and Moore swung into action, embarking on a seat-of-their-pants effort to pirate the airwaves. "When they shut you down, they did it in sequence, so if you were really clever you could stay one jump ahead of them," says Moore. They dug up an old satellite directory and kept dialing, finally managing to contact Sanchini, who took care of the problem by fronting ComSAT $1,000 against Cameron's American Express account.

By T-5 on September 17, life on the *Keldysh* had settled into a comfortable pattern. The dives themselves were beginning to seem routine, the three-hour drop to the bottom just another commute, "like taking the subway to work." The ROV was running properly and they were getting some interesting shots. In one particularly dramatic sequence Cameron, in the camera ship, hovered over *Mir 2,* which had landed on top of the grand staircase, deploying Snoop down to B-deck and inside the ship—what in wreck-diving is called a "penetration dive." In subsequent shots, Snoop slunk all the way to D-deck, four stories down. Though it hadn't been intended as an image procurement device, all ROVs are equipped with video cameras. It's what the pilots use to "fly" them. By chance the ROV caught some interesting images. That night Cameron held an impromptu screening of the tape. "It was spooky," recalled John Bruno. "We realized it had been eighty-three years since anyone had looked down these corridors." An old leather suitcase strewn here, a chair there, a little bit of wood cladding, a column that looked almost intact. "At first you're seeing things you don't understand, can't account for," said Cameron. "Then you start developing theories."

Previous *Titanic* explorers had assumed *Titanic's* wood finishing had deteriorated. Cameron not only discovered that wood still existed, but noted that most of what was left appeared to have been painted white. He said, "Though most of the paint had flaked off, you could see hints of it down in the cracks of the hand-carved patterns on the oak columns and the wall paneling. So they probably used a lead-based white paint in those days that was an inhibitor to the wood-boring mollusks that ate the other wood. When the ship initially landed on the bottom, any organism that could be supported by eating the wood suddenly went into what in biology they would call a bloom. These organisms swept through the ship and ate everything they could. Anything that they missed on their first pass, because it was unfriendly, like some of these painted surfaces, they probably just ignored. Then the bloom died off because the wood was eaten, and then the organisms died off. And when the paint finally flaked off, there were never enough of the wood-boring mollusks around to get a toehold again. That's my personal theory, as a non-scientist who had one year of college marine biology."

Other shadowy images loomed seductively just outside the range of the lights. Cameron was intrigued. He wanted to go further. Tactically he knew it didn't make much sense to take his $400,000 robot and send it deep inside *Titanic* where it might get stuck, never to be seen again. He'd need Snoop later, back in the States, for tank work involving re-creations of the sunken staterooms. "But my curiosity overcame my better sense. I promised myself I would take the ROV back in to explore later, even if I had to pay for an extra dive with my own money."

Dive six was to have been John Bruno's first trip to *Titanic*. Since there was a good chance he'd be supervising the special effects on the film, Cameron wanted him to see the wreck first-hand as a visual assist in creating accurate models. As the only nonessential teammate invited down, Bruno was in an enviable position. This despite repeated entreaties by Abernathy, who was refused on the grounds that this was not a pleasure cruise. He sulked, but seats were at a premium. Bruno was invited to take ROV pilot Jeff Ledda's seat, joining Giddings and Chernjaev in *Mir 2.* The dive was aborted minutes before *Mir 2* reached the bottom due to a total failure of the hydraulic propulsion steering on *Mir 1.* Bruno's first brush with *Titanic* was a fleeting glimpse on the Mezotech. The subs were pulled out of the water in rough seas as a second hurricane, Marilyn, made its way through the Grand Banks.

September 19 was a rainy, cold day with waves rocking at 6 on the Beaufort Scale, the standard unit for measuring the sea state, and twenty-five to thirty miles per hour winds. Whitecaps were everywhere. The subs began diving at 10:30 A.M., with Bruno getting his second chance in *Mir 2.* The *Michael Mariner,* which was off-loading dailies, refused to wait out the dive to transport the day's film, turning back immediately to beat the storm. *Mir 1* was recovered at 8:30 P.M., a relatively short dive due to thruster problems. Upon exiting the sub, Cameron made it clear that he'd be canceling the remaining dives and heading back to shore if the problem was not resolved immediately. Sagalevitch made the mistake of scolding him in front of the crew. "Now, now. There'll be no more nervous dives," said the Russian.

That irked the tempestuous auteur even more. "I'm not nervous!" he thundered, waves crashing for emphasis. "I'm pissed off!"

There were originally to be eight *Titanic* dives. The aborted dive six allowed Cameron to negotiate that number up to ten. The hydraulic problem was fixed for the next excursion. Dives eight and nine went off without a hitch. The weather cleared up enough for another airdrop, this time by a Canadian water bomber, the kind used to put out fires—three days' worth of dailies and two boxes of donuts labeled "Al Giddings," a joke by Ralph. They screened the film immediately and Cameron was pleased to see Snoop descending the staircase and the *Mirs* motoring around the bow and alongside B-deck. If he didn't get another shot, the trip would have been worthwhile. Giddings passed around the donuts, which were gone in thirty seconds.

On September 24, there was an eerie look to the ocean—glassy under an ethereal haze and by far the calmest they'd seen it during the entire trip. The T-10 launch was set to begin at 8 A.M. This time, Giddings joined Cameron and Sagalevitch in *Mir 1* to document the director at work undersea. The lensman brought lights and enough equipment to fill half the sphere. Since Cameron's camera system controls and electronics took up the other half, it was a very cramped dive. Still, spirits were high.

About one thousand feet from the bottom they noticed something amiss. The Mezotech was going crazy, imaging the ship as if they were turning, which they were not. Sagalevitch said that the turbidity was very bad. When they hit bottom, visibility was the worst it had been. There was a strong current coming from the southeast that blew against the starboard side of the ship, the location of all the day's shots. Everything they rehearsed was out the window with the possible exception of Snoop entering the number two hatch. The ship's superstructure might have been shielding the well deck, where the hatch was located. Optimistically, Cameron hoped the "bad viz" was just a scatter layer close to the bottom, and would be clearer seventy-five feet up on the ship.

They decided to wait until *Mir 2* touched down before making a move, and held position a few hundred yards away from the wreck. When the second sub arrived, Cameron instructed them to get into position and report on visibility conditions. Let the better pilot scout the scene. Cameron's dive diary contains a detailed account of what happened next.

> While they're gone, the current continues to increase until it is a virtual gale. The white coral stocks are lying straight out from their rocks, and the legs on all the little albino brittle stars are blowing downwind like streamers. *Mir 2* reports that they are in the lee of the superstructure, and that the situation is manageable on the well deck. Anatoly pumps us heavy but we're still drifting and we go bumping off across the bottom until we fetch up against a steel drop-weight left by *Alvin* in 1985. Thank you, Bob. Fighting against the current, we continue to work our way toward the ship. Small sponges run across the bottom like tumbleweeds, and as the current goes even stronger I am reminded of a sandstorm in the desert. We observe that the *Mir* tracks of a few days ago are being rounded off, blurred, and filled in by the current. I remember that on my first dive I could see footprints from the previous *Mir* expedition four years ago as clearly as if they were made yesterday. Also visible were the distinctive impressions left by the other submersibles: *Alvin*, identifiable by a single skid, *Nautile* by the flat battery compartment that also serves as a skid. This bottom

> current is obviously a condition unprecedented in several years.

They decided to creep along the port side of the ship, assuming the hull itself would provide shelter lee to the current. Within seconds they were in trouble. A vortex caused by the current flowing over and around the ship sucked them toward the port hull, which they slammed against, held there by the vortex. They rose above the rail of the forecastle deck and were blown over and away from the wreck.

> We fight our way back using the excellent imaging of the Mezotech sonar and painstakingly work our way up the forecastle deck toward the bridge, keeping the nose of the sub into the current and crabbing along on the back and forth movements of the stern thruster. It takes us fifteen minutes of hard work to go the one hundred feet to the well deck, and we arrive next to the fallen foremast. I get a brief glimpse of *Mir 2* hunkered down at the hatch on the starboard side of the deck and see cables draped menacingly from the bridge to the narrower port side of the well deck below us. Suddenly we are broadsided by turbulence and swept off the wreck in such a way that we lose all visual and sonar reference.

They were tumbling in the void.

Losing track of the ship was a phenomenon that was surprisingly common even under favorable conditions. It was safer to move in the direction you knew the ship was not, turn around, reacquire it on the sonar and reapproach rather than to drift in random search. *Titanic* was a dangerous mass of tangled wire and jagged metal. Like any true beauty, her charm drew you in despite the obvious fact that familiarity could have wounding consequences.

Possibly even lethal. The Russians nicknamed the camera system "the cannon" because they knew that if the glass failed, the titanium shell was a piece of heavy artillery aimed right at the heart of their submarine. The nine-and-a-half-inch-diameter span of silica supported 1.1 million pounds of pressure. The merest wisp of a fracture would send an explosion of water traveling down the length of that two-foot titanium cylinder at hypersonic speed—several times the speed of sound—almost certainly penetrating the *Mir.*

Mike had warned Jim many times, "When you're maneuvering and you don't need to be filming, always keep the camera positioned transversely, so if the end-cap blows off, it just blows away into the water." Mike believed the concussion of the failing housing would not be sufficient to set off a sympathetic implosion of the *Mir.* You'd actually have to hit the sub with something. "But in practice the thing was almost always aimed away from the sub, pointing at something, which means that the back of it was pointed at us. It was like walking around with a shotgun taped to your temple for about sixteen hours, and just telling people, 'Don't touch the trigger! Don't touch the gun!'"

Cameron held the controls, so it was always his responsibility to keep it aimed properly. As they reapproached the ship, he called out the range on the sonar.

> I was saying to Anatoly you'd better start slowing down, we're going to be able to see it really soon. We were down to like six meters or something like that. And I heard him do the reverse thrust, yet we kept heading toward the hull. I could hear it clearly on the sonar, but we couldn't see it visually, and I thought there was something wrong with the sonar, or maybe he didn't understand, so I told him again, "Slow down! We are heading right for the ship!" And at the last second I looked out my portal and saw that the camera was aimed straight forward.
>
> Of course the one thing that we were never supposed to do was slam the glass housing dome into the *Titanic.* And at exactly the moment I looked forward on the video monitor of the camera I saw a wall of rivets appear out of the darkness. We were literally about to slam right into it.

The camera was set up with a gain control on the pan-and-tilt wheels. It turned fastest on the high gain setting, but if you happened to turn the wheel a little too fast, it would stall, immobilizing the camera. "The trick was, if you wanted the camera to slew rapidly, you'd set it on the high gain setting and turn the wheel very slowly." Cameron didn't know what gain setting he was on and he didn't have time to check.

> I grab the wheel and just started turning, trying to move

> the camera—and nothing happens! It's freewheeling in my hand. The wall is coming straight at us. I stop, wait a quarter of a beat for the encoder to settle down, and turn the wheel very, very slowly. It is probably about the hardest thing I've ever done. And the camera starts to turn away.
>
> There is a crunching noise and we are thrown forward. Through the right port I see the entire pan tilt assembly wobble and disappear in a cloud of dust. I tense for the thunder crack of an implosion of the housing. It has been repeatedly pointed out to me that the implodable volume of the housing is so large that the shock wave from it failing catastrophically could be enough to fail the mansphere of the sub: Lights out in 2/10,000ths of a second. There is no loud bang.

The housing was at a 45-degree angle when it struck. The majority of the impact was absorbed by a polycarbonate matte box shielding the dome port. The remainder was soaked up by Sagalevitch, whose unfortunate proximity made him a target for Cameron's wrath. Unaware of the current, the director thought his pilot had simply driven them into the ship—a not implausible conclusion based on the Russian's track record.

Meanwhile, *Mir 2* had been nestling in the relative calm of the well deck, the only place on the ship where there was not a lot of turbulence. Also known as the shelter deck, it was where passengers in third class, which lacked an enclosed promenade, had been able to take the air in immoderate weather. Once in position, Chernjaev used the manipulator arm to grab a cable and hold position on the number two cargo hatch.

Cameron immediately aborted the dive and demanded a return to the surface. Sagalevitch, incredibly, wanted to try again despite three failures and obviously hazardous conditions, but the director insisted. They informed *Mir 2* that the dive was over and instructed them to head for the top. Just then, Sagalevitch noticed the sub was dangerously low on power. The intense thrust required to vector through the heavy currents had drained their batteries. When Sagalevitch tried to turn on the ballast pump to take them light for the ascent, the inverter failed to kick in. They experienced a complete stall-out at 12,640 feet below sea level. "We were stuck there, and we had already sent *Mir 2* back. We were on our own."

Though theoretically they still had audio contact with the *Keldysh,* the first thing they did when they realized they were low on power was to shut everything off—the camera, sonar, and lights, along with the UQC. There was really nothing anyone could do anyway. "So we're sitting there in the dark on the bottom, and I'm thinking, all right, no problem, we have drop weights. We can get out of this." The drop weights, a cache of nickel pellets, were the subs' last line of defense. In the event of a complete loss of power, they would be automatically released as a result of the break in the electromagnetic charge that held them sealed. Though virtually nothing, including wood, floated under 6,000 PSI of pressure, one thing that did was syntactic foam, which is what the *Mirs* were made of. Freed of the drop weights, they'd eventually make their way to the surface. The *Mirs* were designed to be fail safe, and they were designed well. Optimism prevailed.

They finally got the inverter to come on a little bit to pump some ballast, but not enough. They'd unstick from the bottom, rise about a hundred feet and sink back down. "Now I was starting to get nervous because I thought well maybe there's a pinhole leak in the ballast system—we're pumping out and it's coming back in. We had just hit the ship, so to infer that there might be a technical problem with the *Mir* was not unreasonable." They waited a half hour, hoping the batteries would rebound, and sputtered out another couple of kilos only to repeat the previous pattern—up, then down. "I thought we were really screwed." By the third try, they had bounced some distance from the ship. Coaxing a few more feeble cycles from the pump, they started to rise and this time kept going. But it was at such a slow rate that based on Cameron's calculations from the first fifteen minutes, it would take six or seven hours to reach surface. He was not happy. At last word, the surface was blanketed with fog. Since their Navac went out with the power, they would be rising miles from the ship in a low-power emergency condition with visual sighting impossible. Not a comforting picture. They huddled in the dark listening to the periodic moans from the hydraulic pump. Cameron wrote:

> I wonder why Anatoly doesn't drop the nickel shot emergency ballast to speed us up, and conclude that it is either expensive and he doesn't want to incur the cost or it is a macho sub pilot thing, an admission of failure to come back on the ship with no power and the drop shot used

> up. Finally he mildly asks Al and I if we'd like to go faster. Is this a trick question? We are already freezing, having hardly used the HMI lights whose ballasts give off heat and keep the sub warm during the working phase of the dive. We say go for it and Anatoly mutters something about testing the system, the excuse he needs. He drops a miserly 50 kilos of nickel shot from each emergency ballast system—100 kilos positive, the sub accelerates to 18 meters per second of rise. The ascent will take just under four hours. I get comfortable.

There's nothing else to do for a while. They eat lunch, going light on the food since it will probably be a long recovery. Bobbing around lost in the Atlantic, they are likely to see any items consumed now a second time. They surface finally and the recovery remarkably takes only a few extra minutes, despite the fog and the fact that the *Mir* has drifted a mile and a half from the *Keldysh.* Cameron attributes this to the skillful navigation team aboard the ship, whom they have done nothing to assist. Mercifully, no one throws up this time. Jerked from the water with unexpected violence by the crane, Giddings and his equipment wind up on top of Cameron and Sagalevitch. By 10 P.M. they're on deck telling of their adventure. Cameron looks in amazement at the tough polycarbonate camera matte box, which has been crushed and split by the impact with *Titanic*'s hull. It still has rust from the wreck ground into its surface. A collector's item.

By now, the director's sharp rejoinders to Sagalevitch at the height of the crisis have made their way around the ship. Typically, those who didn't know Cameron well were ready to draw conclusions about his character from such outbursts, but the incident revealed less of his true nature than did the fact he spent the evening drawing flow charts, determined to get to the bottom of the meteorological phenomena that rocked his world. "At the time, we didn't know what was happening," he explains. His calculations revealed in excess of a knot current, four or five times greater than anything they had previously experienced. Water was wrapping over the top of the ship with such force that it caused a huge, cylindrical vortex on the lee side, catching the submersible and actually throwing it forward into the ship. It was only when they had bounced sufficiently far from the wreck that they were able to break the cycle. "Though I'd never heard the term before, I called it a bottom storm," he said, gleeful at coining this new scientific phrase. "It was just picking stuff up and blowing it around the bottom of the ocean."

The next morning Cameron was in Sagalevitch's office, demanding a make-good for T-10. Their last scheduled dive, it had been a complete write-off from a photographic standpoint. The Russian, anxious to bring this adventure to a close, agreed to one more trip. Cameron insisted on two. The cost of a couple of extra dives was trivial compared with the overall cost of the expedition. Sagalevitch demurred, said they'd see. After twenty days at sea, nerves were beginning to fray. Weariness had soaked in, displacing excitement. Ten double dives to *Titanic*—twenty trips in seventeen days—was unprecedented in the exploration of this particular wreck. The million little details it took to support such a mission and the intensity of operating at a level at which human lives hung in the balance had drained the collective spirit of the crew.

Even the ever-cheerful Bruno was beginning to fray at the edges. "Here we are, a bunch of Hollywood assholes driving around the *Titanic* like it's a theme park attraction, bumping into things and generally ogling at the scope and scale of this disaster, creating our own reality of the events. We're voyeurs, staring at the hulk of this great ship as though it was a creature in a zoo under our control. The *Mirs* have made all this as easy as a Sunday drive in the park. But we must remember *Titanic* is a dangerous wreck in a dangerous location. I think she's wearying of our antics."

Cameron was tired too, but the exigencies of physical comfort didn't factor much in his view of the universe. He was satisfied he had some great footage, but frustrated that just when they had gotten good at choreographing their strange bathyspheric ballet, time and the elements were conspiring to shut him down. Instinctively, he felt he had to push it a little further. He was close to something extraordinary. He could feel it, hovering on the periphery. He wasn't going to quit now.

The big question was what to do if bottom conditions were still miserable. He decided to make the ROV dive in *Mir 2*. If turbidity was a problem he could still deploy Snoop in the shelter of the ship. He would put Giddings in the camera sub, and if visibility allowed, he would talk him through some shots from *Mir 2*. Either way, he stood a chance of being in the wrong sub, but there was no way around that.

Cameron was on deck watching when *Mir 1* made waves at 2:00 P.M., witnessing his first sub launch of the expedition. "It is a beautiful sight to see *Mir 1* towed away to the gray limbo of the North Atlantic fog with Lonya—the Lonya Ranger—heroically astride. It seems somehow at once fragile and tiny and plucky and capable. The Russian boat crews and deck crews are so good, so dialed in, the whole thing seems somehow less crazy and marginal for having seen this part of the operation."

Mir 2 went down at 2:45 P.M. Things got crazy and marginal shortly thereafter. The ROV got tangled immediately upon entering B-deck. "Jim and I talked several times and he was sweating," Giddings recalls of the event. "He said, 'Al, we're really screwed up here. This thing's been hung up for a couple of hours.'" With one skid hooked through a pipe, the sub was perched on the edge of the cavity that was once the Grand Staircase. Tugging to reel in Snoop, they were straining an already precarious relationship with gravity, staring sixty feet straight down.

Giddings remembers the occasion clearly. *Mir 1,* which had been hovering in the background, sidled up to offer help. "We started to fly forward and Gena, who was piloting *Mir 2,* said very quickly to Anatoly in Russian, 'You're moving us! Please be careful! You're touching us!' Propellers spinning and all. Anatoly right away backed off, tried a different angle, and got hung up on a cable. That's your greatest fear—white-knuckle stuff." Like a dog leaping at the leash, Sagalevitch powered up, snapping free. He drifted back down, landing nearby on the officer's deck.

"Al, this is Jim. Do you copy?"

"Roger. Copy. Go."

"Are you guys missing anything?"

Giddings answered not that he was aware of.

"Al, the goddam six-foot shroud that covers the main propeller is lying on the deck!"

His steering effectively disabled by the loss of the shroud, Sagalevitch moved off to land on the sea floor and wait out the crisis. Eventually Jeff Ledda managed to rethread the robot back out, and the dive was aborted nine hours after they hit water. As dicey as things had been, Giddings had to laugh to himself on the way up. The scenario of the sub hanging over that pit was strangely reminiscent of *The Abyss,* where Coffey, the good soldier gone bad, sends his submersible tobogganing into oblivion. Six years later Cameron was still a no-fear guy who kept his cool when the going got tough. It would've been easy to cut the cable and run. He was level enough to make jokes at the height of the crisis. Giddings had made many dives in many submersibles, working Woods Hole, Harbor Branch, Johnson Sea Link. It was his living. "The things Jim got through, most people wouldn't have the intestinal fortitude to handle. Not only was he handling it, he was thinking on his feet, directing a film." Before leaving the bottom, Cameron had exacted from Sagalevitch the promise of one more dive.

The Russians worked all night to repair the ailing Snoop. A piece of wood, three by ten inches, was yanked from the port thruster like a bad tooth. Cameron claimed it—a $25,000 piece of wood. That's how much the dive cost. By morning, they had screens on the thrusters, both intake and exhaust. The little videocam was remounted in lower profile and the tether had been extended to ninety-eight feet. Snoop was designed first and foremost to look spiff: eye-like headlamps, a camera that swiveled 180-degrees. It was a happy accident that it happened to be functional enough for a full-blown mission. Cameron meant it to look "big and industrial and kind of butch" so it could recover a safe at the service of his story. In his mind's eye he was already fashioning the ultimate photographic ROV: light and nimble, slim enough to squeeze through tight spaces.

Launch was set for 7:00 P.M., the quickest they could possibly recycle the *Mirs*. The Sub Group meeting began at 2 P.M. Cameron declared that this would indeed be the last dive, brightening the spirits of the crew considerably. "We're down to our last tail shroud," he said with a laugh. "It's enough. *Titanic* would like us to leave." He was going with the shot list from yesterday's dive. They decamped to the conference room to review yesterday's video. The image was snowy. Not as good as last time. Cameron demanded it be repaired immediately. He summoned Millard and Ledda to the room. He was starting to get into one of those moods. At some point it became apparent Ledda had taped over a quantity of footage. This really set Cameron off. On this dive, he would be the only one handling the video recorder. Cameron inquired about the damage to Snoop's tether. Millard said he had checked only four feet. That was it. Bruno left the room, not wanting to see "Jim go postal." After Cameron finished sharing his views on the subject, the bearded, burly engineer thought he'd been through a paper shredder. Asking nicely only got you so far.

When Cameron loaded into *Mir 2* several hours later, everything was in good working order. His new plan was to combine film photography with some of the better ROV exploration footage. He was possessed by the idea that if he went in deep enough, he would find remains of the past opulence and make an emotional connection with the *Titanic* he planned on bringing to the screen. So far, they'd only seen the ship from the outside. Even their existing ROV footage was really just exposed interior around the stairs. He'd gotten to know this wreck pretty well, but she was still holding back. What secrets lay within?

They alighted at hatch number two. The first mission was to snake the ROV down to G-deck to photograph William E. Carter's 35-horsepower Renault. Cameron had written the red touring car into the script in a pretty big way: Jack and Rose make love in the back seat. The car would have been lowered through this very hatchway. Unspooling Snoop into the pit, they lit on D-deck, the third-class open space, setting for another big movie moment: Jack and Rose are joined in exuberant dance on the very hatch occupied by Snoop. In transit it would have been decked over with planking, long rotted out, leaving only the latticework of the beams. They swung the camera around. It looked like a big parking garage, empty but for some posts. Odd to think music and air once mingled here with the happy voices of travelers, excited by the prospects of starting a new life. Virtually all the third-class passengers were immigrants, "People moving lock, stock, and barrel to the United States. They'd packed up their belongings—their family photographs, all their clothing, all their money, all their jewelry." All of it was now scattered across the bottom of the ocean or had long since disintegrated. If they owned musical instruments, they would have been traveling with them, which was Cameron's inspiration for the impromptu dancing scene.

Gingerly, they tried to squeeze Snoop between the planks. It was tight, only an inch of clearance on each side, and the thrusters sent mud swirling, completely obstructing the view. Cameron quickly assessed the situation as high risk, low return. They pulled out and moved on.

The Grand Staircase was without a doubt the architectural centerpiece of the *Titanic* interior. It's crowning feature was a glass-domed ceiling, intricately laced in wrought iron. Eighty-three years ago the gilded railings and carved oak accents glinted richly in the natural light. By night, torchères and chandeliers showed the ship's elegant guests to luminous advantage as they descended to dinner. Now it was just a gaping hole with rusticles lining the sides like moss.

They began the penetration at D-deck, the reception area for the first-class dining salon. The lights cut through the dense blue atmosphere of the room. It was a minefield of wires—the chandeliers, which had rappelled down from the ceiling, now swayed gently near the floor. The furniture had all been swept to the back and lay in a jumbled heap. They snaked around the perimeter and could see that much of the wood paneling was intact, as were a few of the ornately carved columns. Cameron's heart thumped at the sight of *Titanic*'s past grandeur. Previously he'd been photographing a steel shell; now he was seeing what made her special. "It wasn't just that she was a big ship, it was that she was luxurious and beautiful, and the carved woodwork was a lot of what made her beautiful," he thought. They nosed up against a door, still hinged, its latticework of bronze in place. It was a numbing realization that he was looking at a space no human being had seen since the ship sank in 1912. "The last people to set eyes on this door were fleeing for their lives, and most of them didn't make it."

Rethreading out, they worked their way to the forward part of the room, searching for the elevator shaft. The distinctive arched entryway that linked the two areas had crumbled, marked only by a wall fragment. That was intriguing. They explored the floor debris and found a coat rack. At the edge of their lights was the D-deck stateroom corridor. The wood paneling gleamed on both sides. If they could reach one of the staterooms, Cameron felt certain he would see the best-preserved environment the wreck had ever shared. But they couldn't. At ninety-eight feet into *Titanic,* they had delved further than any previous explorer, but their tether was played out as far as it could go. James Cameron was at the end of his rope.

Chapter Seven

> A person who has thought ten times as much as the average person has in a fundamental sense lived ten times as long as the average person.
>
> —Frank J. Tipler

WHEN JAMES Cameron stepped off the *Keldysh* in Halifax in the wee hours of September 30, 1995, there was a private Lear jet waiting to whisk him to the New York press junket for *Strange Days.* The film, an apocalyptic tale of millennial angst that he wrote and produced, was directed by Kathryn Bigelow. The film would be a commercial flop, but for Cameron, it was a mere detour. For the next three years, his life was consumed by *Titanic.*

The studio was impressed enough with his dive footage to encourage further development of the project. Chernin requested that Cameron come up with a budget and left him to his own devices.

Cameron's days were a blur of meetings with costumers and people from casting, budget, and set design. He spent his nights screenwriting, tossing off text for the comet disaster film *Bright Angel Falling* and the futuristic *Avatar.* He also began the process of previsualizing and planning his shots, devising a template from which he could strategize his overall shooting plan.

From February through March, Cameron eyed a twenty-five-foot model of the *Titanic* at Digital Domain. In theory, Cameron's careful preplanning was the smart creative course, and it was economically sound, too. A solid plan—one in which all the moving pieces magically fit—could shave millions off a production budget. In reality, when you got a guy like Cameron staring at something long enough, the mind inevitably strayed toward bigger, faster, better. He was a keen observer, and it seemed no detail eluded his eye. Watching him, one occasionally glimpsed the sheer delight he took in just looking at things.

The *Titanic* model was set up on a stage in the Digital Domain building with sheets of plastic tarp substituting for water. The director and core creative team huddled around the vessel, which Cameron spent much of his time circling with a lipstick camera, the same device he'd used aboard the *Keldysh.* It allowed him to simulate and record camera moves, working toward a blueprint for shot design. Unlike many filmmakers' work, there isn't a frame in a James Cameron film that he hasn't visualized completely. Though he might decide to change it later, nothing is left absolutely to chance. Another nifty planning device, the vid-stick, invented by his brother Mike, was used on set to block or plot the movement of shots.

Aiming the lipstick lens with his left hand, Cameron scrutinized the electronic image fed to a Walkman-sized monitor he held in his right, stepping intuitively about the model ship. Joining him in the dance was the core group that became *Titanic*'s creative A-team, including British production designer Peter Lamont and Los Angeles-based physical effects supervisor Tommy Fisher. Cameron knew both men from previous films. Lamont had worked on *Aliens* and *True Lies,* while Fisher had been a regular collaborator since *Terminator 2.* They were older men, each of few words—Lamont in a courtly, English way and Fisher stony, whether in concentration or contemplation. Fisher regularly took on engineering feats that far exceeded the problem-solving responsibilities of a physical effects supervisor—someone who handled all the practical effects, the unusual things that would happen for real, on the set, as opposed to in the computer. He'd come to have a reputation for large-scale physical effects, a taste developed under Cameron's tutelage.

By far the most important hire was the thirty-five-year-old producer Jon Landau, who'd spent the past five years as executive vice president of feature production at Twentieth Century-Fox and had offhandedly mentioned to Cameron at the *Strange Days* premiere that he planned to go back to producing. Fox had already agreed to give him an independent deal. As casual as he made it all sound, those who knew him were convinced he cooked up this exit strategy in the express hope of working on *Titanic.* Landau came with an impressive resume. His Fox tenure saw him working with director Michael Mann on *The Last of the Mohicans,* John Wu on *Broken Arrow,* and Jan de Bont on *Speed.* Earlier, he had co-produced Warren Beatty's *Dick Tracy.*

Cameron discussed the idea of hiring Landau with Lightstorm

president Rae Sanchini. In her capacity as executive producer, she was the liaison between the studio and the production, and she knew her interaction with Landau would inevitably get pretty intense. Agreeing that the three had enjoyed a good dynamic on *True Lies,* she urged the hire.

Landau rose to the occasion, becoming Cameron's chief co-strategist. "Aside from the specifics of the visual effects done by Digital Domain and by Tom Fisher," says Cameron, "Jon and I figured out how to do everything on the movie—the broad strokes. How are we going to do this? What are we going to build? Are we going to build this side or that side? Are we going to build this length? Are we going to build the forward well deck? Is it going to be attached or is it going to be a separate set? If Jon didn't think of it, I thought of it, and we bounced stuff off each other until we eventually homed in on the answer."

By this time, John Bruno had opted out of the project in order to direct his own film, *Virus,* and a thirty-eight-year-old Digital Domain hotshot named Rob Legato was chosen as his replacement. A few years ago, Legato was pushing model spaceships around on a motion control stage called Image G, doing contract work for "Star Trek: The Next Generation." Then DD president and CEO Scott Ross signed him up as part of his effects boutique's launch team. Working in the film realm was a significant step up for Legato, who up until then had primarily been involved with video. He proved a quick study, landing the company in orbit with back-to-back Oscar nominations for Neil Jordan's *Interview with the Vampire* and Ron Howard's *Apollo 13.* Now he joined the masters around the cinematic campfire, helping to figure out how to create the effect of the plunging ship and breaking, falling funnels and match the models and miniatures, and intercut these images with the action photographed on full-sized sets. A two-part process, the job would also involve detailed re-creations of the modern-day wreck and the free-swimming *Mirs.*

By the end of the shoot, they would build seven ship models, varying from a sixty-foot section to detailed scale models of the entire ship, running anywhere from a one-twentieth to a one-eighth scale mid-ship-to-stern model that was sixty-feet long. The largest complete re-creation, an elaborate forty-five-foot beauty model, would be created over the course of five months at a cost of nearly $450,000.

Cameron also hired the expert historians, writers Don Lynch and Ken Marschall, whose detailed paintings illustrate their book

Titanic: An Illustrated History. They threw open their collections of *Titanic* memorabilia and consulted on the minutiae of the ship and details of the human drama as it unfolded: what was said and who was where, the fine points of circumstance.

There was one aspect of Cameron's *Titanic* vision that would essentially dictate the production parameters: he wanted to invite audiences aboard a sinking ship. To accomplish that, he needed engaging camera moves that imparted a "you are there" sense of action and an up-close-and-personal look at people—characters you actually cared about—sliding into the drink. Prior movies about the *Titanic* disaster isolated the actual sinking into a series of elaborate vignettes featuring models photographed in miniature.

"In the past they've either built a small portion of the ship accurately and used a model for the wide shots, which essentially limited your tighter work to nooks and crannies," explains Cameron. "Or they've shot it on the *Queen Mary* or some other ship that kind of looked like the *Titanic* but wasn't, and hoped nobody would notice. And of course you can't sink the *Queen Mary.* So you've either got big shots of people walking on decks, but they're not the right decks, or you see an accurate area that's much smaller than it really was. In terms of accuracy, they did a pretty good job with the dining saloon in *A Night To Remember,* but it was only a fragment of the real thing."

The main challenge was conjuring a vessel whose very name equaled size. This type of brain-teaser, coming up with the plan, was Cameron's idea of fun. Landau was an integral part of the process. Together, they devised a variety of plausible scenarios. Initially, the two thought they could get away with building only pieces of the ship. The largest of these sections—a 400-foot mock-up of the hull—could be used for the big sailing-day scene at Southampton as well as the lifeboat launch.

They began to think along the lines of redressing a massive container ship, a flat, barge-like vessel, 700 to 800 feet long, used for interocean transport. The idea was to outfit the impostor by placing sets for the bow and poop deck on its flat surface and hanging a false hull off the side. They would dress it with an overhanging deck to allow plenty of room for lighting equipment and camera gear. This would allow them to sail and shoot in open water for the predisaster scenes. The sets could then be transported and reassembled on stages for the interior scenes, and, for the sinking, in tanks.

For his tank, Cameron considered using a dry-dock—essentially a big tank where ships are parked and the water pumped out so that repairs can be made. Cameron wanted everything to look "pretty" and the the quality of every location's natural light was a primary consideration in evaluating locations around the world. Balancing that were economic concerns, primarily affordable labor. "Basically," says Cameron, "we were looking for places that could do the construction cheaper than in Los Angeles, where the cost of construction is extremely high." Union rates and the availability of personnel were factored into every location under consideration, which included settings in Australia and Czechoslovakia. Cameron told Chernin he was prepared to go anywhere in the world to make this film even if it meant being separated from his family. Production scouts were dispatched to Sweden, Poland, and the Caribbean. By January, Lamont had art departments operating in London, Los Angeles, and Mexico City. They were building props and sets without knowing where they would be shipped.

"We began to analyze what the water looked like offshore, in the Baltic, to see if we'd need to go five or ten miles offshore to shoot. We had to figure out the production requirements of the cycle time—going out to the location, how many hours of daylight you could get at a particular time of year. Logistically, it was tremendous," notes Cameron. For the sinking, they were looking at a tank in the Mediterranean country of Malta.

As Cameron had already learned, shooting in water complicates a production. "Water always adds a layer of unpredictability," notes Cameron. "It takes away one element of control." And nothing is as difficult as shooting at sea. With visions of *Waterworld* dancing in their heads, Cameron and Landau refocused their energies on finding an interior space large enough to accommodate *Titanic*'s "at sea" sets. This would allow them some control over the elements, an important factor because the disaster at sea took place on a clear, still night. No wind. No rain. No fog. Since the whole incident happened over a period of a couple of hours, it all had to match. The shots of the lifeboats pulling away from the ship had to take place on glassy, calm water.

Scouring the world for large, open spaces, they came up with blimp hangars—330 feet high and 1,000 feet long with open space, uninterrupted by column support—rock quarries, and a submarine plant in South Carolina. Any huge structure any place in the world was considered. Nothing was quite right.

Landau saw some of Digital Domain's early attempts at creating computer-generated water, and it was as if a cosmic force had snapped the missing puzzle piece into place. "We could photograph onboard without actually having to move, because the only real sense of motion from a ship comes when you look down." Any motion shots that required water could be augmented in the computer. That meant they just needed to build near the ocean, not on it, and could photograph in such a way as to take advantage of the natural horizon.

Cameron immediately responded to the idea. A land-based operation would make access to equipment and personnel much simpler, and they could build a big tank for the sinking scenes. He also began thinking in terms of building his ship in one contiguous stretch, rather than in pieces.

"The biggest decision was to not go enclosed on the *Titanic* exterior set," says Cameron. "We would've had to break it up into too many discontinuous set pieces to put it on stages." The previsualization process showed that the smaller the slices of ship, the greater the number of visual effects necessary to create the illusion of a full-sized liner. Since effects were expensive, this triggered another complex series of cost/value equations. "We decided that the production value of having it all in one piece was greater than the potential problems and costs associated with breaking it up." Cameron was ready to make it, and make it big. He and Peter Lamont designed a plan for a 775-foot *Titanic,* ten stories to the tip of its funnels. Now all they needed was a place to park the thing. It soon became clear that the most effective route, the one that would offer the most control, was building their own studio. But where? It was already April.

Mexico was the obvious choice. The freeway-close proximity to Los Angeles and its world-class crews and equipment were bonuses. Cheap labor and real estate were necessities. They settled on Rosarito, a "resort" community, popular among Southern California college students in the 1970s, that had seen better days.

Initially, the plan was to erect a temporary facility; portable stages and some large cement pits for tanks. Unlike most films, where the technical aspect of directing consists mainly of deciding where to place the camera, *Titanic* now required Cameron to spearhead a major construction initiative.

The geography factor was a wild card in finalizing the budget. The budgetary analysis of projected costs was a financial blueprint for the film that, in theory at least, would dictate production decisions. It was probably the single most important element in the greenlighting process. A good deal of the preproduction planning was geared toward nailing down a defensible budget.

The fact that every film estimate was a projection didn't stop the seven major studios from greenlighting roughly two hundred films a year. On most films, the numbers were strictly plug and play. "Guestimates" for the cost of things such as lighting, electricity, costumes, and labor were the result of some fairly routine calculations on MovieMagic spreadsheets. Sure, there were variables, but the costume drama, comedy, and art film each lived by its own set of rules. The formula was rigid through the early 1990s.

Cameron and crew were having a hard time making the numbers compute. True, there had been other epics but no one had ever produced a film this big. Because of the long period figuring out how to do things—how much to build, what could be shot as models, the number of digital effects—they'd been having a hard time getting final departmental budgets from key areas like wardrobe, construction, and on-set effects. Until they knew what they were shooting and where, they couldn't know what it would cost. The previsualization process took place until the end of March. With the Rosarito site selected, some serious number-crunching could begin. They knew where their sets would have to be shipped which dictated where they could be built. They could begin crewing beyond that core group willing to follow Cameron anywhere in the world.

While in most cases a fairly accurate budget could be generated simply by breaking down a director's shooting script, on a Cameron film the scripts were deceptive. "What are we really going to do? When it says 'Walking the deck of *Titanic*,' I don't think it necessarily occurred to them that we were going to do just that," he said. "I don't think it necessarily occurred to me when I wrote it."

Cameron had been running *Titanic* budgets in his head as early as 1994, before he went to Russia. Back then, he thought *Titanic* could be made for roughly $80 million. At this early juncture, Cameron viewed *Titanic* as a quick and relatively inexpensive detour between *True Lies* and *Avatar*, a futuristic effects extravaganza about genetically engineered life, which he knew would be costly.

He arrived at the $80 million figure by assessing a *True Lies*-scale production and, since he knew *Titanic* would not be a star vehicle, lopping off that film's sizable above-the-line costs. Loosely defined, below-the-line costs covered things like cameras, cable, and special effects—items with sprockets and gears and the folks who operated them, people who worked as much with their hands as their heads. The other major budget item, the cast and things associated with it, fell "above the line." These costs typically included limousines and elaborate trailer-chateaux (nicknamed "honeywagons"), hairdressers, personal masseuses, chefs, and of course, salaries. The above-and-below analogy was not lost on the metaphorically inclined, suggesting as it did a sort of production heaven and hell.

As for his accounting methodology, Cameron would later characterize it as "a wild ass guess" but he was confident enough with the figure to bandy it about to Chernin during those early pitch meetings. Two years and two script passes later, in April 1996, a more scientific budgetary analysis produced a figure of $125 million, excluding the cost of the Baja studio, an investment considerably higher than Cameron's original pitch. Chernin thought the number ridiculously high. He sent Cameron back to the drawing board with instructions to get it below $110 million.

The director tried to accommodate, by cutting roughly eighty digital effects shots. This was par for the course. Preproduction on any big film involved a certain amount of dickering with effects companies. Which shots can you do cheaper? Which can you live without? Fox's internal discussions about how to proceed with Cameron initially involved Chernin, Mechanic, and Twentieth Century-Fox production president Tom Rothman, and eventually even included Rupert Murdoch. In addition to their concerns about the budget and the divergence from Cameron's tried and true metier, the studio was worried about a netwoı miniseries it had in the works. Cameron's original pitch to Fox had been "an idea so old it's new again," but with a TV show airing months before, how new would the idea in fact be? By now, Cameron was more than eager to get an official go-ahead from Fox. He'd had several conversations with the brass about possible release dates. Once that was set everything else would work backwards to meet that date.

Ever since *The Terminator*, all of Cameron's films had been summer releases. Orion had slotted that film in October, where it hit the market with the wallop of a left hook. But that decision had been relatively simple: a small studio counter-programming with a genre film. *Titanic*—a period action-romance, with some modern melodrama thrown in for good measure—defied categorization. Cameron wasn't sure. "I never thought it was a summer movie, particularly. And I had actually asked the Fox executives repeatedly, 'What do you think?' And they were like, 'Ohhh, it could be July 4, it could be Christmas.' I'm like, 'Well, do you see it as a summer movie?' I'm trying to test them to see if that really is what they wanted. I never got a clear answer. So fine, time is going by. I'm doing what's necessary, spending money on preproduction."

Suddenly, the Fox executives looked at each other and realized they had no big summer movies on their 1997 schedule. Some projects the'd been counting on failed to materialize. With little warning, Fox told Cameron they wanted to go ahead with the film, but only if they could have it for a summer 1997 release. "Boom! It was like a rocket going off: 'If it ain't summer, we ain't makin' it!' So I'm like, okay, if I'm supposed to have this film ready for next summer, I'm going to need the green light—a month ago? Two months ago? By that point I'd spent two years of my life on the film, for no pay, so I wasn't about to just write it off."

As insurance, Chernin also greenlit Jan de Bont's *Speed 2,* which also happened to take place on a boat, a similarity that left Cameron none too happy. For *Titanic*'s release, the studio targeted July 4, the same weekend *Terminator 2* had opened in 1991. It felt lucky. As unlikely as it seemed that they could pull together a film of this complexity in a little over a year, Cameron's own experience indicated it was not unthinkable. *T2* was produced, from script to screen, in thirteen months, and that was hardly a trivial film. Of course, it had not involved actually building a movie studio—something a couple of his billionaire friends in the Valley, doing business under the name DreamWorks, had been trying, unsuccessfully, to do for the past two years. Did he think he could make it?

Well, he wouldn't bet on it, but it was possible. Cameron told the studio he'd make his best effort if they in turn would agree to review the matter with him in March or April.

Cameron's original production plan called for five-day work weeks, so he could use the weekends for editing. Request denied. They wanted pedal-to-the-metal filmmaking: six-day weeks. The condensed schedule represented a quick $1.2 million out of the budget. It probably ended up costing them $10 million. On *T2* the shortened workweek actually helped him wrap the film more quickly. It still took five months to edit, but the days were telescoped into the production schedule.

At this point, it could be argued, the green light was somewhat academic. By spring-loading Cameron for summer, they'd tacitly committed to the film. Until now, Cameron had been running the operation on a trickle of development funds and some monies of his own. Now it was just a matter of turning on the money spigot.

Chapter Eight

> The human body is an instrument for the production of art in the human soul.
>
> —Alfred North Whitehead

AFTER THE BUDGET, the single most important factor in getting a studio to greenlight a picture is cast. For his movie, Cameron considered unknowns, newcomers, and even a few stars. At first, James Cameron was reluctant to even consider either Kate Winslet for the part of Rose or Leonardo DiCaprio for Jack. Both actors were the idea of casting director Mali Finn who'd worked with Cameron on *T2* and *True Lies* and knew his taste well.

A quiet, bespectacled woman with a piercingly observant air, Finn poured over hundreds of headshots and videotapes of actors since signing aboard *Titanic* in October. Her Burbank office was wallpapered with photographs of the *Titanic* passengers. Most young actors Finn contacted were desperate to get a meeting, a reading, anything with James Cameron.

Despite Cameron's objections, Finn continued to press for Kate Winslet. "See her, she's remarkable," she told Cameron.

Winslet's initial audition was on a soundstage in Los Angeles. Cameron was testing all his actresses on film and planned to do the same with the actors. Despite his track record, the director was apprehensive about doing a period film. Although he'd created worlds of the future for *Aliens* and the *Terminator* films, *Titanic* felt more demanding because it had to hold its own against actual historical precedent. The past was much more palpable than the ethereal future.

For her audition on a Culver City soundstage, Winslet was dressed by Deborah Scott, who'd been scouring the world for vintage costumes since November. *True Lies* director of photography Russell Carpenter did the lighting. Cameron wanted a polished screen-test. He needed to see his leading actors in period wardrobe and setting, lit perfectly, to make sure not only that they could do it, but that he could do it with them. What he was looking for, he said, was "a chemistry, a chemistry between the director and the actor." Success would largely be a function of finding the right leading lady because the story would unfold mostly through her eyes. "I wanted somebody that could act as a conduit for our present-day emotions, who would be from that time and still be just like us." He described his Rose as "an Audrey Hepburn type: spunky, smart, and elegant." For any young actress this was a once-in-a-lifetime role, with *really* great clothes to boot.

Cameron had indeed limited his options by writing the two lead characters so young. Rose is seventeen, Jack twenty. Cameron felt strongly that the film had to be about first young love. A number of prominent actresses were auditioned for the part including Gwyneth Paltrow, Claire Danes, and the French-born Gabrielle Anwar. Each was thought highly accomplished just to make the short list. "It's not difficult to find good actors," says Cameron. "What's difficult is to find actors who can play that age group with the dramatic range to handle both the intensity and the subtlety of these roles. That and the experience to be able to handle a big long shoot."

Though Winslet had accumulated an impressive body of work for such a young actress, Cameron's initial objection was her close association with period work. The twenty-one-year-old British actress had already done two nineteenth-century films—adaptations of Jane Austen's *Sense and Sensibility* and Thomas Hardy's *Jude The Obscure*—and then she played Ophelia to Kenneth Branagh's Hamlet. Even her screen debut, in Peter Jackson's electrifying and intense *Heavenly Creatures,* was set in 1950s New Zealand, a period of sorts.

The big question at Winslet's audition was whether or not she should act the scene in an American accent. Rose was a complex creature who required some sort of an accent, something Main Line Philadelphia, which they came to describe as mid-Atlantic, for the turn-of-the-century equivalent of a jet-setter. Winslet had memorized her lines for the audition and was given a good stand-in actor to work with. She was feeling confident, so she did the accent. They shot it.

Cameron's first impression was that she was quite beautiful, very engaging, but something was missing. He asked her to act the scene in her natural British voice. "'You've proven that you can do the American accent, now act the scene for me without thinking about that," he told her. The direction worked. "She was stunning. Just stunning. We did many, many takes. I realized it was impossible to find a bad angle for her facially and photographically. She was absolutely exquisite, and from a performance standpoint, very, very flexible. She could take any idea and juggle it, integrate it, and something interesting would come out of it. And we were having fun. It was exhausting, but it was fun." Though he had several more actresses scheduled to screen test over the next few days and he planned to see them all, by the time Winslet left the studio, he had a hunch she was going to be his choice.

She wanted the role badly and was not shy in letting Cameron know. She lobbied the director, ringing up from England. "I was driving around in my Humvee and she says, 'You don't understand. I am Rose. I don't know why you're even seeing anyone else!' She was so positive and aggressive. It cracked me up," says Cameron. "I thought, 'Okay, that's the sort of spirit it's going to take to get through this.'"

Within weeks she was back in Los Angeles, this time at Lightstorm, to read with Leonardo DiCaprio.

When Finn first suggested DiCaprio, Cameron was not terribly enthusiastic, having only seen the actor play the retarded teen in *What's Eating Gilbert Grape?* (which won him an Oscar nomination). Yet DiCaprio, like Winslet, had also accumulated an impressive resume of characters including the sylphlike surrealist poet Arthur Rimbaud in *Total Eclipse,* the heroin-addicted writer-rocker of *The Basketball Diaries,* and, in his most recent role, an institutionalized teen saddled with family trauma, opposite Meryl Streep and Diane Keaton, in *Marvin's Room.*

Cameron first met DiCaprio at an informal meeting at Lightstorm's Santa Monica offices in February of 1996. Cameron, who arrived late, was surprised to enter the conference room and discover nearly every female Lightstorm staffer in attendance. Even his chief financial officer was there. Obviously, all the women wanted to meet Leo. "It was one of those group Hollywood things, which I never do," Cameron laughs, remembering the incident. "Leo must be used to this because he charmed everyone in the room." Looking "slightly adolescent" and just "generally Leo-ing out," the twenty-one-year-old actor didn't much impress Cameron, who thought the kid looked like a slacker punk, albeit a handsome one. But he was impressed enough to agree to have Winslet flown in to read with DiCaprio. Another meeting was set for the following week.

DiCaprio started the next session by saying he didn't want to be taped and he didn't want to read the audition scene Cameron had prepared. It was unexpected behavior, not exactly that of an actor dying to get the part, but Leonardo was too serious about his craft to audition capriciously. Although he was intrigued by the film, he did have misgivings about the role. Jack seemed a bit "light" to him. The young actor favored human- as opposed to Titan-scale drama, where a performance could vaporize in the sights, sets, and sound. DiCaprio brought likability and intelligence to his roles. The fact that they also happened to titillate a generation of weepy teenage girls was something of a distraction to him. When Baz Luhrmann's *Romeo + Juliet* opened in November, DiCaprio would become an unqualified megastar.

Cameron would not be put off. "You're reading!" Cameron informed him. "I've got Kate here from England. Here are the pages!"

The eight-page scene was what's known as a "walk and talk," with the two lovers getting acquainted in their first real conversation after her suicide attempt, when Rose seeks out Jack to thank him for saving her life. Although the script leaves uncertain whether Rose really intended to jump, the implication of having her slip off the rail as she tried to climb back onto the ship is that she would've fallen overboard had Jack not been there to intervene with fate, a recurring Cameron theme.

The scriptment had Rose clambering belowdecks the following day, her first trip to the third-class General Room and Jack's boisterous world, a place lively with emotion. The scriptment reads: "Jack has his back to her, but Fabrizio and Tommy see her coming. Jack, noticing their mouths hanging open, turns." Cameron describes the scene as a gender-bending twist on the Cinderella myth.

During a stroll around the boat deck, Rose demurely thanks Jack. They walk. They talk. A fascination takes hold.

DiCaprio sailed into the six-page scene.

EXT. BOAT DECK—DAY

(Jack and Rose walk side by side. They pass people reading and talk-

ing in steamer chairs, some of whom glance curiously at the mismatched couple. He feels out of place in his rough clothes. They both feel awkward, for different reasons.)

JACK *(looking around)*

So this is first class. Smells better, anyway. You got a name, by the way?

Admittedly, the scene was still rough.

Lines like this gave DiCaprio pause. But it was only a scriptment—an incomplete document, and a difficult one for actors to work from. Actors don't read like other people, which is why screenwriters don't write like other writers. Actors read for the dialogue, their first beat on the voice of the character. Some go so far as to "count" lines.

When an actor connects with the right material, the scene just seems to unfurl magically off the page. "People are always talking about an arc," says Finn. "I think actors are primarily interested in playing a character that goes someplace emotionally."

Cameron adds that, "The hardest thing about this movie is to tell this love story where two people meet, fall in love, and decide they can only be with each other—in the ninety-six hours before the ship hits the iceberg. And you've got to make it believable, make it engaging, make it interesting, make it something you haven't seen before, yet make it universal. Boy meets girl is the oldest story ever told, so how do you make that interesting and exciting and new? And do it in a costume drama, where everybody's wearing silly hats and dresses?"

In this particular scene, Jack is "exulting in his proximity to her and a little intimidated. Meanwhile, she's got the whole thing she's dealing with because he actually saw her maybe attempting suicide, and so she sort of owes him something, but he's from another class and he's kind of rude. There's this whole attraction/tension thing between them." It was a beautiful scene on which to test actors—deep and layered with planes of emotion.

After the scene was over, Winslet got a little weepy. She'd flown over in the middle of shooting *Hamlet,* and the strenuousness of that emotionally charged role, coupled with jet lag, left her feeling wrung out. Despite her own emotional overload, she was hugely impressed by DiCaprio. She pulled Cameron aside and whispered to him, "Even if you don't hire me, you have to hire him."

Cameron invited her upstairs to his office to tell her she had the part.

Elated, on the way back to the airport, she stopped and sent him a single red rose, signed, "Thank-you. Your Rose." She was signed for just under a million dollars.

Cameron's experience with DiCaprio was just the opposite. The actor needed to be convinced that Jack was a worthwhile role. As he read the lines, Cameron found him fascinating to watch, "handsome and incredibly mercurial." Through the course of a scene he'd run ten different emotions behind his turbulent blue-green eyes. "He read the scene once, and then he got up and started goofing around and telling stories, and I could never get him to focus on it again. But for one split second, a shaft of light came down from the heavens and lit up the forest."

After months of searching, Cameron had found his leading man but DiCaprio waffled for months, continuing to press for rewrites. "Leo's process is to push, push, push. At first I was offended by this, because I thought it was a good script and a good character, and this punk kid was trying to tell me why it wasn't right. But ultimately it was really for the benefit of the film because it forced me to think about Jack. Not necessarily to make him neurotic and messed up, but to think about what he was feeling, what his life was like before he got on the ship, how he reacted to these rich people.

"This is a movie about a girl who falls in love with a guy that she is not supposed to be in love with, and it doesn't make any sense for her to fall in love with him whatsoever. Except that the audience has to realize that it makes perfect and complete sense. They have to be as mesmerized by this guy as she is. And so I had to find a guy who had that ability to just suck you in. Leo can do that."

Cameron modeled the character of Jack after the writer Jack London, a self-educated, turn-of-the-century free spirit best known for such works as *White Fang* and *The Call of the Wild.* In researching the role, he had trouble finding examples of how people spoke at "street level" in 1912. The novels of the time—Wharton, James—mainly documented the upper crust. To get a feel for idiomatic speech, he studied the syndicated cartoons of the period.

The actor was resistant to playing the buoyant hero. What would a role like this offer creatively? "He really needed to be chased," says Cameron. "He needed to be seduced. He had misgivings about being in a big picture."

DiCaprio's fey beauty frequently evoked comparisons with James Dean, with whom he shared a certain sullen charm. "I've been mesmerized by him in the past," says Finn, "but I thought it would be wonderful to see him tackle a part that had all that energy and exuberance and love of life. To have him dancing an Irish jig."

Earlier in the process, Finn liked a young New York actor named Billy Crudup for the part. She flew Crudup in, coach, at her own expense because she believed in him for the role. But Billy turned it down for some of the same reasons DiCaprio was having a hard time committing to it. He wanted to be an actor, not a movie star. It was just as well. Crudup was even lesser known than DiCaprio, and Fox would not have been happy. They still wanted Brad Pitt or Tom Cruise for the role.

As the *Titanic* script began circulating through Hollywood, Cruise's agent actually rang up to inquire about the role. The director recalled the incident with no little satisfaction as Cruise is one of those rare commodities: a star with the talent to back it up. Among the megastars, Cruise probably has one of the higher talent-to-dazzle ratios, and the chance to work with him held no little allure. Cameron was flattered and intrigued by the inquiry, though he had his heart set on a younger Jack.

Conversations with DiCaprio continued over the course of the next few weeks during which time Cameron was simultaneously trying to finish the script and get production underway, an absolute necessity if they wanted a chance at making the July 4 date. Cameron had managed to eke a little seed money out of Fox to get rolling on set construction for his underwater wreck interiors.

The sets would be used for present-day scenes involving the recovery of a safe from Suite B-52, the Hockley quarters. Furniture, including a grand piano, as well as wall fittings were torched, resin-coated to bond the delicate, charred surface and then repainted a dull brown to create the look of an interior space submerged for eighty-five years. Burning wood oxidizes its surface, which is basically the same process that would occur after prolonged water exposure.

Cameron considered the wreck sets a key component in creating the link between the *Titanic* then and now. Now that they were nearly finished, he was eager to see them. He and Charlie Arneson hopped into a Jeep and headed for Escondido. (After the deep dive, Cameron had hired Arneson to do research on *Titanic* and its times.)

The set design of Suite B-52 used as reference the Snoop video footage Cameron had shot on his deep dive. Though Cameron had actually photographed the starboard side suite, B-51, it was entirely conceivable that the port side's matching "millionaire suite" was in a similar state. Arriving in Escondido, Cameron wasn't entirely thrilled with the art department's interpretation of events.

"Jim didn't like the finishes," Arneson says. "He saw the *Titanic* firsthand, so he knew exactly how it was supposed to look. They were working from stills, from video reference, et cetera. Cameron grabbed a paint brush and started working. He ended up staying for like a day and a half, with just his Bob Marley T-shirt and one pair of pants. He painted every detail so that it was exact. And Rae was literally pulling her hair out. 'Where's Jim? Is he working on the script? No, he's in Escondido set-decorating!' Actually," explains Arneson, "he'd been working so hard, I think it was a way for him to unwind."

In the final throes of completing his script, Cameron felt as if he was on that uphill climb before the big final descent on a rollercoaster. In the midst of all this, he continued his dialogue with DiCaprio. Finally, fed up, he told the young actor, "'Look, I don't think you should do this film because I'm not going to make this guy brooding and neurotic and I'm not going to give him a hump and a tic and a twitch and a limp and all the other things that you want. And quite frankly, I think you're looking for playable stuff in the wrong place.

"The very toughest thing an actor can do is have absolutely nothing between himself and the audience. No twitch, no hump, no dark secret from the past. Just a clear, open, honest guy who is interesting and engaging. It's the difference between acting the scene with the prop in your hand, and without a prop in your hand. There are very few people who have been able to do it, historically. The Gary Coopers and the Jimmy Stewarts have come along and made an indelible impression doing that, and they're very rare. If you can do that, you can do anything." The character was personal to Cameron, whose own personality type, observers say, falls somewhere between Jack's free-spirited artist—the person Jim wants to be—and Brock, the guy so focused on the logistical details, the mission, that he's lost sight of the big picture.

Finally, DiCaprio relented, agreeing only if Cameron would embellish Jack in other ways. Other young actors might not have felt confident enough to challenge a blue chip director. "Generally," says Finn, "most feel they have to be at a certain level before they can sit down with the director and say, 'Can we work on this character together?'"

Now all that Cameron had to do was convince Fox that DiCaprio had what it took to carry the movie. At that point, Winslet's snooty cinematic pedigree, her cachet with the Merchant-Ivory crowd, actually made her a greater favorite with Fox than DiCaprio—who was currently filming *Romeo + Juliet* for the studio. Chernin would probably have been happier with either Chris O'Donnell or Matthew McConaughey—O'Donnell having established a visible if lightweight reputation as *Batman*'s Robin, and McConaughey coming off the success of *A Time To Kill. Titanic* had numerous speaking parts; Cameron would have plenty of opportunity to cast unknown actors in those lesser roles.

Ultimately Cameron felt that both O'Donnell and McConaughey played too old, though he was willing to offer McConaughey the supporting role of Rose's rich, arrogant fiancé, Cal. McConaughey declined, choosing instead to retread barrister territory in Steven Spielberg's first DreamWorks film, *Amistad.* The part of Cal ultimately went to Billy Zane.

For the rest of the cast, Cameron was seeking to pay "unknown" prices. With the exception of a handful of leads, it was scale plus ten, roughly $2000 a week, the bare minimum you could offer without insulting the actors. Cameron's money was slated for other aspects of the film. "If you look at *A Time To Kill,* for instance, in that supporting cast, Joel Schumacher had Kevin Spacey, Donald Sutherland, Kiefer Sutherland, Ashley Judd, Oliver Platt, and Patrick McGoohan. Those are the types of supporting people that really run a budget out," says Finn. "Their weekly fees or the picture fees are big compared to other supporting players."

For *Titanic,* Cameron indulged himself in one casting luxury: the Academy Award-winning actress Kathy Bates as Molly Brown. Bates was initially reluctant, thinking the supporting role too small. Cameron had actually offered the role to Linda Hamilton when the two were encamped on the *Keldysh,* but she declined. A left-field contender who tested well was Reba McEntire, the country crooner. But it was Bates, with her natural resemblance to the original character, who became his one and only Unsinkable Molly Brown. The studio balked at her salary demand. Even after she came down in price to $500,000, the studio still refused to meet her fee, so Cameron offered to pay the difference of $150,000.

After DiCaprio's success in returning Shakespeare to the masses, the studio brass were heard saying they were bullish about him from the start but that's not how Cameron remembers it. "I called up Peter Chernin and said Leonardo DiCaprio is the guy. You've just got to trust me on this. And they were like, 'Isn't there anyone else?' They wanted a star. It's that studio mentality: 'We can't make a $100 million-plus movie with unknowns. We just can't!' And they were seeing the dailies from *Romeo + Juliet*, so at that point they should've known more about him than I did, and their trepidation was making me nervous," says Cameron, "but I always trust my first impression. It sounds corny, but that's what the audience does."

Of course, Cameron prevailed with DiCaprio and Romeo got the role. When his agents closed the deal in June, they took the opportunity to double his fee to $2.5 million. Like it or not, Leonardo DiCaprio was now playing in the big leagues.

Chapter Nine

> There is only one reason, at least in America, that people put money in film, and that is to make a profit. There is no other reason.
>
> —Curtis Harrington

TWENTIETH Century-Fox was between a rock and a hard place. They had what amounted to a half-greenlighted film, with Hollywood's highest roller at the helm.

Even though Cameron's last two films, *Terminator 2: Judgment Day* and *True Lies,* had made heaps of money, it didn't make it any easier to say yes this time out. "It's scary with him every time," said Bill Mechanic.

Even to the casual observer, *Titanic* would appear a particularly strong departure from Cameron's previous sci-fi and action set pieces. But in fact, the studio responded nearly as hesitantly when he tried to tell them *True Lies* was an action film and a comedy. "Do the words 'Last Action Hero' mean anything to you?" was a question he recalls hearing in a Fox executive suite.

"Peter Chernin was a big fan of the script," says Cameron. "He thought it had substance. He thought it was the kind of movie people should be making. He was nervous as hell about it for all the obvious reasons. He was nervous as hell about it for the same reasons other studios wouldn't have made it at all, just to put that in perspective. He was nervous, but he did it. The other studios were nervous, but they didn't do it. You know what I mean? That takes balls. It takes balls to do something that goes against your own grain as a businessman. But, because he has a literary background, he appreciated what I was trying to do. He had no idea whether it would be commercial or not. He didn't share my conviction that at a grassroots level people would actually *like* the film."

There was a certain cache to being associated with intelligent, award-caliber cinema. Cameron's films had been heaped with Oscar nominations, eighteen among four films, and seven wins, mostly in the technical areas. None of them for him. But Chernin was no patron of the arts. He was a businessman, motivated largely by the desire to maintain Fox's relationship with Lightstorm, though he did see some commercial upside to Cameron's big boat opus. "You can make small movies and be a filmmaker and you can make big movies and be a filmmaker. I think Cameron is in that category of the David Leans, people who tell intimate stories on a grand scale," says Mechanic.

When they finally wrangled Cameron back from set decorating in Escondido, he turned in his finished script. With that and the lead actors cast, the only thing between *Titanic* and the checkered flag was a final budget. Cameron now had set paint on his hands. He could feel the film rumbling to life. The studio was beginning to make noise about wanting to bring in a partner. Someone to share the "risk," which means the expense. Cameron needed money, lots of it, if they were to have any chance at meeting the July 4, 1997 date. He offered Fox four million from his own fees, a last ditch attempt to reconcile the numbers and get the go-ahead he needed. It was the first of three stages that would ultimately see Cameron surrendering his fees and profit participation in the film.

He'd whittled away everything he could while remaining within budgetary parameters that seemed realistic in terms of the film inside his head. Fox wanted to see *Titanic* budgeted at $110 million. With this latest concession, it was close.

The film was greenlit on May 28.

People in Hollywood will say, "Oh, you're making a movie," but it's amazing when a film actually gets greenligt, and it's amazing when a film wraps, thought Cameron. He'd passed his first major hurdle.

Digital Domain had taken over an airport hangar in Playa Vista, the old Hughes Aircraft facility, where a fleet of models was being made seaworthy. Set construction and the manufacture of furniture had been underway in Mexico City since April. More than a thousand articles of clothing were warehoused in Los Angeles with hundreds of mustaches and wigs. Five hundred dining saloon chairs and sets the size of ballrooms were being shipped in from two thousand miles away.

The most immediate effect of Fox's greenlight was groundbreaking at the Fox Baja studios. Cameron and Landau had for the past few months been submitting studio specs and reviewing blueprint plans with Fox chief financial officer Simon Bax. It was hard to get contractors interested in putting up even the shell of a facility Fox had initially envisioned—just the big tank, 600 by 600 feet and the sizable stage two, with its soaring, eighty-foot ceiling designed to allow the shooting and sinking of multi-story sets. Roberto Curiel was initially hired to map in Tank 1 and the foundations that would be used to hold pop-up stages. What he wound up building in only three short months was a fully functional three-stage motion picture studio with the world's largest open-air tank and a filtration system capable of handling 17 million gallons of salt water. The engineering alone, for the rough equivalent of building a sports arena, would normally take longer than three months. Curiel's firm, Maya Curiel, a partnership with his wife, was known for heavy cement work. Arturo Hauter was brought in to do steelwork, putting up buildings and laying the tracks and frame for the 162-foot tower crane.

The twenty-four-acre swath of land where Curiel unleashed a handful of surveyors on June 6 was unremarkable except for a geometric white sculpture posted on the open road, a relic of some abandoned development effort past. Even the locals couldn't remember what it was. It took 10,000 tons of dynamite to blast away the 17 million-gallon hole that would accommodate Cameron's big ship.

By July 1 the site was swarming with a construction force of 1,500 and another 400 set and props builders working under the supervision of Peter Lamont. Sets were arriving daily, parts shipped in from Mexico City and assembled on site. Of course, things were lost in transit, arrived damaged, and had to be repaired. Stained-glass windows got broken. Between 500 and 600 yards of concrete were poured daily. Welders, plumbers, and heavy-equipment drivers simultaneously helped to build a studio and the biggest set in history. Even Cameron was a little awed by the massive scale; it was like erecting a small city.

"When you start any film it feels like this," said Cameron who had the construction foreman send him videotapes of the studio's progress every other day. Watching the little city rise up out of the dust, Cameron had to laugh. "With the exception of D. W. Griffith, who even then probably rented a barn, I don't think *anybody* has ever stood in a field and said, 'I want to build a movie studio here to make a film.'"

Throughout the summer, the art department was assembling the resources essentially to rebuild the *Titanic* from scratch. When Lamont sat down with Cameron for his first *Titanic* meeting, his instructions were: "*Titanic*—no compromises!" And that was the standard to which they held throughout production.

None of the props existed, and since most of them would be sunk and wrecked, none of them could be rented. More than 900 drawings were produced, detailing items from the ashtrays to the ship itself. Some 450 table services, complete with the White Star pattern and logo, 200 deck chairs, and 100 ceiling sconces were running off the assembly line. Carpet patterns were obtained from the original manufacturer, BMK Stoddard. Lightstorm was even able to secure for Lamont the original engineering plans from the ship's manufacturer, Harland & Wolff. Now the problem was how to get all this streamed into the same date and the same place so that it was all there, ready to shoot, with the costumes, the props, the actors, and everything else in place.

Meanwhile, Fox initiated serious discussions for bringing in a financial partner on *Titanic.* The studio had a nice little package to offer: a cast film with a world class director at the helm and a great script.

Split rights on movies was becoming a common scenario. For *True Lies,* Fox had more or less partnered with Universal, which had the lion's share of foreign distribution rights through its CIC subsidiary. Cameron made it clear from the start that if Fox didn't make the film, he was going to take it elsewhere, as he had every right to do.

Back in October, when Fox was blinking, Cameron got pretty cozy with Universal. The studio had desperately sought his help when *Waterworld* was in post-production. Some of the effects shots weren't working. Cameron wound up lending them John Bruno. Pertaining to *Titanic,* Cameron was not adverse to casual, let-people-see-you-having-dinner-together encounters with Universal Pictures chairman Casey Silver, who loved the script. Universal was interested.

Chernin was interested, too. He advocated the material—action-y but not mindless; tragic, yet in its own way uplifting. In a world in which Chernin felt the public was incredibly jaded and suspicious about Hollywood, and particularly big action movies, Cameron's opus was dimensionalized and intelligent. That was, in fact, what he thought to be its greatest strength.

After some internal discussion, the studio decided it could get the most juice out of the film by handling international distribution, since Fox controlled its own foreign rights. The arrangement had worked well for them on *Braveheart,* co-financed with Paramount, who had invited them into the deal. Paramount was serviced overseas through United International Pictures, a joint venture with Universal.

The summer's releases would usher in the era of the $100 million movie season. And that didn't include P&A—prints and advertising—costs. Essentially, these were the duplication costs for getting the actual film cans to as many as 3,000 screens, just in North America, and creating the collateral marketing materials such as posters and trailers for the film.

Lightstorm hooked up Fox with Universal and Silver. Negotiations got underway in earnest just as Cameron was collecting his underwater sets in Escondido, where he was getting ready to hit the tanks for the first stage of principal photography. Universal had, as a result of Cameron's elaborate but shortlived independent distribution plan, serviced *True Lies* in all key foreign territories except Germany and Japan. Silver was seriously interested. "I thought it was a very good screenplay," Silver recalled in fall of 1997. But he hesitated, nervous about hitching his wagon to what he believed had the makings of a runaway train. "Fox was going to run the production. I didn't feel like I'd have any control," Silver noted. He was also suffering post-traumatic-flop syndrome in the wake of *Waterworld,* a film whose very name had become synonymous with seafaring ineptitude. That notoriously troubled shoot had made the studio a media punching bag. When it was all over, Universal's Japanese owner, Matsushita, would take a $60 million write-down on the film as part of its effort to sell the studio to Seagram's.

Silver was not in a gambling mood. "Maybe," he said. Maybe once. Maybe twice. Maybe for weeks on end. "I wanted to say yes, and I couldn't say no," Silver recalled.

The lava wars didn't help. The two studios were head-to-head in a horse race to get the first hot rock natural disaster flick to market. In a nail-biting release skirmish, Universal accelerated post-production on *Dante's Peak* (which in an amusing though incidental turn of events was produced by Cameron's ex-wife, Gale Anne Hurd, starred Linda Hamilton, and boasted uber-effects by Digital Domain). The film was to go out in spring rather than summer, smoking Fox's *Volcano.* Neither Chernin nor Mechanic was amused. Silver had said maybe too many times.

Fox turned its attention to Paramount.

Chairman of production Jon Goldwyn had knowledge of the *Titanic* script through his wife, Colleen Camp, who'd auditioned for the part of Molly Brown. Camp, a perky blonde known best for bit parts in big movies, just happened to be a Titanophile. Goldwyn mentioned to Sherry Lansing, his boss and Paramount Pictures Motion Picture Group chairman and CEO, what a great project he thought *Titanic* was. When an item ran in *The Hollywood Reporter* suggesting Fox was shopping for a partner on the film, Paramount was on the case.

There were multiple calls, at multiple levels. Jon Goldwyn, Sherry Lansing and her boss, Jonathan Dolgen, chairman of Viacom Entertainment Group, began ringing up Mechanic, Chernin, and Twentieth Century-Fox president of production Tom Rothman. Whomever they could reach. Finally, Fox agreed to let them read the script so they'd have an alternative to Universal, which continued to waffle.

"They read it," Mechanic recalls, "and they were enthusiastic. They said, 'We definitely want to do this. Let's work it out.' We went back to Universal, who was going soft. They were already trying to manage some big-budget things like *Dante's Peak* and Sylvester Stallone's *Daylight,* and they were gun-shy."

Mechanic went back to Lightstorm with the offer from Paramount and suggested Cameron and Sanchini meet with them to try and determine whether or not they'd be comfortable working together. The Lightstormers knew Universal from *True Lies.* Silver was a friend. They did not know the executives at Paramount except by reputation. By this time, Fox had the basic structure of the deal down. Fifty-fifty financing for a fifty-fifty split in a revenue pot that would include not only theatrical earnings but all of the ancillaries—the sale of soundtracks and home videos as well as TV rights, both broadcast and cable. Paramount was amenable to servicing *Titanic* to the domestic market. The filmmakers would be working closely with them, particularly on the initial theatrical marketing campaign. Mechanic didn't want to push them into anything.

Lightstorm had no objections to the Paramount team but continued to pull for Universal. At one point, Silver reportedly even agreed to go forward, though it was a half-hearted endorsement: "Yeah, we'll make the deal. It's not that we really want to, but we'll honor our word." Ultimately, Paramount's enthusiasm won them over. Fox invited Dolgen and Lansing aboard. It was a decision all parties except Paramount would at some point regret.

Mechanic, who joined Fox midway through production on *True Lies*—time enough to get a feel for Cameron's production style—said the studio went into this clear-eyed. "We did not go in thinking we were making a low-budget movie," states Mechanic. "We didn't even go in thinking that the budget would be contained, which is why it's the only movie we've split rights on in three years, because you really don't know, and if it went over budget, as it did, you didn't want to be shouldering that responsibility alone." But having a partner doesn't necessarily mean having someone to share your problems, as Fox would soon learn.

Meanwhile Cameron, who'd been in casting sessions as recently as the prior day, was ready to ship out for Halifax and the contemporary scenes involving treasure hunter Brock Lovett's *Titanic* expedition. Finn had approached both Sean Connery and Gene Hackman about playing Brock. By June, with no Brock in place, Cameron secured the services of Bill Paxton. Prior to hitting it big with back-to-back parts in *Twister* and *Apollo 13*, Paxton was best known for his role as the cowardly Marine Hudson in *Aliens*, and Cameron gave his old friend from the Corman days at least a small part in virtually all his films.

Gloria Stuart got the part of Old Rose, the 102-year-old incarnation of Kate Winslet's lively teen. Cameron told Finn he wanted an actress whose face wasn't well known, who would bring an aura of mystery to the role. Stuart, who retired in 1939 after appearing in nearly fifty films, including James Wale's *Old Dark House* and *The Invisible Man*, was eighty-six, and would have to undergo three hours of makeup a day to be transformed into Old Rose. In conceptualizing the character, Cameron visited the 103-year-old sculptress Beatrice Wood in Ojai, California, "to see how vibrant a person of that age could conceivably be." Rose's granddaughter, Lizzy Calvert, would be played by Suzy Amis. Rounding out the Halifax cast was Cameron's old dive buddy Lewis Abernathy as Brock's cynical sidekick Lewis Bodine.

"A role, written by your best friend, specifically for you? It doesn't get any better than this," sighed Abernathy, who auditioned for the role in Cameron's driveway, on Hi-8. The Texan's wife stood in for Bill Paxton. Two weeks with an acting coach and next thing you know he's on a plane to Halifax memorizing lines. About a third of the company's time was spent on soundstages in nearby Dartmouth, where they lensed the *Mir* interiors and the ship's lab, where Old Rose spins her hypnotic tale. They also shot the *Keldysh* at sea.

It was a much smaller company than Cameron was used to, and the group had a chance to bond. First assistant director Josh McLaglen, a Landau hire, was new to the first string team, and he was working out great. Director of photography Caleb Deschanel was the other new recruit. Cameron had always had a tempestuous relationship with his DPs. The more creative among them usually had personalities to match. As the person responsible for the lighting, they usually had the most technical job on the set, and they were used to being masters of their own domain. Their second in command was the head electrician, the gaffer. Below that, the grips. In the usual chain of command, the director would not directly instruct these staffers. He would issue commands to the DP, who would then direct his own crew. As far as Cameron was concerned, they all worked for him.

It was no secret in Hollywood that Cameron could light his own films. He didn't, though, and he encouraged cinematic experimentation—to a degree. Color, but stay within the lines. He knew what he wanted it to look like, and he knew what it should look like. He was picky about practical things like the "logic" of light sources as well as interpretive things like color palette. Cameron liked Deschanel. They were on the same wavelength on things like books and art. But he could see their filmmaking was at odds.

Cameron gleaned through their discussions that Deschanel wanted to do the period lighting for the Rosarito shoot using a muted, traditional color palette. The director wanted the era to blaze with color. He grew up loving the *Wizard of Oz,* still on his short list of favorite films, and he approached the present day Halifax scenes as monochromatic punctuation not unlike the black and white Kansas sequences that "bookend" the 1939 Technicolor extravaganza.

Bright color was in fact accurate to *Titanic*'s 1912 period, but only among the upper classes; it was a luxury, a sign of wealth. The common assumption of a gray turn-of-the-century is due, he discovered, to the fact that photographs of the period are sepia. Would Deschanel know how to light his big ship? A respected artist he might be, but a set 775-feet long was not something anybody could wrap their mind around. Cameron was nervous.

There was a lot going on. The production had immediately fallen behind schedule due to weather related problems with the *Keldysh.* Not a good sign only weeks into a six-month shoot. Shooting at sea was a challenge, particularly on days when they had to coordinate the activities of two ships and a chopper. A naval vessel was brought in to augment the Russian ship, which did not have the capacity to land the Sea Stallion helicopter that transports Old Rose to *Titanic.* The Sea Stallion is the only helicopter in existence capable of making the 1,400 mile round trip to the *Titanic* site. As always, Cameron liked to write in the coolest toys for his films.

Before they left Halifax Cameron told Landau to fire Deschanel. "He's used to working with people who are like, 'Oh, Caleb, blow us away with your magic!' Well I don't want anyone blowing me away with their magic," he says, turning the words over like something sour in his mouth. "I don't like surprises." This was apparent when, on a starry North Atlantic night, Cameron—starved, after uninterrupted hours at work—was served soup by a catering girl making the rounds of the set. The director, still behind the camera, took one sip and steam came out his ears. It was scalding. His soup went flying overboard. Deschanel, preparing to take a sip, found his soup sailing over too. "Don't you *ever* serve me boiling soup again!" he told the stricken service woman.

Stuck with a wedding caterer in a backwater town, they had some memorable mealtimes and none more so than on the evening of August 8. What Lewis Abernathy remembers most about that meal on their last scheduled night in Halifax was how quiet the set was when he returned to the Dartmouth stage at 11:00 P.M. It was not an unusual time to be taking a break. Film crews were pretty much summoned to the set in twelve-hour intervals. A few hours overrun in the early week led to midnight lunches on Friday. On Sunday, the day of rest, the clock got reset.

Abernathy poked around, finally coming upon Cameron sitting in an abandoned laboratory set, a Medic and his first assistant director Josh McLaglen hovering over him. "What's wrong with you?" he inquired. Cameron said his stomach was acting up. Probably something he ate. That wasn't unusual. He had a pretty sensitive stomach and he'd been running around like crazy, eating all this weird food. Some Pepto Bismol and he'd be fine.

Abernathy, conscientious for his first turn in front of the camera, had been taking his meals at the hotel. The catered food sucked, and he wanted to avoid belching, bad breath, or gas—"all the things that occur in my natural state." He went back to his trailer and spent another ten minutes primping.

Bored, he returned to the set, wondering why no one had called. "Hell-oooo? Hell-ooo?" he hollered. Nothing. Entering the cafeteria, he was hit with a wall of suffering not unlike that of Scarlett O'Hara in the infirmary scene of *Gone With the Wind.* Eighty-five people rolling around, completely out of it. He heard some of them talking about seeing streaks and psychedelics. "That's when it hit me: food poisoning! We're going to be knee deep in vomit soon! Really bad seafood can make you hallucinate a little bit and this caterer was big on clams."

He saw Cameron across the room, and arrived at his friend's side as they were ushering the director out. Abernathy followed him to the parking lot where they loaded Cameron into a van. "I said, 'Jim! Jim! Where you goin'?,'' Abernathy recalls. "And he turned around, and I was just shocked at the way he looked. In the fifteen minutes since I'd seen him sitting in the chair, he had completely deteriorated. One eye—and this is where life imitates art—one eye was completely red, just like the Terminator eye. A pupil, no iris, beet red. The other eye looked like he'd been sniffing glue since he was four. When you see someone like that that has changed that dramatically in that short a time you think the next stop is death. I'm looking at him goin', 'Jim, are you okay?'

"And he says, in this slurred voice, 'Fuckin' caterer poisoned me! They're taking me to the hospital.' And I'm like, 'Jim is there anything I can do for you?' And I'm thinking call an organ donor bank, next of kin, mortuary... Who do you want me to call in your last hours? And he puts on this big ol' grin and says, 'Finish the movie, Lewis, you know what to do!' He said it in such a clear tone, and he sounded so happy, I said, 'Now I know you're fucked up, take him away!' And he went willingly with them."

Fifty-six people were transported to the local emergency room where they were put under immediate quarantine. When no nausea occurred, it became apparent this was no ordinary case of food poisoning. Abernathy developed another theory. He sprung into action, joining forces with the show's medic, who'd been so bored they set him up as an extra. "But when crisis struck, he turned into like super-medic," marvels Abernathy. "He kept everybody calm, took their blood pressure, kept them from freaking out." Abernathy took a different tack, putting on mood lighting and popping in

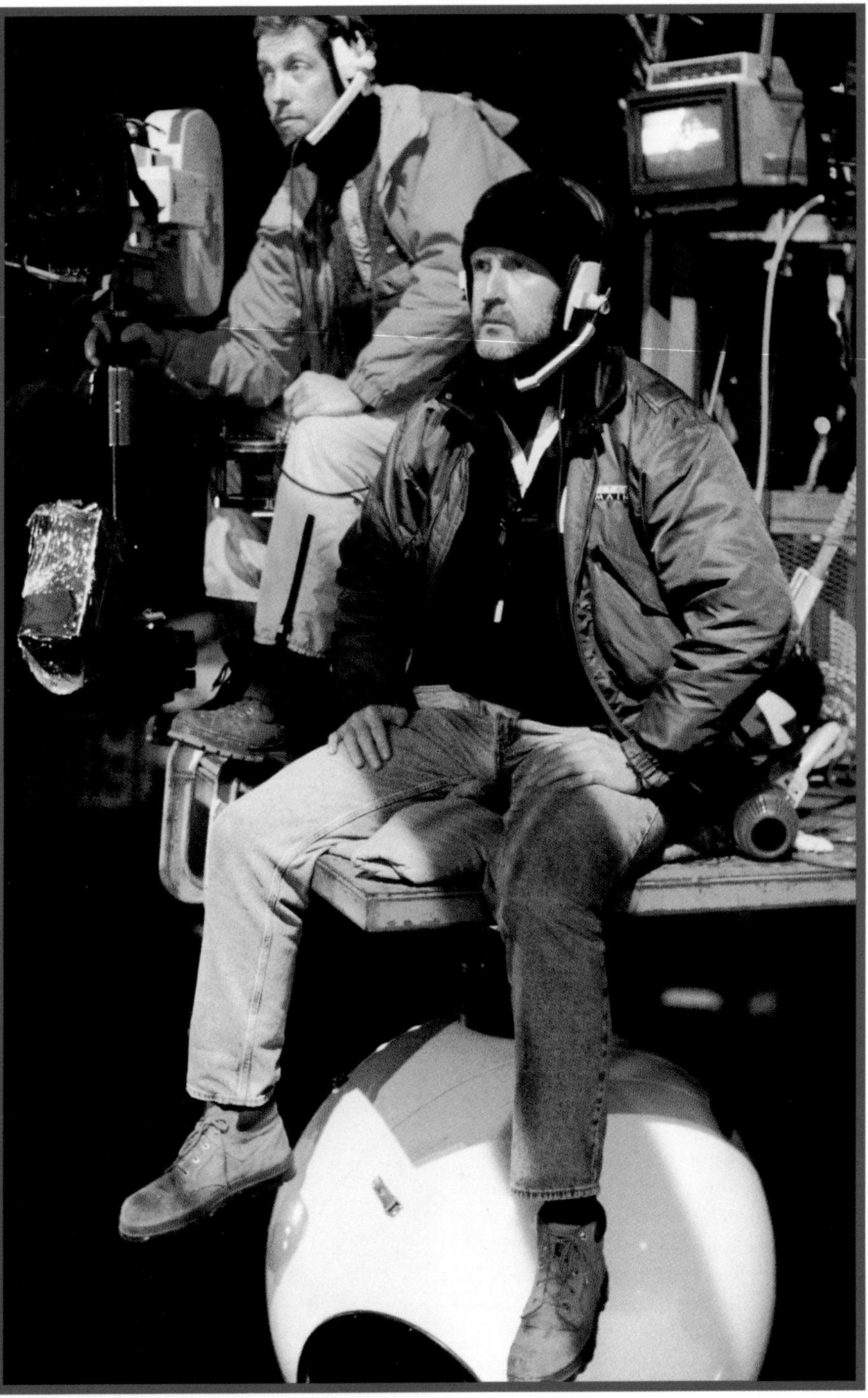

Steadicam man and A-camera operator Jimmy Muro joins James Cameron in the tower crane, a 162-foot construction crane used as a camera and lighting platform.

Above: The *Mir 1* is one of two submersibles on the *Akademik Keldysh;* there are only five submarines in the world capable of diving to the depths of *Titanic.*

Right: James Cameron (right) joins Russian submersible pilot Anatoly Sagalevitch (center) and a Russian engineer in *Mir 1,* which would take them two-and-a-half miles to the ocean floor and the wreck of *Titanic.*

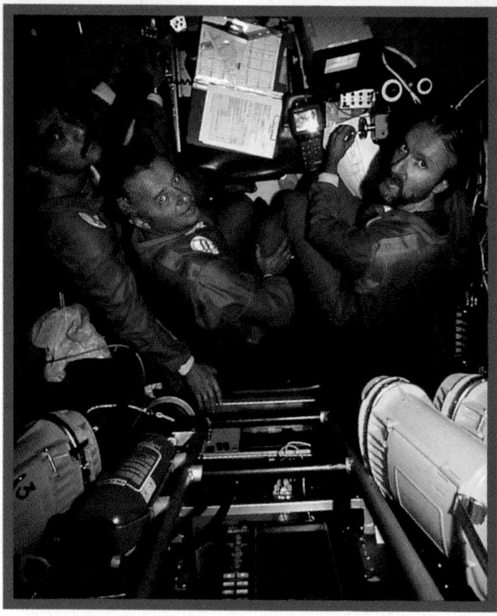

Al Giddings Images, Inc. ©

Al Giddings Images, Inc. ©

Above: Cameron with photographer Al Giddings (at left) planned his shots of the wreck using a model of the wreck. *Below:* With smoke and mirrors, the model appears underwater.

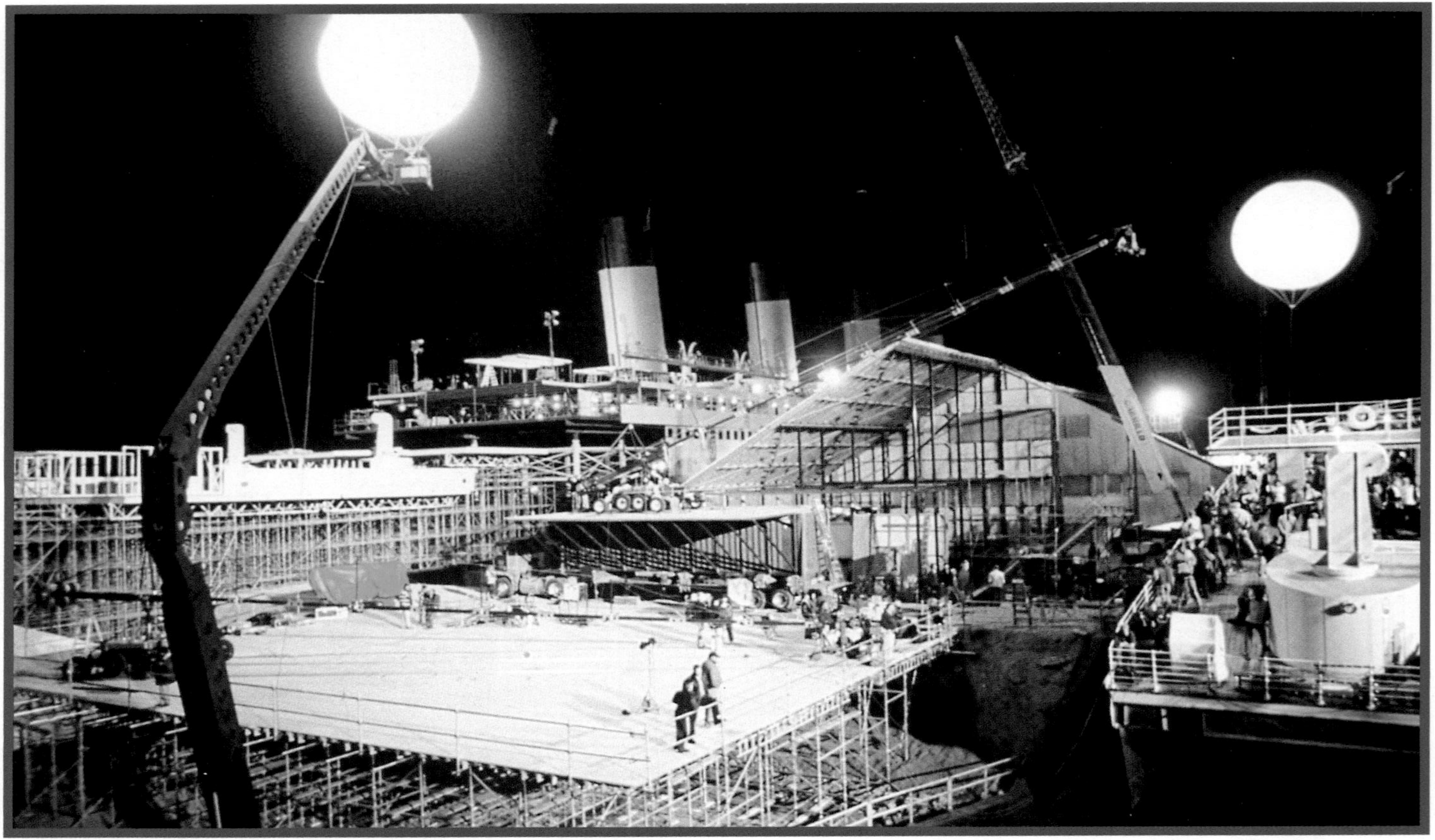

By night, the 775-foot, 10-story re-creation of *Titanic* lit up the Mexican coastline, visible for miles along the winding Autopista.

Cameron's *Titanic* spanned the length of two football fields. To save money, it was completed on its starboard side only. A skeletal visage of scaffold and iron faced the sea. The port side was filmed on starboard and later "flopped" as a visual effect.

The motto on the show was "we either do it right or we do it till we get it right." Here Cameron goes over video playback of a scene in progress with leading man Leonardo DiCaprio. They'd routinely do ten or twelve takes to nail the nuances the director was looking for.

[T]he "flying" scene where the lovers exchange their first kiss was shot on four different [l]ocations in and around the set. The pieces were then edited together to form a single, [s]eamless sequence.

Above: Rose *(Kate Winslet)*, escorted by Jack Dawson *(Leonardo DiCaprio)*, talks with her fiancé *(Billy Zane)* and her mother *(Frances Fisher)*. *Below:* Molly Brown *(Kathy Bates)* with Jack.

The lovers' embrace is broken by a surprising jolt from the infamous iceberg. After puzzling through various ways to create the iceberg using effects, Cameron finally persuaded his special effects team to use real ice.

©1997 by Twentieth Century Fox. Photo: Merie W. Wallace.

bove: Winslet lounges on an Empire sofa, preparing for the scene in which Jack sketches her nude.

pposite: Cameron filmed DiCaprio sketching Kate Winslet, but the cutaways close-ups of the drawing hands were filmed months later, as "inserts," with Cameron himself doing the sketching.

NOTICE
THIS VESSEL HAS
TRIPLE SCREWS
KEEP CLEAR OF
BLADES

)pposite: Though it was only a 12 foot drop from the stern to solid ground, it felt much further to leading lady Kate Winslet.

bove: Shots like this one of the Jack pulling Rose toward the stern were filmed on the decks of Camerons life-sized *Titanic,* which was cantilevered at six degrees.

'elow: Cameron fearlessly manned a hand-held camera and joined the stunt crew sliding down the tilting poop deck.

Above: Actress Linda Hamilton relaxes with Cameron on the set of *Terminator 2* in 1991. They were married during the making of *Titanic.*

Right: The Abyss was Cameron's first taste of filmmaking as extreme sport. He spent ten to twelve hours a day under forty feet of water, then had to decompress for ninety minutes, which he did hanging upside down in a ten-foot tank, watching dailies through a plate glass window.

ove: Cameron on the set with fellow producers Rae Sanchini and Jon Landau.
low: DiCaprio, Cameron, Fox's Peter Chernin and Bill Mechanic, and Paramount Chief Sherry Lansing had a lot to smile about at *Titanic*'s December 1997 US premiere.

Hordes of screaming fans evoked Beatlemania for Cameron and DiCaprio at the Tok
world premiere of *Titanic* in November 1997.

some Roy Orbison tunes. Paxton and a teamster made a daring hospital escape and got back in time for the party. The conga line, he told Abernathy, was still going when he left.

Landau, for one, was not amused. He found the incident frightening.

A police lab report would later confirm Abernathy's suspicions: somebody spiked the clam chowder with PCP. "The first thing we did was get everybody together in a big room," says Landau. "When you turn around and a twenty-three-year-old, healthy young woman sort of faints for no apparent reason, that's scary. I thought, Jonestown." The producer saved samples of all the food.

The local authorities launched a full investigation, but it was pretty much written off as a prank by some locals who wanted to have a party on the last night of Hollywood in Halifax. The most unfortunate effect of the incident was they had to shoot in Halifax an extra day.

As outrageous as it sounds, the poisoning incident was only one step removed from what would have been a fairly routine catering crisis. "It looked like the white, goopy stuff that poisoned us on *Dolores Claiborne,*" says script supervisor Shelley Crawford, disdainfully. "I couldn't even think about eating it."

Bill Paxton was later heard inquiring as to how he could get "the soup" written into all his contracts.

By the time they returned to Los Angeles on August 9, they were a week over schedule and commensurably over budget. "There were signs," says one observer, "that things were going a little haywire. Paramount got nervous." Dolgen called up Chernin and threatened to pull out unless Fox renegotiated their deal, putting a ceiling on their investment. There were threats of a lawsuit. Chernin, up against the wall, agreed.

With a budget hovering around the $110 million mark, Fox agreed to a 20 percent allowance for overages and capped Paramount's stake at $65 million. Anything over that amount would be paid by Fox.

It would later be described in the press as "one of the better deals since the Indians sold Manhattan."

Chapter Ten

> Directing is an instinctive thing, like the question of pitch for a singer... it's like lion taming or being the conductor of an orchestra. You have to come in and know where the camera is, or there are all sorts of evil demons that will attack you and the doubts will show up on the screen.
>
> —Orson Welles

CONSTRUCTION dust hung in the air. The studio in Baja was evolving much more ambitiously than planned. Early in the process, they discovered it was cheaper to erect steel than rent pop-up stages and to outfit dressing rooms than lease honeywagons. In mid-August, some Fox executive glanced around and decided it didn't look at all temporary. A bit more attention to things like electricity and Baja could become a permanent asset on the Fox balance sheet. With four indoor stages and the world's largest open air tank, the 100 Day Studio, as it became known, was the first movie studio built by one of the Hollywood majors since the 1930s.

The site had been carefully planned for the launching of *Titanic.* In May, Cameron and Landau and various department heads lugged the twenty-five-foot previsualization model down to Baja. They parked it on the coast and spent a day looking at it from different angles, paying particular attention to its position relative to the sun and prevailing winds. This meeting determined where to position Stage 1, the A tank, which was three feet deep for most of its 600-by-600-foot area. This was where the lifeboats would be deployed. To accommodate the big ship itself, a forty-foot deep pit ran through the center of the tank, slanting along the coast in a southwesterly direction. Next to it, a fourteen-foot-deep trough would accommodate the stunt divers.

Cameron landed in Rosarito on September 9, 1996. They had a little groundbreaking ceremony on August 10, attended by the mayor of Rosarito, Arnold Schwarzenegger, Tom Arnold, Bill Paxton, and the governor of Baja. Cameron uncorked a bottle of champagne, probably his last distraction before fully immersing himself in the movie. He rented a house on the ocean, seven miles south of the new movie studio.

Cameron rehearsed his principal actors for a week in Los Angeles and a week in Rosarito. Half the time was spent on the eight-page walk-and-talk scene from DiCaprio's audition. "We all knew there was a better scene there," Cameron says.

In Mexico, they collected in the office quad, a low-slung, sand-colored building near the entry gate. Cameron manned a video camera and had them do improv versions of the scene, first as themselves. Then he had them play it in character but in their own words. Play it mad, play it sad, play it like it's your first date, like you hate him, like you think he's the most beautiful man in the world. Later, the director would synthesize the various emotions in his rewrite, an all-nighter the day before the shoot.

One of Cameron's first orders of business upon returning from Halifax was to replace his fired director of photography. Cameron had a reputation for being tough on crews, and none more so than his DPs. *Terminator 2* cinematographer Adam Greenberg was not shy in sharing his harsh assessment of the director, even though he received an Oscar nomination for his camerawork on that film, an honor virtually unheard of for an action flick. Asked a few months after wrapping *True Lies* if he would work with Cameron again, Russell Carpenter sighed that had he been asked a week after wrap, the answer would have been no. Yet he knew the director had coaxed some of his best work out of him. Carpenter went on to lens both *Terminator 2/3-D* and the screen tests for *Titanic.* As a result of his work on *Terminator 2/3-D,* Carpenter—with his familiarity with huge sets—was an obvious replacement choice. When he arrived at Baja in early September, all Carpenter could think was, "How are we going to be ready to shoot?"

By some miracle, they actually began their first day of principal photography at Fox Baja studios on September 18. The first scenes they shot were in Rose and Cal's suite—Rose unpacking her French impressionist paintings. Two days later, DiCaprio arrived on the set, and for his first day of filming was charged with the formidable task of sketching Winslet's voluptuous form. She disrobed and posed—impudent, like Manet's *Olympia*—on an Empire divan. "Like Cleopatra," reads Cameron's script.

Having just enjoyed her first impassioned kiss with Jack at the bow of the ship, Rose invites Jack to her room to "Draw me like your French girl, wearing this," she says, waggling a sizable diamond necklace. "Wearing only this!"

DiCaprio, as Jack, stammers and rubs charcoal against paper, looking, as Cameron describes it in the scriptment, "so stricken it is almost comical." Eighty-five years forward the drawing sets the movie into motion when discovered in a salvaged safe. It is dated April 14, 1912, the night *Titanic* hit the iceberg. Cameron photographs DiCaprio drawing, but the cutaway close-ups of the drawing hands are actually his own, shot much later, in September 1997, as an insert, as the director traced his own sketch of Winslet, made from a photograph, while talking on the phone.

It just happened to work out that the first scene Kate and Leo shot for *Titanic* involved her dropping her clothes, but the timing, he says, was fortuitous. "It created a kind of a tension and nervousness between them that served the scene very well. I give them enough credit as actors that they could have created that even if it was the last day of the shoot, but I think the fact that it worked out that way actually gave the scene a certain intangible something, makes it a little more fun."

Though there would typically be at least one hundred people in Cameron's immediate vicinity on any single day of shooting—and up to twelve hundred at the height of extras—only a handful were present on Stage 3 for the drawing episode. Next, they moved on to the confrontational breakfast between the affianced Cal and Rose. Comparatively speaking, it was a small set, put up in one of the first structures ready for filming. At this point, the short term shooting schedule remained malleable as the moving pieces fell into place. The walls of Stage 2 were going up as they built the set inside.

It was obvious early on that to meet their schedule, the big ship would have to be under construction before Tank 1 was finished. The scaffolding started going up while the cement was still wet on the tank. Lamont and Cameron decided during the planning stages that the ship could be shortened by 10 percent without audiences noticing. Rather than scaling down the entire ship, however, they simply removed parts of it: an eighteen-foot span between each smokestack and a twenty-foot piece of the poop deck. It was 90 percent the real ship's length, but with few exceptions, everything on it was full scale. The funnels, davits, and lifeboats were all reduced by roughly 10 percent. At 1:1 they overwhelmed the shortened ship.

"If you think of the *Titanic* as a loaf of Wonder Bread," explains Cameron, "we took out slice five, slice eight, slice twelve and twenty-two. So it was four slices shorter, but if you looked at it, you saw a loaf. But we did it in a way that the doorway to the first class lounge still lined up with Boat 7, like it was supposed to, so everything agreed with itself." The intimacy Cameron afforded himself with the ship paid off in movie magic tricks like this. "Just because you want something to be accurate doesn't mean you have to reproduce it perfectly. It just means you have to make it look like you have, which is different," he says. "*Titanic* was 100 percent scale, shortened by sort of recombinant gene-splicing in a way even the experts who walked the deck didn't notice."

He loved to hear them admire his ship. It rose, beam by beam, on a forest of steel legs.

Tommy Fisher had his truck parked out back, on a service road between the tank and the sea. In eight weeks he received shipments of 300 tons of steel, arriving in units. Tommy and his team would fit the pieces together as if they were playing with a giant erector set. They worked from trussing plans drawn up by two teams of engineers, bolting the *Titanic* superstructure together. Welding would've been preferable, but welders were skilled labor and more costly. Fisher supervised his own crew of fifteen, imported from the states, and another fifteen local Mexicans.

Cameron made extraordinary demands of Fisher. The fact that he was able to meet them explained why he was still around for his third film. For *Titanic,* the director had some pretty unusual requests. The ship had to be designed to tilt at two angles—three and six degrees. In addition, Cameron and Fisher designed the ship to split between funnels two and three. The 200-foot forward section was built on a "riser" that traveled the forty-foot depth of the tank like an elevator, allowing it to sink on command. It was actuated by eight seventeen-foot-long hydraulic rams.

Figuring out how to sink a set the size of a building was enormously complicated and difficult. The hydraulics were Cameron's idea. He drew Fisher a thumbnail sketch during a brainstorming session at Lightstorm. The system would have to be custom built and, of course, it wouldn't be cheap. To economize, they decided they would amortize the hydraulics by putting them to more than one use. In addition to sinking the "riser" portion of the *Titanic* ship set they would be used to lower and raise the dining room. When the unit arrived it was installed at Stage 2, an enclosed structure with twenty-nine feet of subterranean space that could be filled like a tank or shot dry like a stage. Cameron would use the giant pulley system to raise and lower the 1.3-million-pound Grand Staircase-dining room set, an environment three stories at its height, that he would load up with actors and then flood.

Tom occasionally took jobs in which his main job was to file a new camera part. Cameron's shows were hard work, but the challenge was fun. He was glad there were people crazy enough to make films like this. His worst fear? To be trapped in a world of *My Dinner With Andrés*, two people talking at a dining table and Tom at the unemployment office.

While waiting for the completion of Stage 2, Cameron killed time by filming two weeks' worth of post-sinking scenes in a small tank on Stage 4. The availability of anytime, anyplace shooting that can make for a productive work day in the event that regularly scheduled scenes are postponed due to weather, illness, or whatever other inconvenience is known as "cover," and two weeks' worth is a lot to burn through.

The gentle lapping of water in the 100 by 100 foot tank lends Stage 4 the feel of a moody grotto. Sounds echo from the surface of the four-foot pool, which casts rippling reflections off the indigo walls. First up, the big "death scene." The lovers cling to a jagged sheet of floating oak. Cameron nixes the debris. It doesn't look substantial enough to float two people. He orders Lamont to manufacture detritus based on a piece of actual wreckage he'd seen at the *Titanic* Museum in Halifax.

They move on to group shots of the thrashing masses; their first sizable sequence. Cameron, wearing waders, walks through belly-deep water, cutting a swath between the cameras and his "video village." The little cluster of monitors that displays electronic feedback from the cameras is parked in the water. The electrical supply to this and everything else on *Titanic* was specially engineered for water safety.

There are three cameras shooting today. They've done a few run-throughs, to give him an idea of what the lenses are seeing. Cameron picks up a cordless microphone and addresses the crowd: "I want to be able to hear you scream, like you mean it. Fifteen hundred people are going to die tonight. That's the entire population of the town I grew up in," he says dramatically. Then adds, "We're going to be doing this a few times. Don't waste all your energy on the first take." They look thrilled to hear from him.

First assistant director Josh McLaglen's job is to get them in shooting shape. "You're freezing," he barks, "drowning in the middle of a pitch black ocean. Just *think* about what those people were going through!" All instructions are immediately repeated in Spanish for the benefit of the local extras.

A few days later, they shoot Fifth Officer Lowe, the *Titanic* hero. His was the only boat among twenty to go back to try and rescue passengers from the freezing ocean. "Ha-looooo!" Lowe calls, probing the darkness with a flashlight. "Is there anyone alive out there? Can anybody hear me?" Between takes, Cameron informs the actor, Ian Gruffud, it's unlikely the real officer Lowe had a flashlight. "He was going by sound at that point," and only managed to rescue five people, though two died later.

The oak paneled flotation device comes back from Lamont, much more to Cameron's liking. Winslet wades out and calls flirtatiously to DiCaprio, "Darling! Come and join me on the debris!"

Cameron felt you needed "to see breath to sell cold." These people were freezing to death. Nobody was coming up with a gun and shooting them. After talking to Fisher about practical options, such as refrigerating the set, Cameron and Landau make a decision to put the breath in digitally during post-production. No one had ever done that.

The scene is shot on the same night that Bill Mechanic decided to visit the set. His boss, Peter Chernin, had just received a huge promotion. Formerly the chairman and chief executive of Fox Filmed Entertainment, Chernin was in early October named president and chief operating officer of the studio's parent News Corporation, effectively becoming number two in North America to one of the century's biggest media tycoons, Rupert Murdoch. Chernin was happy to hand off a number of things to his own number two, Bill Mechanic, since Chernin lured him away from Walt Disney, where he ran worldwide home video and international theatrical distribution, to found FFE in December 1994.

Up until then, Mechanic's involvement with Cameron had been minimal. Now it would all be on his plate. By December it would be official and he'd have Chernin's old title, FFE chairman and CEO.

Mechanic now had a lot of expensive movies to mind, including Jan de Bont's *Speed 2, Volcano,* and *Alien Resurrection,* a rather daring attempt to resuscitate the franchise under the auspices of French art-film director Jean Pierre Jeunet. Mechanic had been following *Titanic* closely enough, however, to know it would require special care and handling. A misstep on *Titanic* was an international incident. There weren't many films about which you could say that. Tonight Mechanic was just there for a friendly look-see.

Cameron, a natural storyteller, perches like a genial camp counselor on the edge of the lifeboat, which is tied to the bottom of Tank 4. With the sweeping gestures of a symphony conductor he unspools a terrifying tale of desperation in the face of death. "You've just been lowered sixty feet. The descent was terrifying. And now you're watching the ship go down by the head. An hour ago this was unthinkable."

A few hours later they're setting up the next shot: a sweeping pan of humanity. Fifty dummies are floated in the tank. McLaglen addresses the extras. "Those of you to my left, you're dead. We just want you laying there. People on my right, you're . . . let's call 'em the half-deads . . ."

Titanic was already behind schedule, but the ship wasn't ready anyway, so not even shooting quick was going to help. The sets they did have they were still painting. The joke was, don't wear any clothes to work that you'd like to wear again. They were finishing "to camera." Cameron would tell the art department, "This is what we need. Finish it while we light." Lighting a set could take anywhere from an hour to six hours, if they had to rerig a complicated setup.

There was an eleven o'clock call on October 14, the first day of shooting in the spectacular dining room. At 4:00 A.M. Charlie Arneson, who had more or less taken over physical plant ops, found himself trying to deal with a freak storm that sent three feet of water coursing through the untested filtration plant.

Five hours later, more than one hundred actors, extras, and crew members would file through the entrance to the hangar-like Stage 2 of the Baja Studios, past the crafts services table packed with licorice, crackers, and snacks, down a pipe-worked metal stairway, and two flights through a maze of dusty scaffolding to another world altogether. Here, crystal glints on chandeliers and creamy white light hangs in the air. *Titanic*'s first-class dining room is like an elegant tableau eerily frozen in time. One hundred tables are meticulously set for a dinner that will never take place. The symmetry and perfection of the room are as awesome as anything out of Kubrick's *Barry Lyndon* or *The Shining.*

The hub of action is the far side of the room, where Cameron is shooting the first-class guests arriving for dinner. The air is thick with smoke and the smell of Juicy Fruit gum. One hundred and fifty mouths chomp out the tension between takes. There's no fidgeting allowed when the cameras roll. People of stature simply didn't fidget back then, notes etiquette coach Lynne Hockney. A slight British woman with bobbed hair, she moves with casual elegance. A dance historian, Hockley will also choreograph the steerage reels. Her daily manners classes, held in a nearby tent, cover everything from the proper way to eat a seven course meal to rising gracefully from a deck chair while encased in a whalebone corset.

"Cut!" Cameron cries on DiCaprio's dining room entrance. This is his Cinderella-at-the-Ball scene—the dinner to which he was condescendingly invited by Cal in gratitude for saving Rose's life. However, to the surprise of Rose's fiancé, the ragged steerage artist has been made over into a gentleman, complete with pearl stud cufflinks and a tux, by Molly Brown.

They try the scene again. "You're a little too funky chicken there, Leo," Cameron says of the actor's jerky greetings to the other guests. They try it again. "Cut! Leo, don't nod to the waiter!"

"But that's what I've been doing!" Leo complains.

"I know. It's getting too mechanical," the director says. Cameron's gaze alternates between the actors and his video monitors. He approved the lighting from what he saw on the monitors. His eye was calibrated to video, whereas most cinematographers had to look through the camera lens to light. Between takes he sweeps through the room, making adjustments to the table lamps, the chairs, instructing this or that actor. He boomerangs back to the monitor. His script supervisor shoos away anyone who comes between Cameron and the video, maintaining an open path at all times. He perches in his director's chair. "I like to pretend that I'm home with a beer and a rented tape, so I can react naturally," he says with a smile to the group around him.

They run through a few more takes. Bernard Hill, who plays Captain Smith, doesn't seem to be getting to the table quickly enough. "Bernard! Where's Bernard? You're late! You're late every time.

You've got to get in earlier. I don't care who you have to slug to get there!"

Cameron turns his attention back to the monitor. He instructs his camera operator, Jimmy Muro, to tilt the lens up a touch. "I want it to look like the Palace of Versailles, lots of height."

"I only think one thing when I see all this—make comedies!" laughs Tom Sherak, Senior Executive VP of Fox Filmed Entertainment, kicking up little puffs of dust. Landau escorts him across the lot, playing host, pointing out the sights. The men are dressed casually, Landau in khakis and Sherak in jeans and a blue denim workshirt. It's a bright, sunny day, and the *Titanic* commands the horizon, looking less like a skeletized leviathan and more like a ship. The three funnels are up and one more is lying off to the side, chained and ready for transport by crane. Baja Studios hums with the energy of a small city. Lights are beamed up to warn low flying planes.

"See these Quonset huts," says Landau to Sherak, pointing to some corrugated steel units that housed lathes, welders, and other noisy, spitting machines. "We bought them from somebody who built them for *Die Hard 3*."

"You mean we bought back our own stuff?" Sherak chides, as they pass the props building, the door held ajar by two dead "bodies." Bare-chested Mexicans in cut-offs and workboots are hammering away at lifeboats.

The exec is clearly excited about being on the site. One of the few holdouts at Fox since the *Aliens* days, Sherak is a particular favorite of Cameron's. Even though he professes to hate set visits, Sherak is here today after being personally summoned by the director. Cameron's invitations are infrequent, at best, and certainly not to be ignored. There are only a handful of people Cameron just had to invite to share the experience—his parents, Hamilton, the immigrant owner of his favorite Greek restaurant. They got a kick out of it, and he enjoyed their reaction.

Sherak stops in the middle of a dusty intersection, spinning on his loafers. "This is NAFTA at work!" he says with a flourish, indicating the flags of Mexico, Canada, and the U.S. flying above Stage 2. For the benefit of the reporter trailing along at his side, the executive explains that this couldn't be more appropriate since the director is from Canada and has shot scenes in all three nations.

A construction vehicle caterpillars by, beeping them out of the way. The reporter sidesteps the vehicle, scribbling notes as they resume their stroll to the stage. This was the first press visit to the site although eventually *Titanic* would have a steady stream of visiting reporters and journalists. Cameron's relations with the print media have always been somewhat strained. Electronic was okay. They'd cover the opening of his films and feature him on the occasional geek-hour effects special. Journalists were another story. He gave them plenty to write about, and he mostly hated what they wrote. Despite that, he was probably the only major Hollywood figure never to have hired a publicist to try and spin the coverage his way. He believed that if he was honest, they'd print the truth, though in the past his experiences had been less than satisfactory.

So Cameron's open-door policy was something of a surprise, considering the volatility of his sets. Many directors, with much less to manage, closed their sets to the press—just one more unnecessary distraction. But Paramount, which was handling domestic publicity on the film, knew what a spectacular promotional asset it had in a set the size of a Roman circus. Anyway, Cameron was still smarting from an incident involving *The Abyss* when he'd allowed only one writer on the set and the guy trashed him. Never do that again.

As Sherak and entourage arrive, Cameron is still lensing the scene in which the actors descend the Grand Staircase to dinner. The women sashay in their finery. "Give 'em plenty of room," Cameron orders, warning the men not to step on the trains. He doesn't want his actresses tripping down stairs.

Cameron sees Sherak and breaks away for a greeting, clapping him on the back. "It's an action movie, really!" he says with a chuckle. The men pose for photographs, looking oddly misplaced on the elegant marble and oak stairs. Sherak is dressed identically to Cameron, in his production uniform of jeans and blue workshirt, with the exception of script pages sticking out of the director's back pocket and Cameron's brown suede workboots.

The next day, they're back in the dining saloon, shooting the big dinner scene. They rehearse it a few times, actors reading from the script, just to get the beats down.

"Tell us of the accommodations in steerage, Mr. Dawson," says Frances Fisher, launching the exchange. "I hear on any other ship they would be first class."

Jack responds, "The best I've seen, ma'am. Hardly any rats." The comment prompts hearty laughter.

Cameron plants his palms on the table, leaning in next to

DiCaprio, and explains to the twelve actors seated there, "It begins with Ruth going out of her way to trash Jack, then a number of subtle digs from Cal, who thinks bringing the monkey up from steerage will be for the amusement of one and all. They're feeling pretty good about their stations in life, when Jack, quite honestly, and without any artifice or pre-thought, winds up turning the tables by just being himself, dropping his role-playing of trying to be a gentleman."

By his second champagne, Jack is exhorting them to seize the day. "He's giving his speech; he's just sort of eating while he's talking, and having them give him another champagne." Cameron instructs DiCaprio to grab the wine glass incorrectly, by the globe rather than the stem, in contrast to everyone else at the table.

"He's giving this philosophy which actually strikes everyone as quite poetic and profound and valuable regardless of your station in life." The scene ends up with Rose leading a toast to Jack. "Here's to making it count!"

Jack is celebrated. Ruth's attack backfires.

Cameron squats beneath the camera, between Canadian actor Victor Garber playing shipbuilder Thomas Andrews and Kathy Bates. His eyes sparkle as he watches the actors breathe life into his lines.

A white-haired waiter asks Jack how he takes his caviar.

"None for me, thanks," Jack says, waving him on. "Never did like the stuff much."

Winslet launches right into her line with Garber, but Cameron interrupts. "How are you playing that? The 'No caviar' thing?"

"I should glance at him, shouldn't I?"

"This whole scene is about you and Jack looking at each other." He pauses a beat for emphasis. "And I'm not getting a lot of that now."

"You will," Winslet assures him.

"I know I will," he says with a laugh. "The question is when."

She blinks back her surprise and launches into a dead on delivery, complete with the most fetching glances.

Satisfied, Cameron rolls film and they do numerous takes. Each time, they're serving real Beluga and the caviar budget alone is sizable. By the end of the evening, the waiter's near-useless arm has been encased in a quick-dry plaster cast, freezing his elbow at the 90-degree angle required to carry the tray.

On the set, *Titanic* historians Ken Marschall and Don Lynch are received like royalty. Pointed at and whispered over, their reactions are scrutinized. The videographers doing the "making-of" focus their lens on them. Cameron himself is eager to gauge their reactions to the vision he has conjured.

The low-key Lynch quietly takes it all in while the more animated Marschall has a visual epiphany. When he was approached to consult on the film, Marschall knew it would be ambitious, but he had no idea of the lengths to which Cameron and crew would go to achieve perfection. Up until now, the high point for them had been the 1959 *A Night to Remember,* which Titaniacs revere for its technical accuracy. Marschall must have seen the film a hundred times. *Titanic* made *A Night to Remember* look like a child's production, he thought excitedly. Looking around, it seemed to him that no expense had been spared.

Cameron even had them detail the ceiling, something many directors wouldn't even bother to show. In the farthest corners of the sizable dining room, tables are set with patterned plates and silver. The ornately carved wall paneling on the grand staircase is not typical movieland plaster of paris but oak. Real oak. Acres and acres of it, deck after deck. The details are truly mind boggling. Newel columns are molded from real fittings lent from Marschall's collection, acquired from *Titanic*'s sister ship, *Olympic,* which was scrapped in 1935, its pieces sold at auction.

Cameron enjoyed few things more than hearing the experts gush over his ship. They were among the few who would appreciate the trouble he went through. Compromises could have—and, it was argued, should have—been made. He even tried making some of them. For instance, economics dictated that the ceiling sconces be molded plastic, but the high-wattage bulbs required for the photography caused them to melt and they had to be remade in glass. When a decision had to be made about the chandeliers, Cameron had Lamont skip the Lucite and go directly to crystal, so they would tinkle and tilt just so during the ship's demise.

Cameron introduces his experts to the actors.

"Hello. I'm Colonel Gracie!" says actor Bernard Fox.

"Indeed you are!" agrees Marschall.

During a break, the director shows them how he photographed the Grand Staircase at the wreck site, his index finger extended in imitation of the Snoop Dog. "We came down through here," he says, retracing the camera's path, "then we hung left on D-deck and we ended up right here." Bam, his finger jabs a hapless, lacquered door. "And there should be a little brass sign right there that says 'Push,'" he says, tapping the wood accusingly. He calls for someone from the art department to fix it immediately.

Even Cameron's dreams are infiltrated by *Titanic.* He is haunted by the nightmare that he is on the ship, headed for the iceberg. He knows of the freezing black fate that awaits them, yet it is the ship's decor that torments him. "We got that door wrong!" he screams. "That door opens in! We thought it opened out!" He wanted to be able to say, to the best of his ability, that this was exactly what it would look like if you went back in a time machine and stood inside the *Titanic.* Though it wasn't necessary for people to know the difference in order to enjoy the film, he wanted the experts to be awestruck.

"Ahhh! It's amazing," Marschall marveled.

In reality, when Lamont ran the numbers, it was only marginally more expensive to work with real oak than to paint plywood or plaster to look like wood. Besides, when the ship sank and when several tons of water roared through those stairs, Cameron didn't want some cheesy piece of foamcore falling off the wall. He wanted, of course, to see splintered wood.

The company worked in the luxurious dining room set for a total of ten days, and half that time was spent underwater.

Chapter Eleven

There are rules, many rules, in Hollywood's power game.
—Martin Scorsese

THE TILTING poop deck was a stunt coordinator's dream, or nightmare, depending on your perspective. It was definitely the most elaborate operation Simon Crane, age thirty-five, had ever orchestrated. With his perennial tan and megawatt smile, Crane looked like a rugged, slightly timeworn Tom Cruise. Like most coordinators, he got his start as a stuntman. He'd acted in *Aliens,* but since he'd been wearing an alien mask the entire shoot, he didn't expect Cameron to recognize him.

Crane had worked steadily since then, but given that it was in Britain, where action films aren't exactly a cultural staple, his profile remained low. He was perhaps best known within the industry (and to audiences, though they didn't know his name) as the guy who does the daredevil jet-to-jet transfer at the beginning of *Cliffhanger.* With the success of Mel Gibson's *Braveheart* and its acclaimed battle scenes, which Crane coordinated, he finally earned himself an international reputation. The timing was fortuitous.

Cameron had made his two previous films with Joel Kramer. Kramer began his career as Schwarzenegger's stunt double and was a great favorite of the actor. No one could deny he'd done some brilliant work on *Terminator 2* and was a logical choice for *True Lies.*

But there was an accident on the set. A stunt man suffered serious burns on his arms shooting a scene in which he was filmed leaping from a fiery explosion. Cameron wanted the actor in regulation stunt wear, but Kramer thought a new body gel would be safe. It was the first time emergency medical treatment was required on one of his sets, and Cameron was devastated. He prided himself on his safety record. While he didn't blame Kramer for the incident, when Crane's *Titanic* bid wound up lower, it was an easy decision.

Titanic was packed with stunts, but in broad terms, the two biggest deals were sending the jumpers over the ship's side and the "tilting poop deck," a ninety-foot span of stern that tilted skyward.

During the final death throes of *Titanic,* the stern reared up very slowly to 45 degrees—time enough, it is believed, for at least half the remaining passengers, as many as 1,200 people, to congregate. When the ship split in two, the stern splashed down quickly, then stabbed up again, very fast, to 90 degrees. This dramatic event would be the action climax, the ultimate James Cameron moment in the three-hour-and-twelve-minute film.

The effect would be achieved using 250 people—150 extras and 100 stunt performers—lashed or tumbling along the tilting deck. Their number would be heightened by digital stunt people, added during post-production as a visual effect. The churning ocean below would also be added in the computer.

In planning the shot, handfuls of toy army men were dropped down the deck of an upended model. They also tried it with marbles, studying the dynamics of the fall, and how things piled up. "Like skittles or ninepins or whatever you them call in America," says Crane. "One person would fall, hit someone else, the two of them would fall, hit something else. Kind of like a giant pinball machine. But you don't want it to look stunty, you want it to look realistic."

The extras would be harnessed off to the side with the stunt people tumbling through the middle. Most free-fell, but some wore descender rigs. Crane had padded the set as much as he could. Objects that looked like metal were actually foam so people could hit what appeared to be capstans or benches and then bounce off them. Cameron jokingly called it "the Nerf set." By all appearances, it seemed impossible that anyone would get hurt.

The scene was minutely planned and continually rehearsed. Boring work, to be sure, since safety is not a particularly exciting goal. At the end of the day, though, safety was what mattered most. Danger, like everything else on a movie set, is supposed to be an illusion.

"No smiling," Crane admonished the 250 people assembled on the tilting deck under the bright afternoon sun. "We're videotaping these sessions." Cameron would view the tapes in the evening, after shooting all day in the dining room, and instruct Crane to change this or that. Finally satisfied with what he saw, the poop-deck scene was ready to shoot.

When the cameras started rolling, there were immediately problems with stunt people falling onto and hurting other stunt people. Falling down a flight of stairs is a pretty simple stunt, but if you do it a hundred times, you're probably going to get hurt at least once. Each take on this scene had 100 stunt players, 100 stunts that they did ten times over a three-day period. Cameron's POV varied—hovering above in the crane or sliding along the deck with a hand-held. Much of the work was shot when the ship was at 30 degrees, with the camera dutched to make it look steeper because at a 90-degree angle, the stuntmen dropped like stones, falling out of frame too quickly.

"Anything above twenty-five degrees and you were holding on for your life. Forty-five degrees felt like a straight drop," Cameron notes.

So ingrained, evolutionarily, is the sense of "level" that even slight changes are hugely disorienting. In all, there were three broken bones: an ankle, a cracked rib, and a broken cheekbone. No one was hurt badly, but any injury was of concern. When Cameron realized what was happening, he halted the falls and had everyone harnessed down and dangling. The free-falls would be inserted by computer.

By October of 1996, Cameron and company had run through some $75 million and would go through a matching sum before wrapping on March 23, not even including bank interest, marketing, distribution, and certain effects-related costs. It put them well over budget and on track to becoming one of the most expensive films ever.

The news had not gone unnoticed by Bill Mechanic, who made his fateful set visit earlier that month demanding cuts.

Cameron felt bad, but what could *he* do? He hadn't made up the erroneous numbers. That's what he was told it was going to cost by the experts, the people who do the bids and sign the contracts. Then you get into the game and the ground rules start to change.

Before the film was even greenlit they'd already gone through three rounds of scene cuts on the script. Plenty of notes. Nibble, nibble, nibble. Early on in production Chernin followed up with a five page list of cuts which Cameron had reasonably gone through and said, "I think I can live without this, this, this, and this."

By the time of Mechanic's second, fateful set visit, "I had already been through that cinching process," says Cameron. "The knife was getting a little close to the bone."

In the last three or four weeks cost reports showed significant variances. Worse, nobody seemed able to say with any confidence what they had spent or what the ultimate cost of the film would be. Managing a film with the logistical and budgetary requirements of a small city was a more complicated undertaking than anyone had anticipated. Purchase orders were arriving on the desk of unit production manager Grant Hill at the rate of hundreds per day.

Landau, theoretically in charge of the purse strings, was in over his head, handling much more than could humanly be expected of one person. Though Landau's contract was technically with Fox, the studio had no illusions that the producer could rein the director in. Landau had gone native. His loyalties were with the film. And anyone who'd seen the early footage, Mechanic included, knew *Titanic* was something special. Who wanted to stand in the way of that? Certainly not Mechanic. He just wanted to bring some order to what had become an "uncontained" situation.

But Cameron wasn't exactly open to suggestions. His priority was getting the film made and he made it emphatically clear he would not be reading memos from middle management Fox executives. The director showed a disinclination to speak to anyone at the studio other than Chernin, who was unwilling to confront him, and seemed barely tolerant of Mechanic, even after he was named chairman of Fox Filmed Entertainment.

A low-key guy of medium height and build, soft-spoken and bespectacled, Mechanic was easy for some to write off as a lightweight home-video guy—until you realized that he virtually invented the priced-to-sell business, building the $30 million Buena Vista Home Video into a $3 billion business by the end of his eight-year tenure. A renegade in his own way, Mechanic was a USC film school graduate who substantially wrote the rules of the video game during that industry's scrappy formative years. During his three years at Fox he rebuilt the company.

Although he knew it was a risky move with someone like Cameron, whom he perceived as a control freak, Mechanic decided to install his own lieutenant on *Titanic.* He didn't want to upset the delicate balance that kept James Cameron spinning with enough force to keep hundreds of millions of dollars in orbit, but he had to do something. By this point Mechanic knew that the only hope for Fox was to have a great film at the end of the day, and he didn't want to do anything to jeopardize that. But if firing Cameron wasn't an option, gaining control of the spending was. He called Marty Katz.

Mechanic knew Katz from his time at Disney, where Katz had spent eight years supervising production for the studio's motion picture and television divisions. He had a reputation as a tough, no-guff administrator. A former U.S. Army first lieutenant, he ran his operation with militaristic precision. On any other show he would be the studio enforcer. But Cameron wasn't one to be enforced. Katz became Fox's "facilitator." Though he signed on with the loose designation "production consultant," he would in fact function as a sort of supervising producer, working closely with Landau, whom he knew from his Disney days, when Landau was producing *Dick Tracy.*

Katz was enormously impressed with what he found underway at Fox Baja Studios when he arrived in late October. In twenty years of motion picture experience, he'd never seen quite anything like it. Getting the studio built for $20 million must have been an incredible challenge. Building it for $20 million while multiprocessing the production was an extraordinary achievement. The operational scope of the set was enormous. It was the first film Katz had ever seen that ran twenty-four hours a day, seven days a week. Simple things like communications were a tremendous logistical feat. Everyone was on a walkie-talkie. Hundreds of them were being used.

A huge amount of work had gone into getting the film to this point and it would be foolhardy, he thought, for anyone to come in expecting to "take over," lecturing about how to "fix" things. He'd heard enough about Cameron to know someone like that would last about five minutes on his set. Yet anyone too passive wouldn't get the respect necessary to do the job. His was a precarious position. But Katz sensed they could use his help.

Of all the agents Fox could've dispatched to Rosarito, Katz felt they were lucky to get him. Many in his position were just dollar-watchers, men who charged blindly down the path of least economic resistance. Katz prided himself on the ability to balance the needs of the studio with those of the filmmaker and, ultimately, the best interests of the film. The relentless momentum of *Titanic* had everyone in a reactive mode, trying to get through from one day to the next while managing a crushing workload. Katz put in several twenty-hour shifts trying to keep up with it all.

It was overwhelming. There was a million dollars a month in heavy equipment—cranes, generators, forklifts. The production didn't just have the departments found on any film. Here were departments like marine, engineering, outside engineering, housing coordination, and motor pool. And while you could probably find any one of these on a lot of movie sets, no single film—not *Cleopatra,* not *Ben-Hur,* not *Gone With the Wind*—had all of them.

When Cameron wasn't shooting, hundreds of craftsmen and technical support were mobilized, preparing for the time when he was. When he shot nights, the legwork would run from 6:00 A.M. until 5:00 P.M. When they were shooting wet, the swing shift would come in and find sets that were totally destroyed by water, stunts, and practical effects. Department heads from art and effects would be standing by at 6:00 A.M. to receive the director's hand-off notes, which detailed what was needed for the next day. Rooms, soaked to the ceiling, had to be restored to meticulous splendor; eighteen hundred pieces of flatware had to be removed from the floor.

Costumes had to be repaired and dried. The amount of work a department like wardrobe could do in one night was astounding. It was a factory. The big Southampton dock scene posed its own problems. More than a thousand extras waved off the ship, requiring at least eight thousand articles of clothing, from suspenders to hats. The wardrobe building seemed to run for miles, rack after rack of jackets and ball gowns. Next door, the hair and makeup department brandished walls of mustaches, beards, and wigs.

The props department was a factory that could manufacture ornaments, furniture, and molds, often on a moment's notice. Things destroyed by acts of God or acts of James were replaced overnight. It was like magic. Magic that cost money.

Contrary to what was being reported, it was tough on Cameron to see the cost reports and realize, at a certain point, that he could never cut enough scenes to make up for the overages. Money he'd planned to spend a certain way was being spent on things like transportation, cables, and lights. Granted, they were serving his requests, but he'd been told such expenses were going to cost half as much. The fact was, nobody had ever done this stuff before, building a tilting poop deck or a riser deck to sink a full size ship. That meant nobody really knew how much it was going to cost.

The press loved to write that he was behind schedule; the irony was that had he been running on time, he'd be cooling his heels anyway because the ship was finished a month late. For a major construction job, that's not a lot, but nobody wrote that.

And the arguments with the executives. He was so tired of the same conversations, over and over. There was too much story, more than he needed. He disagreed. Eventually you'd think they'd just get it, figure out that that's why they hired him, because they thought he knew how to make a film better than they did. Everyone said he had a huge ego, but he viewed this as an empirical statement. He reasoned that the studio executives had thought about ten thousand things for the past three years, while he'd thought of nothing but the movie.

Cut this, cut that. They hated the spitting scene, where Jack teaches Rose to spit overboard. They wanted to lose the flooding of the third-class corridor, where the immigrant and his son are bowled over by a torrential gush. Could he eliminate the lengthy tour through the inner workings of the ship—the boiler room, the engine room? After all, Jack and Rose don't even go in the engine room. Cameron's answer was always the same, "I think I know what the film needs. In my opinion we can't do without this. There will be a diminishment."

"We're losing light," cries Jimmy Muro, a slight man with a shock of brown hair and world-weary eyes. In addition to being the A camera operator, he has mastered the duck-walk of the Steadicam, a stabilized camera more or less worn by its operator that allows very free tracking shots. Muro was a great favorite, and veterans marveled at how "nice" Cameron was to him. There were lots of people who could operate the A camera; Cameron let him do that more or less as a favor because finding a good Steadicam man was a whole other problem.

Muro's first Cameron film was *The Abyss*. He remembered arriving on the set, where he'd been summoned from his home in New York. The first thing he noticed, aside from the fact that it was being shot in a nuclear reactor, was that Ed Harris, one of the film's stars, was sleeping on the floor in a cement corridor. Well, he thought, this is going to be a challenge. The experience of shooting that movie changed his life. Now he lived in Los Angeles and was one of the core team of creatives that would follow Cameron to the end of the earth to make a movie. And here they were, on the Baja Peninsula.

November 15 marked the completion of the 750-foot *Titanic* set. For the next nine days, she was the focus of shooting the Southampton scenes. To see the big ship jacked up to full height—five stories from deck to dock—painted and detailed, every lifeboat in place, was a heightened experience for Cameron and the cast and crew. The sight made them all feel as if they were on top of the world.

The ship was planted with its nose facing north, starboard side to the dock. This allowed them to take advantage of the prevailing winds with smokestacks that sent billows of smoke tufting aft—a minor bit of environmental engineering that enhanced the illusion of motion in the sailing scenes. Cameron's attention to detail was such, however, that he wanted his ship docked with her port side to the pier, as was historically accurate. To adjust for this, the uniforms and signage, including the four-foot words "White Star Line" on the terminal building, were printed backwards. In post-production, the film would be "flopped," reversing the orientation.

With *Titanic* in full glory, they were prepared to begin. First assistant director Josh McLaglen yells, "Background!" and activates a thousand extras, nineteen horses, ten carriages, three dogs, and a burgundy Renault that soars skyward as it is hoisted into the cargo hold by crane. Scenes like this really test a first AD, whose job, among other things, is to wrangle crowds. With the background players moving, McLaglen calls "Action!," animating the principal players. Amidst the throng, the Hockley party descends from their touring car like a pageant of peacocks. The scene is composed of a hundred tiny moments, unfurling in a series of well-timed vignettes. Winslet, adorned in white pinstriped travel suit and lavish purple hat, is a sumptuous visual anchor in the sea of gritty humanity. "A crowd of hundreds blackens the pier next to *Titanic* like ants on a jelly sandwich," Cameron set the scene in his script. The Hockleys have arrived late and must enter on the dock instead of through the terminal with others of their class.

Cameron moves quickly between his cluster of principal actors and the video village, some twenty feet away. In the flickering black and white of the playback monitor, the scene has the eerie authenticity of an old newsreel.

The last cut is called. Cameron asks an assistant to grab him a cappuccino—decaf. He's sworn off caffeine for this shoot. Associates say the stimulant has a pronounced effect on his kinetic demeanor. During *Terminator 2,* when they were filming on location, one crew member recalls Cameron getting so keyed up he'd stalk the corridor of his hotel at night, burning off extra energy.

Digital Domain's Rob Legato is down from Los Angeles to discuss the effects shots. They chat briefly about how a model will be substituted in for the real ship when *Titanic* leaves port. Then Cameron herds him into the crane basket and they're hoisted a hundred feet in the air, doing a fly-by over the bow of the ship. The wind speed, Cameron notes, is about twenty knots—exactly what the passengers would've felt on the deck of the *Titanic* the night she sank.

The setting sun shoots pink and orange rays across an improbable lavender sky. The quality of light on the ship is dazzling. The moon appears, a perfect white disc. From the vantage point of the crane, the moon looks like just another magic prop, requested at a filmmaker's pleasure. Cameron absorbs every detail of his ship. Southampton would mark the last time the *Titanic* team saw daylight for quite some time.

By Thanksgiving the press was having a turkey shoot with *Titanic.* Cameron couldn't understand it. Maybe they were just lazy. His film was a big target, easy to hit. There had been several reporters to the set since that first visit, and the early indications were not great. He felt faint stirrings, the ineluctable hum of bad buzz. *Newsweek* ran an item headlined, "A Sinking Sensation" while *Time* checked in with, "Glub, Glub, Glub... Can James Cameron's extravagant *Titanic* avoid disaster?" The budget was reported at anywhere from $120 million to $180 million, enough to put *Titanic* in contention to be the most expensive film ever made.

Cameron's response was, "We're doing spectacle. Spectacle costs money." This seemed fair enough, but only incited them further. Comparisons were gleefully drawn with *Waterworld* which, at $170 million, held the record for what amounted to excess.

The first speculation began on how unlikely it was that cofinanciers Fox and Paramount would earn back their investment. To make matters worse, Sumner Redstone, chairman of Viacom Inc., the parent company of Paramount, went bragging to Wall Street analysts about how well the studio had done for itself, capping its investment. He'd financially overextended himself to buy Paramount, and Viacom stock still hadn't recovered. In fact, it was taking a beating. Redstone was willing to claim whatever bragging rights he could get.

At this point, it wasn't even a matter of who looked smart, it was who looked less stupid. Fox was in the unenviable position of being forced to assume a defensive position against its own business partner. It even appeared that the Paramount side was leaking tales of Cameron's excesses, escalating rounds of internecine studio one-upmanship. It would be a full year before the film's early reviews triggered confident predictions that Paramount, at least, was guaranteed to make some money.

Chapter Twelve

> Any sufficiently advanced technology is indistinguishable from magic.
>
> —Arthur C. Clarke

THE MOVIE WASN'T in control, but it wasn't totally out of control either. Marty Katz knew from out of control; that meant not moving forward but moving laterally or, even worse, moving backwards. Things aren't getting done. Sure, it could be argued that Jim was too much of a perfectionist. Did he really *need* to be such a perfectionist, eating up time with take after take? But those things do not an out-of-control movie make. Cameron was doing backbreaking, diligent work, and he was doing it in an organized fashion. He was leading the troops, doing every bit of what they were doing, plus another hundred percent.

Katz remembered one night when they were shooting the post-impact sequence. The ice arrived in hundred pound blocks. Cameron hoisted an ax and began hacking away. Getting over their initial disbelief, the crew followed suit. Thirteen men hammering with axes; an evolutionary one-up on the opening of *2001.* Giving up his ax, Cameron stepped back and watched for thirty seconds, then he just couldn't stand it anymore. He pushed a puny guy aside, taking his ax. It was just too much fun. The director was setting, in Katz's words, "an unbelievable standard," showing that he knew full well the film was going to be hard work, but no one would work harder than he would.

Such dedication generated strange rumors. The Hollywood gossip mill was, predictably, humming with reports of Cameron's excess. "He's gone Kurtz," they whispered, alluding to the renegade military man in Francis Coppola's *Apocalypse Now.*

The installation and operation of the tower crane—the Cam crane, as it was dubbed—could easily be misconstrued as the conceit of an egomaniacal director. A holdover from the construction phase, the crane was used to build the ship, and maybe could be used as a lighting platform. However, when Cameron got up there to eyeball some camera angles on the tilting poop deck, he noticed how smoothly the crane operated, so he planted Muro and a Steadicam up there. Because of the wind, they put gyros on the Steadicam. One thing led to another until they made the cognitive leap, "Let's get a Wescam! And bolt it to the basket!" The Cam crane became an invaluable tool for capturing the swooping pans and zooms of the ship, and saved a fortune in helicopter rental fees. This was one innovation that didn't come out of *American Cinematographer.*

Katz notes that another film with significant engineering challenges was *Waterworld* and perhaps, he adds, if they'd approached their problems in like fashion, the movie wouldn't have been so out of control. That's not to say *Titanic* was all smooth sailing. There were problems. For instance, the original electrical budget on the film was short by $9 million. Initially, they'd planned to relocate equipment from set to set. But once the lights were placed and the wires laid on the ship, it seemed illogical to move them back and forth. Here were miles of portholes and a light behind each one, manually installed, pane by pane; more cable and more lights than had ever been assembled on one production. At the cost per hour they worked the crew, it didn't make sense to spend two hours relocating a generator. Since it was cheaper to get another generator, they soon had virtually every available generator on the West Coast working their movie.

Where they could cross-collateralize between departments more efficiently, they were prevented from doing so because nothing was centralized. If the electrical department needed a crane they'd rent one, though there might be five such machines sitting on the effects stage next door. In a way, Katz admired each department's unwavering focus on being ready for the director's shooting needs. The problem, from his perspective, was that there wasn't an overarching administrative plan.

He didn't blame anyone. If he had to offer any criticism, it was that it should have been apparent earlier on that they couldn't keep going this way. "There's no crime in saying wait a minute, we have to slow down here, even if it means a delay of a couple of weeks, to figure things out, make sure we have the right systems in place, get the studio finished." Landau had asked for two extra weeks before the move to Rosarito so that the studio would be more complete and they could take some time to catch their breath after Halifax. But the Halifax filming had already put them behind schedule and the studio wanted a summer movie. Fox said, "Denied." There was simply too much work to get done before Christmas. The production started at a wild gallop and had a hard time hitting its stride.

Katz, a dead ringer for Joe Pesci, right down to the vocal cadences and cowboy boots, was realistic about his job. Knowing full well his particular skill set—keeping fiscal mayhem at bay with cold objectivity—was not going to win him any popularity contests, he took things in good humor. On the wall of his office in Santa Monica was a framed note he'd sent his Disney boss, Jeffrey Katzenberg, "Said the hemorrhoid to the asshole, what would I be without you to look up to?" To which Katzenberg scribbled back in the lower right hand corner, "Marty, how right you are!"

Within a few weeks of his arrival in late October, Katz embarked on an administrative overhaul. Though not uniformly impressed with every department manager, he thought the majority of them only needed a little extra manpower. The only casualty was a production supervisor in the construction department whom Katz felt had no sense of what it took to manage the production's multifaceted needs cooperatively. Overseeing two major outside companies, dealing with the inner and outer areas of the ship, and keeping a handle on costs and deadlines was impossible with this guy. Katz hired an expert he knew from Disney.

He brought in more production managers, freeing up Landau to devote himself to Cameron as a creative producer. "Jim needed a contrapuntal person who was there, whether he listened or not. Jim needed it, and Jim demanded it. Jon had developed a relationship, and I basically said, 'Jon, go ahead and spend your time with Jim. I'll take over cost reporting, management of the departments, and communications with the studio. I'll deal with everything other than your making sure that Jim has what he needs creatively and schedule-wise.'

"In a very short order we at least knew what we were spending," Katz claims. Now there were some hard decisions to be made. The money had gone out fast and freely. That was an unfortunate fact but, on the positive side, it had gotten them to this moment. The first three months of principal unit work had produced some amazing imagery.

Had Cameron known earlier that he wasn't X amount of millions over but Y, could he have done things any differently? Would he? Directors are allowed to be wacky and artistic. Producers have very definite fiduciary responsibilities to the studio or financing entity. Cameron had been busy directing his movie. If no one—not his own producers, not the studio—could tell him how much he was spending, how did they expect him to make informed choices? Any one incident—a union problem or a customs issue—could keep Landau tied up indefinitely. He spent his days in meetings, his nights on the set, and was working twenty hours a day.

Michael Eisner once told Katz there were two kinds of mistakes. There's a mistake and there's "The Big Mistake." Everyone makes mistakes. You recover. The big mistake is one you don't get over. Katz saw a big mistake looming on the horizon and it was tilting in his direction. In addition to sitting level, the big ship was going to be pitched at Angle 1, three degrees, and Angle 2, six degrees. Three degrees might not sound like much, but the procedure for hydraulically jacking a wood and steel superstructure four blocks long is hardly small. Not only did it involve draining and filling the 17-million-gallon tank, but securing the reconfigured ship would be a Herculean feat. Then there was the little matter of redressing it. The initial plan was to go to Angle 1 before Christmas hiatus and Angle 2 when they returned.

Had things gone according to the original plan, this might have been possible, but things changed. The completed ship weighed twice as much as was originally estimated. "They kept putting stuff on it," Fisher shrugged. Since no one had ever built a life-sized recreation of a luxury liner before, they couldn't be blamed for missing the mark. The estimates on how long it would take to jack the ship went from six to thirty-six days.

Katz was bothered by the plan the first time he saw it because even if they got the ship to three degrees, there was no guarantee they'd get the work done by December 21. Weather, an actor getting sick, any number of things could cause a delay and there was no way the crew was staying beyond December 21. They'd already put in more than ninety days of shooting, the length of an average shoot. They'd had it. They wanted to see their families. So that would mean keeping the ship at three degrees until after break and jacking it to Angle 2 after production resumed. Killing time on stages while they jacked the ship would burn through all their cover. Katz had nightmares of the film shutting down, of people being paid to do nothing to avoid the risk of losing them. How long would that be? Two weeks? A month?

He was faced with a dilemma. Sure, Fox could tell Cameron, "We're not doing that. Move on." As the money investors, they had every right to. On the other hand, as a proven filmmaker, Cameron would be equally justified in saying, "Hey, that's fine! Let somebody else finish this. I'm not doing it." If Cameron were forced into something he didn't feel good about, Katz had no doubt as to what he would do. Walk. Then the movie shuts down—indefinitely.

The only hope was to convince the director that eliminating Angle 1 was a good idea. "Jim is a tough guy, but if you could explain it in a way that makes sense to him, and if it's not a compromise—because that is not in his vocabulary—but a trade-off, it might work," mused Katz. Landau approached Cameron. "We've got a big crisis. We don't think we can do the jacking. The only way to make it happen is to skip the three-degree angle and start disassembling the set immediately to go to six degrees."

Cameron initially resisted. The construction firms were telling Landau they could meet their deadlines. "Jon is a great cheerleader," says Katz. "He makes people want to perform for him." Katz was a cheerless pragmatist. Pressed, the builders began to hedge.

"You're spending a quarter of a million dollars a day shooting," mused Cameron. "Suddenly overnight the rules change, but you've already committed to the path. You're already making the movie." Instinctively, he felt he should trust his original plan, conceived in the objectivity of pre-production. Once shooting began you developed tunnel vision, focusing on the matter at hand. It was easy to lose sight of the big picture.

"I thought, 'Oh, it's just going to look like the ship goes from doink to doink,'" the director says, demonstrating a comedically quick sinking ship with his hand. "Nothing in between." But he started to think about doing some of the three degree shots with models. Would it be possible to do them on the level deck, dutching the camera slightly? Would audiences know the difference? "And I'm thinking, ahhh, it's a big compromise. But maybe we can do it."

Cameron commuted home to Los Angeles every Sunday, his one day off, to spend time with his family—when he could get out of the editing room. He'd intended to commute by helicopter. They built a helipad. His fantasy was to shoot the movie out of the country, with all the cost savings that entailed, but be only an hour commute from home. When the helicopter was grounded by a rainstorm one morning, he was forced to drive, arriving at the set one hour late. He decided to stick with a standard issue carpool van. The three-hour commute gave him time to revise shot lists or catch up on his sleep.

This Sunday Cameron reviewed his script, noting all the wide shots at three degrees, cutting some and massaging the rest. "I figured, that can be an effect, that can be a model, this shot I think we can do as a split screen—I can shoot the boats in the foreground, I can shoot the ship in the background, and I can split-screen the background and rotate it and angle it." Some of the shots could be pulled forward onto the level set, some faked at six degrees. But Angle 1 was essentially replaced with visual effects. "You've got to roll with the punches," he sighs. Cameron began shooting his scenes on the big ship November 22. Two days later they started detaching the poop deck. Cameron had to laugh. They build one of the biggest, most expensive movie sets in history, and he has two days to shoot on it in one piece.

The dome implosion was originally planned as a model shot, which common sense dictated would be cheaper. But then, because they had to build the set anyway, it seemed less expensive to do it real. The price difference between a set that could survive that kind of pressure and one built simply for normal use was nominal and good models were very costly. They built the set so that they could flood it.

The entire dining room set was built on a platform that raised and lowered like an elevator, controlled by Fisher's eight hydraulic actuators. When it sank, water would come pouring in. The only problem was, it didn't drop quickly enough. "I told him, 'You're off by a multiple. You need to be two or three times as fast.' I was trying to scare them," Cameron snickers, "but it needed to be twice as fast."

Water is uncontrollable, and that was the precise feeling James Cameron wanted when he flooded the dining room.

At first, everyone was nervous to be working with the strange gravitational dynamic of the moving set, 1.3 million pounds of heaving wood and steel. But after working there for a few hours, people were beginning to get comfortable. Then suddenly, the set let out a heaving groan and, for no apparent reason, plunged five feet. "Pieces started falling off the ceiling and water started rushing in, and man, I'll tell you, it got *real!*" recalls Cameron, who with McLaglen took charge.

"Everybody out of the set, now!" There was an orderly evacuation. They had the safety drill down cold, with escape hatches on the ceiling and other marked exits. No one ever knew for sure what happened. Some kind of computer glitch, it appeared. "But from then on, everyone understood the set could sink and we could really be on the *Titanic,*" said Cameron, noting, "Nobody ever dozed through the safety briefings again."

The water on the set was a luminous green, lit from beneath. The room dripped with lacy, liquid beads; the walls seemed to sweat. Cameron wanted to create a "strange space," unnatural, not of this earth.

Landau, wading around in a wet suit, coined the phrase, "Elegance submerged."

For most of the dining room work, the crew wore black neoprene wet suits. For some of the more intense shots, Cameron commanded the set in full scuba gear, complete with mask and compressed air tanks: the Director from the Black Lagoon. On the set, he plodded through the water, awash up to his chest. Mask pushed back on his head, Cameron checks the monitors. "Martin, stop helping people," he admonishes a minor character. "I hate that. It's every man for himself."

The dome implosion destroyed the Grand Staircase and is the climax of the flooding sequence. The scene took Tommy Fisher two weeks to prep. By the time they started shooting, he had spent eleven hours putting on the finishing touches. The scene was "a oner," no second chance to shoot it. Cameron hedged his bets by loading sevn cameras into the room. There were two positioned downward from the dome, two pointing in a window. Cameron himself was operating a hand-held; Muro on Steadicam. They had a "bungee cam" hanging from the ceiling. Rather than getting each individual camera up to speed, Cameron called a "roll," and each operator had seven seconds to shout out if they were having technical problems. After seven seconds they launched into the countdown that would trigger the liquid avalanche.

Three cargo containers send 45,000 gallons of sea water crashing through the elaborate filigree ceiling. Stunt people thrash about in the whirlpool below. Chairs and tables swirl by. It's all over in less than a minute.

The cameras rolled for less than a minute.

Cameron immediately planted himself behind the bank of monitors, reviewing the take, camera by camera. The playback filled the air with piercing shrieks. Cameron watched the screen, as one magazine described it, like "a man reading the fine print in his contract with the devil."

Cameron made them stick around for one more shot—water crashing through some dining room windows—before signing off on his cordless microphone with, "Merry Christmas to all, and to all a good night." Everyone would get an extra week of holiday so there'd be ample time to jack the ship to six degrees.

There was no Christmas cheer for Bill Mechanic. The neophyte studio chieftain was wringing his hands over *Speed 2,* which was also slipping behind schedule, and *Alien 4,* which was having problems of its own. Another little project of his was building an animation division to rival that of his alma mater, Disney. He'd sunk millions of Fox dollars into a fully staffed studio in Arizona. Its first project, three years in the making, was a romantic riff on the story of the Romanoff princess *Anastasia,* due out Thanksgiving. If the movie flopped it would be a major public embarrassment. All these concerns buzzed around Mechanic's head, but the blinking red light on his radar was *Titanic.*

Over the Christmas hiatus, Cameron, Landau, and Sanchini were hauled into Mechanic's office by Katz. It was December 23, and Mechanic was feeling Scrooged. The group delivered a status report. The film was clearly way over budget and two weeks over schedule. They still had another sixty days to shoot. Mechanic was interested in future plans. Would Cameron be sticking to the schedule? Could Mechanic count on him to make the revised budget? Would Cameron make more cuts? Reduce the shooting schedule? End the pain? But you couldn't cut enough scenes to make up for these overages. "If we stopped shooting today we could remove enough production days to offset the overage," Cameron told Mechanic. "But of course we haven't sunk the ship yet, and I don't think anyone's going to want to go see a movie called *Titanic* where the ship doesn't sink!"

Cameron did not view the situation lightly. He was a good soldier and these problems had occurred on his watch. Fox's pain was real to him.

Cameron asked the others to leave and pulled Mechanic aside. "Look," he told the executive, "I'm not happy this has happened. A studio shouldn't be put into a situation where even in a success scenario, by everyone's standards, they don't make money. I feel responsible. I will not compromise the film, but I'll do what I can to make it easier for you to see a return on your investment by removing the only gross player—me. I'm reassigning my profit participation back to Fox."

Cameron's offer was more than unusual, it was unprecedented. Let's put it this way: across town, in a trailer, another A-list director was shedding tears, literally weeping, as he shared the news with a studio bigwig that his big summer film had gone over budget. He was crying, but he wasn't offering to give back any money.

Some studios build in penalties for directors who go over budget. The most common course correction is called a "double addback" and it means that for every dollar over budget, the director pays back two from the back end. So if the film goes $100,000 over budget, for example, the studio would have to see a profit of $200,000 before any profit participation kicked in. Considered a somewhat insulting addendum to have attached to a contract, the double addback was rarely tolerated by A-listers. Cameron did not have such a clause in his contract.

Mechanic appreciated the director's offer but said it didn't matter since *Titanic* was not likely to make it past the break-even point and profit sharing was therefore irrelevant. Fox was more interested in halting the hemorrhaging.

At this point, Fox was within its right to fire him. However, although Hollywood executives probably spend a good deal of their time fantasizing about it, in reality they can't go around kicking directors off their pictures unless they gomore than 10 percent over budget, according to the rules of the Directors Guild of America.

Cameron believed *Titanic* would do well commercially. His guess was about $400 million in box office receipts worldwide, which was certainly a healthy sum. When you factored in home video and TV rights, he thought, the film would be profitable, though not wildly so. Cameron's profit participation equalled 10 percent of the studio's first dollar gross. Under this scenario, his offer to Fox amounted to a gift of between $10 and $20 million.

Yanked out of his movie world in Rosarito, Cameron was faced with the fact that even his mildly optimistic revenue prognosis was the minority view. Tension had risen considerably between the partners, Paramount and Fox. There was an air of desperation in their dealings. The concern was not who would make more money, but who would lose less.

In September, Paramount had undergone an executive reshuffling, appointing Robert G. Friedman vice chairman of the Motion Picture Group of Paramount Pictures, in which capacity he supervised marketing and distribution. Robby, as he was known throughout the industry, began his career in the Warner Brothers mailroom and worked his way up the ladder over the course of twenty-six years, ultimately named president of worldwide marketing and publicity. A compact man with silver hair and ice-blue eyes, he was known as a savvy marketer with a knack for rubbing people the wrong way. He was having precisely that effect on Mechanic, with whom he had been having regular and rather pointed discussions about setting a *Titanic* release date.

Paramount had to show a seven-minute presentation reel of the movie to the National Association of Theater Owners at their annual ShoWest convention in March and an availability date was integral to that process. Friedman was pushing the July Fourth weekend that Fox had mentioned in their original discussions to partner on the film. They pressed Fox to press Cameron to reel the film in fast.

Already behind schedule, it was questionable whether Cameron would be able to pull together a film this complicated so quickly. With everything that had transpired during the first half of the shoot, he felt it unlikely that they could meet a summer release. But they were unwilling even to discuss other dates. "At that point, they had so much money in the picture that they absolutely lived in denial that the film could not be made for summer," explains Cameron. From Fox's perspective, the earlier Cameron delivered, the less expensive the movie would be.

The six-day weeks meant very little editing had taken place since shooting began. Cameron began requesting an additional editor in September. The unbudgeted item became an issue. No one wanted to pay. Fox finally agreed to the hiring of editor Richard Harris, who'd worked with Cameron on two previous films. Harris was set to join in January.

But Mechanic was losing patience. There are certain areas of responsibility in which a domestic distributor takes an active role, and setting the North American release date was one of them. Fox was already invested at a level in excess of Paramount, and Mechanic felt the partner studio should be taking a more equitable stance. Paramount, meanwhile, resolute in its philosophy that a deal's a deal, was responsible for $65 million in negative cost. The studio would also be picking up a sizable print and advertising tab. Fox was stuck for the production overages and delivering it as a summer movie was its problem.

Mechanic felt Paramount needed a big summer movie more than Fox did. The hottest thing on Paramount's dance card was *Face Off,* the John Wu-directed action flick opening June 27, which starred John Travolta and Nicolas Cage. Fox had its summer tent pole film in *Speed 2,* which was releasing on the July Fourth weekend. For obvious reasons, Mechanic was not eager to see *Titanic* competition land there, but it was Paramount's contractual right to select a North American release date for *Titanic,* though Fox could approve it. When Mechanic finally came around to approving July Fourth, his attitude was, okay, but Paramount should pay for those acceleration costs. A line was drawn in the sand. Mechanic thought he was calling Friedman's bluff.

An extra week had been built into the vacation schedule to allow extra time to jack the ship. They had run through so much cover that there was little left if the ship wasn't tilted on time.

After some perfunctory festivity, Cameron spent two days on an effects stage with Legato at the Playa Vista studio and the remaining nineteen days of his hiatus in the editing suite. Initially, he concentrated on the model shots, but toward the end he brought in some principal actors. Winslet and Zane were there to film one of the past-present "dissolves" in which Cal collars Rose with the diamond necklace, which she clutches at her throat. Moving in for a close-up, the shot dissolves eighty-five years forward to pull back off Gloria Stuart's hand as Old Rose.

DiCaprio and Danny Nucci were also there to do greenscreen work for the scene at the bow, where Jack delivers his flamboyant proclamation, "I'm the king of the world!" Joined by his Italian sidekick, Fabrizio, they watch dolphins and Fabri pretends he sees the Statue of Liberty. "Very small, of course." Since the shots of the ship in motion at sea were done using models, the actors had to be filmed separately and composited into the scene later. This is done by photographing them against a background of electric hue, in a shade so odd that when you run it through a computer asking that the color be removed, it doesn't alter anything natural to the scene (blue was in fashion for a while, but now it was green). A photographic element like this might be combined with fifty other images to form a complete picture, like fitting pieces into a puzzle.

Cameron designed some exceedingly complex shots in *Titanic,* some costing up to $400,000 to combine as many as two hundred elements—shadows, smoke, and birds, for example. The scene with Nucci and DiCaprio starts simply—the actors against a fake background of sky and sea, a wind machine mussing their hair. But a moment later, when the camera pulls back for a giant "reveal" of the entire ship, the image is created almost entirely in a computer. With the exception of the ship, which is a model, everything else, right down to DiCaprio and Nucci and the people walking the decks, is generated by computer image. Cameron had had many of his principal actors, including Winslet and DiCaprio, "scanned" into the computer the previous summer in anticipation of shots like these.

The actors sat in a contraption not unlike a fast-photo booth, hair pulled back, perfectly still, while what appeared to be a vertically positioned fluorescent light bulb slowly whirred around their heads, circling a full 360 degrees. The laser beam mapped the data into a digital library that would also include the "captured" body movements—things like walking, stooping, falling—that would be utilized to create digital extras to populate *Titanic's* decks.

By the time the troops reconvened in Rosarito, Cameron had taken off all of two days for the holidays.

Chapter Thirteen

Fear is not an option.

—James Cameron

WHEN THE CAST and crew returned to Rosarito after the holiday hiatus, they found the *Titanic* plunged by its bow beneath the waterline. The foremost 150 feet of the ship was removed and its likeness was painted on the bottom of the tank. Even in the overheads it was impossible to spot the deception.

A 600-foot-long set, elevated three stories high and stacked with an army of extras, was big filmmaking, as big as it gets.

Their first task was to shoot the frenzied deck action and deployment of the lifeboats.

It was time for James Cameron to sink the *Titanic.*

Through the miracle of movie making, the night of January 19, 1997 was about to merge seamlessly with April 15, 1912 at 1:30 A.M. as *Titanic* thrashes through its last hour of life. Wisps of smoke pant from three stacks as the ship groans into the sea. They're prepping for the shoot. The ship glitters with the bravura of 40,000 amps, ablaze like a baseball stadium. Three thousand lights are joined together by seventy miles of cable. Chief Lighting Technician John Buckley had been gulping back his anxiety for months, waiting for the day he'd hear, "Okay, switch 'er on! Let's see the Titanic!" One of the biggest challenges of the whole film was sculpting the big ship with soft lighting. They had four eighteen-foot diameter Solaire balloon lights for that purpose. To position the lights, they had two construction cranes and eight "cherrypickers."

They built a forty-by-sixty-foot reflector—silver overlaid with muslin—that they hung from the tower crane. It made nice light, but caught the wind like a sail. One night, seventy-mile-an-hour gusts came up, shredding $120,000 worth of lighting gear. That's when they invented the "master cylinder," a twenty-foot diameter piece of culvert pipe they hung from the tower crane when the director wasn't riding in it. If it got really windy they used freestanding hard lights—a Night Sun and a Musco—but that was a last resort. Cameron didn't like the look.

During the day, the rigging crew would position the cranes and heavy lighting gear. It took hours to prep for the night's shoot. And if Cameron wanted to change the plan during shooting, it was an ordeal—forty electricians running nonstop for up to six hours.

They were using eight thousand lights on the movie—four thousand movie lights, and four thousand "practicals." Many of the lights had to be immersed in water, which complicated matters. Filmmakers doing water work typically use DC, or direct current, which is safer when wet. But it prevents them from using the more desirable HMI (Halciogenic Mercury Iodine) and Xenon lights. AC current can kill a man at .5 amps—it's stop-and-start spurts create fibrillation in the heart. Exposed, the body becomes a filament, a conductor of heat and electricity.

When they were sinking the dining room, Buckley had an electrifying encounter with a table lamp, taking about twenty amps as he yanked it from the water. His arm was numb for three days.

You could feel the voltage running through the water when it leaked. It would usually dissipate after a few feet. Buckley did spot checks, walking around, slapping at the water. There were 650 portholes on the ship, and Cameron was particularly interested in getting a perfect halo of sea green around the ones that sank beneath the waterline.

Director of photography Russell Carpenter and his techies zip around the tank in Zodiac boats, moving lights. Carpenter receives his lighting instructions via headset from Cameron, who is scouting the ship from 162 feet above in his Cam crane. "Lose the underwater light at the bow. We can see it," says the director. "Give me a little more light on the deck house, just aft of the number three funnel."

"We have a 5K on the other side, we can move it over. It'll take ten minutes," says Carpenter.

"Fine," Cameron responds. "Do it now." Now, as opposed to waiting until the next roll. He wouldn't initiate any act until he knew how long it would take, because at any one time he had ten such operations cascading through his mind. One might take ten minutes, another an hour. That meant he was an hour away from shooting.

On steel wheels bigger than a man, the crane slides the length of the glistening hull, sending ripples of water through the tank. The crane takes approximately ten minutes to make a pass the length of the ship, announcing its intention to move with the fast, hollow ring of a fire alarm. The crane operator, a brawny Texan who more or less came with the equipment, sets the basket down lightly. Cameron leaps out and is off in a flash. A little crowd collects in his wake—Landau, McLaglen, Carpenter—all waiting to take orders. They've learned to walk quickly to keep up with the director as he charges over to video village, on the eastern side of the A tank.

Meanwhile, on the deck of *Titanic,* tuxedoed extras mingle with the dungareed crew. Costumed dummies are lashed to the rails. The sound of satin rustles in the wind. Of course, when the real *Titanic* sank, such aural luxury would not have registered above the screams. Some of the dummies move—extras placed for effect.

There's a refreshing snap to the air, and the folding chairs, circulating cappuccino, and expectation of fireworks give the set a festive feel, like a evening picnic by the lake. Cameron seems oblivious to the niceties, focusing on the task at hand. "Shelly," he says to the script supervisor, whose job it is to maintain continuity. "Have you told them who's rowing in one-ninety-five?" The scene has Molly Brown arguing with Quartermaster Hitchens in Lifeboat 6, the hysteria of full evacuation playing in the background on the big ship. Close-ups for this scene had been shot months earlier on Stage 4 and, of course, needed to match this shot.

Cameron lines up his first shot. Tonight he has five cameras at his disposal, though right now he is using only two, a Technocrane and the Steadicam. Muro is balancing on the edge of a camera barge, getting a little more shake than he bargained for as he frames the occupants of Boat 6. An octopus of people stands behind him, proffering booms that hold lights, reflectors, and microphones. Hair and makeup people remain poised, at the ready. The Zodiac is more crowded than the lifeboat.

The two boats float roughly twenty feet from shore. Cameron examines the images on the monitor.

The buzz of preparation has its own momentum. He tells McLaglen to get over to B-deck and wrangle the extras through a rehearsal so he can see the crowd action at the front part of the ship.

"Wouldn't this just ruin your night, thousands of miles in the middle of nowhere?" Cameron asks no one in particular.

It's midnight, and they're waiting for the wind to die down. Eighty-five years ago, the *Titanic* slid into a perfectly calm sea. "Like a mill pond," Captain Smith says in the script. Cameron looks into the black sky and imagines it filled with digital stars. His film will have more digital effects than any film, ever.

The extras are mobilized and Cameron is unhappy with the mild activity on deck. "They're not reacting to what's happening, they're just strolling around," he tells McLaglen via the headset. They do it again. It's better.

"What's going on with the boat?" he inquires. Fisher and Bates are playing cards. "Molly Brown strikes again!" Bates cackles, laying down her winning hand. There are three lifeboats in the water and four strung from the side of the ship. One careens lopsidedly against the hull. It's historically accurate. "Having now worked with these lifeboats, I can say that twenty lifeboats launched in two hours is not bad," offers Landau, critiquing the historic rescue. "But they probably could have saved five hundred more people if they'd been more efficient."

"This wind blows!" Cameron deadpans. At 12:30 A.M., nature finally cooperates and he calls action. The extras dart purposefully with a high degree of nervous expectation.

EXT. OCEAN/TITANIC/BOAT 6

(The hull of Titanic *looms over Boat 6 like a cliff. Its enormous mass is suddenly threatening to those in the tiny boat.)*

HITCHINS

Keep pulling—away from the ship. Pull.

MOLLY

Ain't you boys ever rowed before? Here, gimme those oars. I'll show ya' how it's done.

When filming begins it's like throwing a switch and Cameron operates at a different level than those around him. He's a supercomputer processing a thousand tasks. His eyes sweep the set, locking finally on the monitors. He absorbs the information—the visual cues, the headset data, the nearby chatter—with the quiet intensity of a tightrope walker. He is jazzed.

A white flare explodes over the ship.

"Cut! Jimmy, the drop was too early. We're supposed to be meeting the boat." After each take a wet-suited minion tugs Boat 6 back into position. By the third take, it's apparent that the flares are exploding too high and taking too long for the camera to follow them down.

"That one went off at four hundred feet. It needs to go off at two hundred feet. Can you cut down the charge?" he asks Tommy Fisher. "How big a charge is it now?"

Fisher doesn't know.

Cameron presses, "Do you have a scale so you can cut them all down the same?"

Fisher says yes.

"Russ, you're not keeping enough water in your frame."

"More water, sir!"

Cameron decides he'd like more contour on the hull. "Sidelight it," he says slowly. "Do it now." His voice has a dreamy urgency and he does not look at Carpenter as he speaks. He stares at the ship, though his tone of voice implies that to *not* do it now could be dangerous.

Carpenter mobilizes the tower crane, attaching a twenty-by-forty muslin bounce card that will gently redirect illumination.

Visiting the set that night are the studio contractor, Roberto Curiel, and his wife Maya. They sidle up to the back of Cameron's chair. "Couldn't you build us a better ship?" Cameron asks. "This one's sinking."

They break for lunch at 2:00 A.M.

Cameron goes to his trailer to review his shot list, figuring out how to play the game during the last half. "Usually the problems of the day are going to manifest early on, lunch is where I regroup and try to save the rest of the shooting day," Cameron says. "On a big complex shoot like this, you'd walk in first thing in the morning, not knowing: Do I have my actors? Can I even shoot the scene on the call sheet? Have they got the sets done? Do the hydraulics work? There are thirty questions that have to be answered before you can even shoot a frame of film."

Landau joins Cameron in his trailer to give him an update on the studio line. Fox is insisting on the removal of the "flooding corridor" sequences, as well as the scenes in the boiler room and the engine room. This is not the first time they've asked for these cuts.

Cameron dismisses the request, as he has in the past. He's keeping the scenes.

But he agrees to one concession on the interior ship scenes, allowing them to be shot as second unit, under the direction of Steve Quale. This was a major concession for the director, who in principle doesn't believe in second unit. "It's like an artist agreeing to let someone else paint the corners of his canvas."

By 3:00 A.M. they're on to the next setup: the mad, swelling rush of humanity towards the bow. McLaglen supervises the activity on deck, where Kate and Leo race through the throng. Winslet is vaulting over railings, descending full deck levels in high heels and a gown. This might be considered a tea party compared to what James Cameron usually does to his action heroines—Jamie Lee Curtis dangled from a helicopter in *True Lies* and Linda Hamilton ran through blizzards of broken glass in *Terminator 2*. Still, it's a bit more than most actresses are expected, or prepared, to do. There are stunt jumpers going over the side—a fifty-foot free jump into water.

Cameron is filming them from the crane, where he is joined by Carpenter. Boyish and bespectacled, the director of photography is, at over six feet, one of the few people on the set who can stand next to Cameron and look him straight in the eye. Between these two and the Wescam operator, there is little room to maneuver in the small basket.

While most directors would stick an insurance camera off to the side, locked off and boring, as security, James Cameron has a knack for complicating shots. He'd hire the best person for the job and assume he'd get his master shot—invariably some big, complicated crane move with rack focus. Even his B cameras would be on the move, the Steadicam weaving about, some dolly action on the sidelines. It made for awesome shots that he'd cut into great sequences, but it also made for some tense moments.

On big scenes of the boat evacuation, people were spread out for acres, and everyone communicated by a radio system, the Clearcom. Channel One was limited to the A team—Cameron and an inside circle that would change somewhat from setup to setup but always included McLaglen, Fisher, and the camera operators. Everybody else went on the walkies, fifty open channels. Tom Fisher's son, Scott, often found himself on Cameron's wavelength. There was some high-decibel action. Cameron had a standard repertoire of insults and the veterans were well acquainted with his favorites, which ranged from "Any idiot could figure this out!" to inquiries as to whether the listener had finished high school.

Fisher's personal favorite was a line aimed at B-camera operator Memo Rosas. Cameron was riding around in the crane basket doing big, wide shots with the Wescam. In a situation like that, he really couldn't place other cameras, though he'd sometimes sneak Muro in with the Steadicam off to the side somewhere. Memo wasn't doing anything for a couple of shots. He wandered off and Cameron broadcast his displeasure. "Get Memo back! We're all down here working and he's off getting a pedicure! Let him do that on his own time!" Pedicure! Where did he come up with that stuff?

Sometimes the admonitions were well deserved. Cameron was not stingy with expletives when making a point. At first, it could be shocking for anyone with limited exposure to teamsters, newsrooms, or moody filmmakers, but after a while most people got used to it. Everyone had their turn in the barrel, got past the sting, and laughed it off. Those who couldn't didn't last long on his sets.

Traversing several hundred feet of hull in a single shot is not a simple matter. That Cameron, in the crane, now had a way to get his camera anywhere on that ship within minutes created certain challenges for Carpenter. The DP remembered one night, just as the sun was about to come up. Cameron wanted desperately to get a shot that swept down the whole length of the ship. "We had electricians, gaffers, everybody—it was like throwing ballast out of a sinking hot air balloon. We were just heaving lights over the side to get them out of the shot, out of his way. It was like, 'Here comes Jim with his Wescam!'"

In fact, they weren't using a special kind of crane. It was a construction crane—a *used* construction crane. Cameron would instruct the Wescam operator, who would work the shot while talking the crane driver through the moves via headset. They would do a few rehearsals. When filming began, the director would provide a running commentary of instruction. "Faster! Faster! Faster! Pan right! Pan right! Now slower! Slower! Okay, zoom in!" The moves were so complicated that they would only work once out of every three or four times. And then maybe you'd hit a bad streak. Trying to hit your marks with Cameron in one ear and the crane guy in the other, it was pretty easy to get screwed up. Cameron wasn't known for his high tolerance for screwups.

On this particular night, everything seemed to be going wrong. The director's headset ran out of batteries. (He had a pet peeve about batteries. They were small and cheap and there was no good reason they shouldn't always be in plentiful supply.) Cameron's voice was cutting in and out. On the deck of the ship, Josh yelped, "I can't hear Jim! It's like sabotage!" The Wescam generator ran out of gas. The operator was repeatedly missing his marks. "Miss it again and you're fired!" He missed it again. He was fired.

"A film is only as good as its extras," Billy Zane says, standing off on the sidelines, watching the action as he awaits his next scene. "Think about it. If you've got an extra who's just looking into the lens, or looking uninformed, or ill-dressed or allowed to keep blue eye-shadow on, it's like heh-heh. You blow the reality of the moment no matter where the shot ends up."

All the extras on *Titanic* were required to read up on the period with material provided by Finn, so their conversation would be authentic, even if they were only talking in background. That Cameron put a lot of stock in that kind of effort, creating "atmosphere," impressed Zane, who aspired to direct. Cameron would take time to tell extras the motivation in scene 171, what's going on in the scene for him, if not emotionally, at least logistically.

It's time to roll action. Cameron hoists a hand-held camera with a wide-angle lens, and heads straight into the crowd of leaping kids. With the camera on his shoulder he appears to have achieved some happy natural state. The cares of the previous hours melt away. Bobbing head and shoulders above them, he looks like the Pied Piper leading them through a gleeful dance.

"All the technology invented by the crew members, the amount of juice you have on this picture, and at the end of the day, God's still got a really great show," says Billy Zane, settling into a director's chair. His legs rest on *Titanic*'s port rail, facing the sea. The end of Zane's day is the beginning of the day for most. "Just when you think you've cornered the nice light—" As the sun sends its first cool rays over the Mexican hills, he reminisces about all the beautiful sunrises and sunsets he's seen from these decks. He's pensive, philosophizing about the inspired madman leading the show. "He's a daredevil of the highest order, off screen and on. It's really fascinating to feed off that energy and give it back. There's a kind of film magic that occurs when there is risk, when there's a lot to be lost. And you throw yourself out there as a performer and, I think, as a director. You need that sense of risk. The danger."

Zane reveled in Cameron's ability to balance the technical and emotional aspects of the acting craft. The director was generous with takes. "Film," he liked to say, "was the cheapest thing on the set." He'd shoot a scene twelve times, twenty times, to get it right, playing through all the emotional beats. To the casual observer it might seem like a lot of extra work, the same lines again and again, but to Zane it was heaven, a luxury in the cost-conscious world of big filmmaking.

"The first few takes," Cameron told Zane, "are just to find out what the scene is about. The next few we'll use to focus in on certain ideas, and the last take will be to refine it, to close it." This process took the pressure off the director (and the actors) to figure it out right away, made filming more of an exploratory process.

A typical shooting day on a big movie like this costs $300,000. For what? One take? Two takes? "I don't think so," says Cameron. "You're not going to stop until you know you've got it nailed."

The breakfast scene with Cal and Rose is one for which they did many takes. Cameron averaged seven or eight takes per shot, and rarely went above fifteen. Here, Zane attempts to intimidate Rose, his fiancée, who has just spent the previous night with Jack. The director wanted Zane seething with the perfect touch of desperation.

INT. ROSE AND CAL'S SUITE/PRIVATE PROMENADE—DAY

(SUNDAY, APRIL 14, 1912. A bright clear day. Sunlight splashing across the promenade. Rose and Cal are having breakfast in silence. The tension is palpable.)

CAL

I had hoped you would come to me last night.

ROSE

I was tired.

CAL

Yes. Your exertions below decks were no doubt exhausting.

ROSE *(stiffening)*

I see you had that undertaker of a manservant follow me.

CAL

You will never behave like that again! Do you understand?

ROSE

I am not some foreman in your mills that you can command! I am your fiancée.

(CAL explodes, sweeping the breakfast china off the table with a crash. He moves to her in one shocking moment, glowering over her and gripping the sides of her chair, so she is trapped between his arms.)

CAL

Yes! You are! And my wife—in practice, if not yet by law. So you will honor me, as a wife is required to honor her husband! I will not be made out a fool! Is this in any way unclear?

Cameron carefully modulated Zane's outburst. After a few early takes, he said to Zane, "The problem I have is I'm not surprised when he turns over the table. I think it should be fucking *shocking*. The way I conceived the scene is... this control, it's the difference between conventional tires and radial tires. Conventional tires break away slowly and then they slide out. Radial tires hold the road perfectly right until the moment they give. In a world of control, Cal can create that facade up to a certain point. When it breaks, it breaks abruptly and catastrophically. It's not a smooth slide."

"No hydroplaning," asked Zane.

"No hydroplaning. That comes later."

"Tires. You're bringing tires into this!"

"My tire metaphor doesn't work for you?"

"White walls, with a..."

"Racing stripe..."

"Racing stripe and a meaty tread. Tread lightly."

"Yes," Cameron agreed, gazing at Zane in the monitor. "Does he give good frame or what?"

They did six takes. Cal overturned the table, and two grips squatting just out of picture dragged it off the dolly track as the camera rolled by. After each cry of "Cut!" a half-dozen production assistants picked up broken china, which they tossed into blue plastic buckets.

"Cal is an archetype for a dying era," says Zane. "The Edwardian upper class inventors of the iron age. The shapers, co-creators of our country, our economy. We witness a change in a character that we love to hate. For better or worse, Cal does care about Rose. But he has to get to the point where he realizes he does. Initially, he does not know what love implies, that it could mean anything more than possession."

Zane's character was defined largely as a foil against Jack, the "bohemian ambassador" representing the new American spirit, the movement in art and social programs. "To see the beauty and the romance of this avant-garde aesthetic, of the bohemian, who Cal thought was slime and never gave the time of day, to suddenly see, through Rose's eyes, that one pair of boots could outshine the cleanest spats, the most manicured hands, is shocking to him," claims Zane. "It's the girlfriend dropping the prep and going for the grunge boy, totally blowing the Ivy Leaguer's world by forcing him to see the beauty and relevance of a rougher edge."

Zane points out, "One of Cameron's favorite phrases on the set was, 'I don't know how I'm going to get out of it, but we'll find a way.' To an actor, that's a challenge."

As both the screenwriter and director, Cameron feels he has a certain advantage. "The great thing about director-screenwriters is," he explains, "they know what they don't know." There are scenes in the script, in every script, that for whatever reason don't quite work, and as a director, he has the luxury to indulge his probing nature. By contrast, directors for hire are handed finished scripts and there is a certain expectation that they'll color within the lines, deliver what the studio is paying them to deliver.

According to Zane, the thrill of adventure lurked between the time Cameron called "Action!" and "Cut!"

"It's exquisite, really, to have a voice like his and the will to make it heard," says Zane, staring over what is now a fully lit morning. The crew is wrapping it up around him. "This is the slice. This is the tale he wanted to tell. I think it's going to be an amazing film, because the passion behind it is so extreme. You'd really have to look to a labor of love, independent film for this kind of vibe. You just don't get it on the larger budgets. They're not that kind of animal. Because the studio wants everything that spills out of his head, they'll humor him to the tune of $200 million dollars, but it's the rarest of circumstance. This is Cameron's baby."

Despite such enthusiasm, by February, even the most stoic actors were beginning to fray at the edges. All that night shooting on the ship, the waiting in the cold, ocean air in corsets and tuxedos, was getting to them. As far as Scott Fisher could see, it wasn't that Cameron was so tough, it was just that the actors had been spoiled by the industry standard. "They're used to, 'Hey, I come on the set, I work, I'm going back to my trailer.' On this film it was, 'Okay, you can come to the set and you can sit around for a while, and you can be in shots where you're way in the background and we don't really see much of you. I'm paying you to work on this movie. We're all going to be here for sixteen hours.'"

Working on the ship was an ordeal. The dressing rooms were not twenty feet away, as they'd be on a sound stage, but fifteen minutes away and the trip involved automotive and freight elevator travel. Since they couldn't just pop in, Cameron was inclined to keep them hanging around if he might need them in a few minutes. But then if he had problems, a few minutes could turn into forty-five minutes.

The grueling exertion of this shoot had a profound effect on the actors both physically and emotionally. Their talent was a resource for Cameron, a precious resource, but as with every tool at his disposal, he squeezed every last drop of performance from them. In the same way that his lighting had to be perfect and his effects had to be state of the art, he wanted everything those actors had, and he was not afraid to wrest it from them, if necessary. Winslet and DiCaprio were getting quite a workout.

Cameron introduced Winslet to "squibs," little explosives that simulate a bullet hit. For the dining room chase scene, he took pains to point them out so she wouldn't be surprised as they popped in the water around her; an experience she'd never have doing Jane Austen adaptations. And then there was that scene in the labyrinth, where she's carrying an ax to rescue her handcuffed lover. The water was freezing! Winslet initially requested the authentic touch, to help her "process," but the reality of it was a little too much. They shut down shooting very quickly and returned after the water was heated.

Rolling onto the lot each day, Cameron would break out his radio and ask, "Is everybody here?" Then, "How's Kate feeling?" They lost practically a day a week to her. It was a big deal. There were times it came down to "Show me the doctor's note." Cameron hadn't missed a day of work to sickness in eighteen years. Is she sick, and do we get the insurance claim? Or is she not sick?

"Oh, she's not *that* sick."

And there were a few days Cameron indulged her and allowed her to call in sick.

But when Kate was on the set, she was great. She was never tempermental. She cared. She worked hard.

Leo was felled by tonsilitis once. The worst you could say about him was he was a dawdler, always ten to fifteen minues late to the set, preoccupied by the latest shipment of video games.

Turnaround time for the actors—their guaranteed downtime from the set—was twelve hours, according to the Screen Actors Guild. Early on in the shoot many players—particularly the actresses who had two and three hours of hair and makeup—waived this clause and returned after ten hours so they could work the first shot of the day. But by the middle of February, as fatigue set in, they changed their attitude. If it wasn't required by contract, they didn't do it.

When he arrived at the studio each day, Cameron often thought to himself, "No movie should be this hard."

Nobody was working a more punishing schedule than he was, a fact his detractors tried to use against him. "Cameron loves pain," they'd say. But he didn't love pain, he loved results, and sometimes results required pain. Nothing good was ever done easily, so he accepted that if you wanted to do something good, you had to work hard.

In February, the Sunday workload expanded. In addition to editing, Cameron began meeting with composer James Horner about scoring the music.

Born in Los Angeles, Horner speaks with a British accent, having spent his formative years at the Royal Academy of Music in London. Back in Los Angeles, he found employment at Roger Corman's New World Pictures, where he met Cameron. By the time they got around to working together in 1986, the composer already had garnered some big name credits—*Cocoon* for Ron Howard, another Corman graduate, and *48 Hours,* directed by Walter Hill, who was also a producer on *Aliens.*

Cameron's compressed post schedule on *Aliens* turned the two-week scoring period into a creative pressure cooker that their relationship barely survived. Cameron went on to use Alan Silvestri for *The Abyss* and brought back *Terminator* composer Brad Fiedel for *T2* and *True Lies.* By *Titanic,* the director was ready for a change. In September, he made a run at composer John Williams, who'd become wildly successful in Hollywood scoring Steven Spielberg films. In fact, he now did nothing *but* Steven Spielberg films. He had his own private bungalow at Amblin Entertainment, Steven's adobe utopia, nestled into an idyllic corner of the Universal Studios lot. In the fall of 1996 Williams was busy scoring *The Lost World.*

Williams' agency, Gorfaine/Schwartz, was the hottest music shop in town, and Michael Gorfaine also happened to represent Horner. He slipped his client a copy of the script. While Horner had no particular interest in working with Cameron again, he responded strongly to *Titanic.* "I wasn't interested in doing one of Jim's action movies," says Horner. "I wanted to do a film where Jim was taking a huge step out on a branch and everybody could hear the wood breaking."

Gorfaine prevailed upon Lightstorm music supervisor Randy Gerston to put in a good word for Horner, who was also a client. Gerston, whose tastes ranged from Nine Inch Nails and Portishead to Puccini, admired Horner and thought he'd bring something interesting to the mix. And it didn't hurt to have Michael Gorfaine owing you a favor.

Horner had by this time amassed five Academy Award nominations for work that included the *Apollo 13* and *Braveheart* scores, both of which Cameron loved. When Gerston brought the idea up the director needed only a little coaxing to agree to meet with him. Horner was summoned to the Malibu Hills.

Music is an integral part of any film, particularly an epic, and Cameron had a strong sense of what he wanted. His vision was defined largely through what he didn't want—a precious, string-driven accompaniment that screamed "period film." As with the casting, the dialogue, and the lighting, he wanted something that, without being inappropriate, would be contemporary. Cameron liked to screenwrite to music and had written *Titanic* to the Celtic stylings of new age singer Enya, whose ethereal music could move him to tears. It was perfect for the effect he was after, creating an emotion, but not through strings. At one point, Cameron actually hoped Enya might score *Titanic.* Gerston convinced him to approach her with the idea of a "musical project" that would team her with an established composer. Enya had never done a film score, and the fact that it took her two years to record an album made Gerston nervous. An album is thirty minutes worth of music, and Cameron needed three times that amount in six weeks. Enya sent back word that she did not do "musical projects."

Cameron still planned to use Enya on his "temp track," a rough mix of off-the-shelf or "source" music assembled with the work print to suggest mood in broad terms. Temp tracks are the curse of composers because directors tend to fall in love with them, and composers wind up competing with music their boss has already used for six weeks.

Stanley Kubrick temped *2001* with a classical repertoire and liked it so much he wound up using source music in lieu of a score to create one of the most compelling music marriages in movie history.

Randy Gerston never actually spoke to James Horner. But he did share with Michael Gorfaine some of Cameron's musical predilections.

"I've got this wacky idea," Horner said to Cameron at the interview.

"What?"

"You're going to think I'm crazy, but I'm keep hearing something that's a little bit—I almost don't want to say it, but a little bit like Enya."

"Bullshit! Somebody told you to say that!" Cameron laughed.

Horner got very innocent. He also got the job.

During that initial two-hour discussion, they talked about how they might better work together. Cameron stressed that he didn't want any surprises, and would Horner be so kind as to please mock up the key themes on a synthesizer?

Horner guardedly agreed. It was not something he warmed to doing. At this point in his career, why should he? The schedule was tight and it was one more thing to worry about.

Cameron was intrigued when Horner suggested the use of Celtic instrumentation. The ship was built in Belfast and there were many Irish aboard when she went down. It was an unusual choice for something like this but Cameron was challenging him. An oboe playing three notes, no matter how exquisite, is still an oboe playing three notes. Horner wanted to find something that didn't have that baggage. Relying primarily on synthesizers and vocals would allow him to go contemporary or elegiac in the overall "color" of the score. Only a few scenes would require the force of a full orchestral presentation.

Cameron stressed that he wanted tunes. Great love stories need memorable themes, like "Lara's Theme" from *Dr. Zhivago.* It was all about melody that could be hummed. He'd heard so many scores, beautifully recorded at a cost of millions, but completely unmemorable; lush, overproduced junk, as far as Cameron was concerned. "Crack the melody and it doesn't matter whether you play it on solo piano, it'll work," Cameron advised. He sent the composer thirty-six hours of daily selects, and told him, "Steep yourself in the footage and write Jack, write Rose, write the *Titanic*—however you want to break down the melodies in your mind. And when you have those, you'll have done ninety percent of the work."

Three weeks later Horner was ready to demo for the director. He invited Cameron out to his studio and with no preamble launched into the *Titanic* theme on his piano. Cameron's eyes were tearing up by the time Horner finished. The music was everything he had hoped and prayed it would be, gliding from intimacy to grandeur to heart-wringing sadness. Effortlessly, the music seemed to bridge the eighty-five years between then and now.

"That's great. You've got it!"

The composer had two more melodies. One, more bittersweet, with a deep, melancholy underpinning, would be linked with Rose's sadder moments and Jack's death. By the time Horner finished, Cameron was crying. Horner then played some of the pipe tunes on his recorder. Eventually, they decided to minimize the bagpipe sound, which the director felt was too ethnically specific. Ultimately, they were used to evoke the spirit of steerage, with its exuberant dancing.

Horner had secured the twenty-seven-year-old Norwegian pop chanteuse Sissel as his "vocal instrument." Though virtually unknown in the United States, her records have sold millions in Scandinavia, and she had an international hit dueting with Placido Domingo on the official 1994 Winter Olympic song "Fire in Your Heart." Horner tailored the score to her keening voice.

By mid-March, the composer was incredulous that Cameron still seemed determined to make the July 4 date. Horner had serious reservations about whether the work could be done. Composing, orchestrating, dubbing, and recording the music required eight to ten weeks, minimum. Then there were the effects and the editing. And Cameron, zealous in his new pursuit, was showing a fondness for re-editing scenes.

By now, the pressure from the studios was enormous. Oddly, in the thick of filming, it hadn't seemed to affect Cameron. Now, with the end in sight, it squeezed in.

Digital Domain, which had been focusing largely on models, was now eager for cut sequences that would enable them to begin the computer animation. There was barely anything to give them. Here it was March 1 and it was all they could do to get a seven-minute trailer cut together for the ShoWest convention that week.

Preparation for the annual convention of exhibitors had somewhat forced the issue of a release date. As the domestic distributor, Paramount would present the clip, and Friedman felt it imperative to put an availability date on it. When you were steering *Titanic* into port, "Coming Soon" just wouldn't cut it. Friedman wanted to say July 4, to stake out the turf. Every other studio in town was watching to see where *Titanic* would dock so it could steer its own summer offerings clear of its wake. Whether the film was good or bad didn't matter. It would "open," meaning it would dominate the box office upon release—a combination of the curiosity factor and the loyalty of a core group of fans. Cameron's films always opened at number one; even *The Abyss* held that position for two weeks.

Cameron didn't want to sign off on the date. He knew there was a very real possibility they'd miss it. The agreement all along had been they'd reevaluate the date at Christmas. No real discussion had taken place, yet almost by default there was now a lot of pressure to make July 4. Even Fox was pushing now that it was apparent *Speed 2* was a clunker and was moved up to a less competitive June date.

The irony of being shoehorned into the date vacated by the "other" boat movie was not lost on Cameron. The director had found it dispiriting back in the fall when he learned Fox had given his *Titanic* date of choice to the Jan de Bont sequel.

Lightstorm president Rae Sanchini had been dividing her time between the Rosarito set and the company's Santa Monica headquarters since filming had begun, a task complicated by the fact that she'd given birth to her first child, a daughter, shortly before filming began—a feat that earned her a full five days off. As the executive producer on the film, she shared liaison duties with the studios with producers Landau and Cameron. However, since she was spending most of her time in Los Angeles, working with the studios became primarily her responsibility.

After viewing the first cut of the trailer, Friedman called Sanchini at home on a Sunday night and said, "I just saw your ShoWest trailer and I threw up all over my shoes."

Sanchini, who hadn't seen the piece yet, recalls that the Paramount reaction triggered a "weird panic," as if they were saying, "Oh my god, is this the movie?" Paramount had not been privy to the footage on any ongoing basis. As the producing entity, Fox was the studio with access to dailies. When the relationship with co-financier Paramount deteriorated, Fox revoked every courtesy they could.

Apparently, Paramount had been functioning under the notion they were getting a slam bang summer action piece. The trailer, with its emphasis on the character of Old Rose and the period love story, came as a shock.

For the trailer, Cameron created a linear piece that unfurled the story of the film, beat by beat, in five minutes. Conceptually, this was vastly different from the abstract trailer style used to sell most films, Cameron's in particular. Typically, the trailer didn't show too much of the film, but this was the entire movie in miniature. They didn't show Jack dying, of course, or who ended up with the diamond, but everything else was fair game. And in fact the piece ended with the awesome crane-out over the tilting poop deck—the climactic last gasp of *Titanic* plunging into the sea.

A tape was messengered to Sanchini the next day, and after viewing it, she only saw one problem. "It had one obvious flaw—it kept bringing old Rose back in, like a Greek chorus, and she was really slowing down the momentum." After discussing the matter with Cameron and Landau, Sanchini had Rose, the narrator, cut out, so the trailer relied on dialogue to unfold the tale. This revised version was delivered to a very nervous Paramount as the ShoWest piece.

On March 4, the *Titanic* trailer was shown at ShoWest and the audience responded with jubilant cheering and thunderous applause.

Chapter Fourteen

> This Hollywood guy dies and goes to heaven. Peering through the Pearly Gates he glimpses someone riding overhead in a crane with a movie camera and says, "I didn't know James Cameron was dead." Saint Peter replies, "No, that's God. He only thinks he's James Cameron."
>
> —Quentin Tarantino, on "The Howard Stern Show"

THE NEXT HURDLE was gravitational. The "riser" was the 200-foot section of the ship that began between funnels two and three and ran just forward of the bridge. Designed by a company called M Industrial Mechanical, it was built to the specifications of Cameron and Fisher and structured like an elevator—a 1.4-million pound elevator. MIM came in roughly double its estimated weight, the result of a decision made during construction to use more steel. The eight seventeen-foot-long hydraulic cylinders had been relocated from Stage 2 and attached to the riser in a pulley configuration that allowed them to lower the section thirty-five feet underwater. By hiking up the back and lowering the front, they could play with the angle of descent, tilting to about 12 degrees, and even rolling a little.

Preparing the riser took ten days, so during that time Cameron filmed Jack and Rose running through the ship's interior and their love scene. In a daring, imaginative stroke, Cameron set his love-making scene in the back seat of a car—a witty reworking of the time-honored teenage tradition. Here the familiar becomes exotic, since this particular car, William E. Carter's burgundy Renault, happens to be in the cargo hold of a ship. The scene was inspired by the fact that the real William E. Carter, a playboy traveling in Europe to buy polo ponies, had purchased the luxury car for $3,000, a considerable sum in 1912, when a Model T cost $400.

Readying the riser required draining and refilling A tank. The hydraulics were actuated by two laptop computers, controlled by Fisher's men. The first time they lowered the set, they found it almost impossible to raise. It was too heavy. Fisher rigged up steel cages which he then filled with huge blocks of Styrofoam, positioning them under the ship to create natural buoyancy. But then it didn't sink quickly enough, so Cameron had them peel back the plywood decking to weld in metal grating, which cut down the resistance. The platform would be raised and lowered forty times over seven days, beginning March 6. They were the seven most intense days of the film, and the most expensive shooting days in the history of motion picture production.

An average big action film like *Die Hard,* for example, will cost between $100,000 and $150,000 a day. Cameron's shooting days on *Titanic* averaged about $225,000 to $250,000 a day. Two extremely complicated scenes, however—the dome implosion and the South Hampton dock—hit the astonishing rate of $500,000 a day.

At the height of the action, Cameron was shooting with seven cameras. Muro was on deck with his Steadicam, which provided the up-close and moving-through-space feeling Cameron wanted for the sinking scenes. He wanted to put audiences in the middle of the action, with wide lenses, of the ship going down around them. In addition to manning his own hand-held unit, the director recruited every other available operator, including Steve Quale, who was hauled in from second unit.

They were shooting scenes of Collapsible B—one of four compact lifeboats stowed near the bridge. Fabrizio and Cal and some others were tugging at it, trying to get it launched as the ocean roils at their feet. Quale recalled the sequence. "Jim had several cameras up front, and Jimmy Muro was shooting the band playing toward the rear, maximizing the number of times he will sink the set, because you could only do it so many times during the day. This was the very end of production, and he was running out of time."

Quale got into position for the shot; the camera, bagged in plastic, rested on his shoulder. As the set submerged, he climbed a ladder, staying two heartbeats above the water line. The water was supposed to stop before it reached his neck. Quale wore a dry suit—a rubber outfit that would look appropriate on the Michelin Man. So he won't bob and float, his ankles were weighted with two hundred pounds of lead.

Cameron called action. The water rose steadily and Quale backed up, moving up the ladder. On the very top step of the small stepladder, the currents were catching him in their sway. He was holding the camera above his head but Cameron had not called "Cut." The film was still running. From where he stood, the shot looked amazing. He was a man on a mission. The water was up to his chin. He inhaled deeply, prepared either to start hollering or hold his breath. Then he heard "Cut!"

Quale knew the set would only sink as high as his chest, the results of strict computer pre-programming, but with the water rising around him, he was feeling a little nervous. "They had safety boats and divers everywhere," he adds. Safety divers who would've easily found Steve Quale—he'd be the guy under the camera, sticking out of the water like a bamboo shoot!

Yet no one would think of interfering with Cameron's shot. Though he might make an exception if it meant life or death, doing so would, for the most part, invoke hearty wrath. Quale was amazed by the difficulty of making a film of this complexity. There was so much going on and the littlest things could cause huge problems. A few nights ago, they were shooting several hundred people running along the riser, and one of them—one among hundreds—ran in the wrong direction, ruining the shot. Cameron swooped in on his tower crane, right up over the deck, and, wagging his finger like the hand of God, admonished, "You there! You! Don't run that way next time, run this way!" Then he swept off. On the next take, everyone got it right.

It was the last shot of the evening. The riser was plunging into the deep. A cadre of stuntmen were trying to right Collapsible A. The launching of this particular boat had become something of a *Titanic* scandal. The last boat to leave the ship, it was loaded up with women, but it was recovered filled with men. Circumstances surrounding that turn of events are unclear. The way Cameron chose to play it, a wave washes up over the deck, capsizing the boat as the men try to cut it free. A mad scramble to right the boat ensues, and those who are lucky enough to clamber back into the half-flooded vessel just happen to be men.

It was nearing dawn and the shot had to be finished before the sun rose. On the first take, the stunt men can't get the boat righted; it capsizes and sinks. No good. Next time, same thing. Third try, they flip it over, but the boat comes up empty. Cameron wants to see people clambering aboard on the spin. The director, who was perched on a ladder operating a hand-held, loses patience with Crane. "You said you could do this! What's wrong with them? Do it now!" he shouts across the tank.

This was no simple stunt. Each take took two hours to prepare, due to the logistics of sinking the riser. Six consecutive stunt errors had cost them over $500,000 over the course of a day and a half.

Crane, exasperated, says, "You're lucky they got it over!"

The remark set Cameron off. "What do you mean we're lucky? That's their job!"

Crane, who's been simmering to a slow boil since Christmas, has had it. "Go fuck yourself!" he shouts back. It isn't on the headset but in front of thirty crew members, enough to undermine the director.

"What did you say?" Cameron asks, incredulous.

Crane was the kind of guy who didn't vent, and the insurrection was more astounding to onlookers than the sensationally sinking ship. "You heard me," he says, holding his ground.

"Yeah, well you're fired!" Cameron counters.

A lively discussion ensued, concluding with Crane stalking off the set. In a show of support, the sixty stuntpeople working that evening followed him.

By now the sun was coming up and everyone was ready to call it a day. Cameron and his key lieutenants broke for their daily "micro-meeting," where the subject of stunt coordination was the main focus.

Situations like this assure that producers earn their millions. Landau knew losing the stunt coordinator and his crew at this point in the shoot would be a disaster. Many of them had been established as characters. Wouldn't Jim reconsider?

"What do you think?" Cameron was indignant. "Should he be able to say that to me?" Clearly, he didn't think so. "Say anything you want to me in private. Just don't break the chain of command on the set."

Every person in the room had exchanged heated words with him at one time or another. Take McLaglen, for instance. Out of 165 shooting days, there were probably a hundred in which the AD walked away from the set kicking dirt and cussing the director.

Earlier this week, doing lifeboat deployment, Cameron decided he wanted to see one of the boats flooding as it rowed away. Well, it took time to get the extras in wet suits and get a stunt man on the tiller. Finally McLaglen climbed into the boat himself, trying to make it happen and having to listen to Cameron screaming in his ear the whole time on a private channel. "Do you know how much money you're wasting me right now?" *Wasting!* He was killing himself. But it was just heat of the moment. Then Cameron would see you at lunch and tell you what a great job you'd done. Would McLaglen work with him again? In a second.

The way Josh saw it, Cameron was a true leader in the sense that he motivated people. He did it in different ways. Sometimes it was through aggression.

"You work on other shows, and there are these little hierarchies," explains Scott Fisher. "The camera department has it's chain of command. You know, 'We've gotta do a little work on the camera here. We're shutting down for a little bit.' Or the producer will come over and say, 'Do it this way.' On Jim Cameron shows there is one guy, Jim Cameron. There's no us and them. There's Jim, and there's everyone else, and that's it. That's the way he likes it. But it's good, because it's a level playing field. It's simpler."

Cameron said the only way he'd have Crane back was with a public apology, and Crane was refusing.

"Let him walk," said Cameron, "and his stuntmen too." He could recruit the lifeguards to continue shooting. Plenty of stuntmen were sitting around Los Angeles watching "Jerry Springer" and would love the work.

Landau didn't relish the thought of having to explain this to the studio. He was determined to make peace. A compromise was reached. The next day, while Cameron was going over some logistics with the department heads at the side of A tank, Landau came walking up with Crane, who said he was sorry, things got a little out of hand. It wasn't in front of everyone, but it was good enough. Crane was able to save face by avoiding an apology in front of his own stunt crew and Cameron was appeased.

The last thing they did to the big ship was split it apart. It took a whole ocean to take down the original *Titanic,* but it took only James Cameron to demolish this one.

The Fishers rigged it, removing a piece of hull and relocating it to ground level, where it was placed in two sections that could be pulled apart. They tried to simulate the effect for Cameron by videotaping a model. The boards twisted apart painfully. He liked it.

But when it came time to shoot it, he didn't seem as pleased. He thought only one side of the ship was going to move. Since it was already set up, he'd shoot it, but the Fishers should plan on rerigging it. He shot it. He loved it.

The ship now lay crippled in its giant tank, strewn in parts about the lot. Industrial-scale magic.

When the dining room set was struck from Stage 2, a labyrinth of corridors rose in its place. These halls were flooded with ferocious intensity through February and March. The exploding steerage door was one scene the studio lobbied heavily to cut from the script. An immigrant Russian and his son are blown fifty feet down a corridor by the torrential gush—one of Tommy Fisher's practical effects. To create the illusion, three cargo containers full of water sat poised above the set, a funnel running to the door. Cameron calls action and a stunt man scoops up a dummy child and runs toward the door, which creaks and moans, straining its hinges as water oozes through. Then it's "Go!" and the doors are sprung open, unleashing the 40,000-gallon payload of the tanks.

Cameron, who is operating a hand-held in the corridor below, is unimpressed. "It never went much above three feet," he sniffs, explaining patiently to Scott Fisher, "I want a wall of water, not a shrubbery of water." He tells them to fix it. They scratch their heads, then he tells them how to fix it.

He wants them to triple the number of dump tanks. The corridor as built would never accommodate that volume of water; the walls would blow right out, and with other sets abutting this one, there wasn't enough room to backbrace it. And a set breaking apart in fast moving water is very dangerous. Take it outside, Cameron said, and build it like a channel. Stack the dump tanks higher and use the gravity to force the pressure.

Scott Fisher couldn't believe it. Even with the two studios breathing down his neck for more than $100 million, Cameron had the nerve to go back and reshoot. On the one hand, Fisher admired the inventiveness of less influential directors who had to find ways to make do. On the other, he respected Cameron's visionary zeal. He fought to keep the shots he wanted, and he'd fight to reshoot them too, if need be. It was all about making the movie the best it could be. If he saw a way to do something better, even if it was only a little better, that's what he was going to do.

The last day of shooting on *Titanic* began March 20 and ended March 22. The uninterrupted roll of days and nights began on Stage 4, where they'd hung a giant backdrop to simulate the natural sunset for the kiss between Rose and Jack. A wide-angle shot, dead on into the painted canvas, which Carpenter thought looked phony but Cameron wanted to shoot anyway. "If it doesn't work, we won't use it," he said.

When the scene broke, "It was sort of like the end of a Super Bowl," recalls Landau. "Jim had everybody take a moment of silence in memory of the lives that were lost and the lives that were affected by the disaster, to try and put into perspective what it is we were doing." Landau and DiCaprio arranged for an equally dramatic end to the arduous production journey.

Then Kate gave Jim a big hug. The minute the actress broke away from the embrace, Landau gave Leo his cue and the actor soaked Cameron with a bucket of ice cold water.

Now only the die-hards remained—the core contingent, with another forty-eight hours to go. "The best days on a Jim Cameron film are the last days," says Arneson. "They're unbelievably long, but Jim cannot give up the camera. He's totally into filming. He knows it's going to end, but he doesn't want it to. As tired as he is, he doesn't want it to end."

The next day at dailies they viewed the kiss at the bow, and Carpenter thought the background looked great. "You'd never know it's just a big painted wall. It's amazing what worked on this film."

Day 162 of a 163-day shoot, they found themselves in the outdoor labyrinth, once again facing the flooding door. This time there were 120,000 gallons of gushing water. The force going through that tunnel was torrential.

On March 22 they finished with Captain Smith's demise on the bridge of the *Titanic.* The British actor Bernard Hill remembered the scene as a personal high point. In breathing a historical figure to life, Hill found it quite extraordinary to have a perfectly recreated bridge for his character. But Hill was nowhere to be seen that last night of shooting. He'd filmed his "death" weeks earlier, when they sank the bridge on the riser. Since then, the bridge had been detached and reassembled in a tank on another stage. A stuntman stood in for Hill as a half a million pounds of water poured through the pressurized glass. Cameron, wearing a wet suit, helmet and full scuba gear, was the scene's sole camera operator. "That water hit me like a bulldozer," says Cameron, "and slammed me against the wall. I remember thinking, 'Lord, take me now because post-production is going to be a bitch!'"

Chapter Fifteen

> You love your work. God help you, you love it! And that's the curse. It's the brand on your forehead for all of them to see. They know they have you. A man who loves his work is the only kind they fear.
>
> —Ayn Rand, *The Fountainhead*

NATURE ABHORS a vacuum and so do newspapers. *Titanic* wrapped on March 22 and was followed by a blistering streak of press coverage.

Called the "*Waterworld* of 1997," the very name *Titanic* had the irresistible ring of self-fulfilling prophecy. Cameron had known all along he'd be taking heat over the title, but he thought they'd save their digs for the film. Not so. This was a blood sport with three recurring themes: the wobbly release date, abusive working conditions, and budget overages.

It started with safety issues. There was an incident involving the tilting poop deck when a cable snapped, freezing the platform at a 90-degree angle with roughly fifty stunt people and extras harnessed aboard. Reports swirled, and the mishap was merged with the stunt-related accidents for a singular tale of high-rise terror. In fact, the crew broke for lunch while Fisher fixed the problem. The hostages were freed in forty minutes, none with anything worse than mussed hair. Landau's wife and eight-year-old son had been lashed to the rail. How bad could it have been for the producer to have put his family on the line? Like the children's game "telephone," where a whispered secret will emerge unrecognizably after making its way round a room, everything having to do with *Titanic* seemed to get twisted.

When a cameraman, Brent Hershman, died driving home after a nineteen-hour workday on the New Line Cinema film *Pleasantville,*

Time ran a story on "Hollywood's sweatshop-style work practices" with a photo of Cameron beneath the headline.

The director, who prided himself on his safety record, was galled by what he felt were distortions. They built the first movie studio in modern history, to produce the biggest film ever made, with only one serious mishap—a construction worker was injured when he backed off a scaffolding on Stage 2. The accident required an emergency splenectomy. A movie medic, not the contractor, got the injured man to the hospital. The story should've been that they'd saved the guy's life. The Medivac helicopter stationed at the studio was never even used.

A particularly bruising *Los Angeles Times* article described Winslet brandishing an "ugly gash" on her knee, incurred during filming, and quoted the actress as saying about Cameron that, "If anything was the slightest bit wrong he would lose it. It was hard to concentrate when he was shouting and screaming." Though she was careful to point out he never screamed at the actors. "I think Jim knew he couldn't shout at us the way he did to his crew because our performances would be no good."

Cameron was hurt by the remarks. He fought back, firing off a defiant letter that ran in the *Los Angeles Times* on May 5. "Just as it does not serve a mountain climber, in the retelling of the tale, to suggest that the mountain conquered was a gentle grade, it does not serve those who have been tested by fire on one of my films to describe the experience as routine," he argued, going on to state, "For me, *Titanic* has been a work of pure passion unlike anything I have ever done."

Winslet, contacted in London, said her words were twisted and wrote her own rebuttal letter to the *Times.* It was understandable. She'd done the interview too soon. After working a Jim Cameron film, the cast and crew felt as if they were coming off an extended march. It took about six or seven months for the dull throb to turn to a rosy glow. Ask them a year later and they'll say they considered it the most incredible adventure of their lives. Kate's interview came a little too early. At twenty-one, she was still new at the game.

The cost overruns had the same effect on the media as a red flag on a bull. *Titanic*'s final tally was $200 million—66 percent over its original budget of $120 million. The Baja studio added another $20–30 million to Fox's debit sheet. Surpassing *Waterworld, Titanic* was now the most expensive movie ever made; a dubious distinction in a year where indie films like *Sling Blade, Shine,* and *The English Patient* dominated the Oscars.

Cameron tried to ignore the press and concentrate on the post-production process. Upon completion of principal photography he was faced with editing a daunting 1.3 million feet of film—about twelve days worth—and more than five hundred visual effects. Everybody knew what no one was saying—July 4 would be an impossible date to meet.

Executives at Fox and Paramount were monitoring the director closely to determine how quickly he could pull *Titanic* together. In April, theater owners were told that July 18 or early August were more likely dates, and that there was even a chance the film would be pushed back to fall. On April 15, *Variety* ran a story headlined "That Sinking Feeling," reporting that despite "round the clock efforts" to complete *Titanic,* Cameron was unlikely to make the July 4 date and ascribed the blame largely to the extraordinary volume of visual effects. The story hinted that the director was stringing his two financiers along, having "apparently postponed his decision several times."

The article had an unexpected effect. It had incensed Rob Friedman because it quoted Bill Mechanic, who made it seem the release date was Fox's call, not Paramount's. At this point, Paramount was feeling pretty good about buying half of the world's biggest movie for a thrifty $65 million. Friedman called *Variety,* livid, and the paper followed up with a news grabber entitled "No word from helm of *Titanic,*" which began with the carefully chosen words, "Two major entertainment companies are still waiting to hear." The story—the first to sport the breathless logo "*Titanic* Watch"—quoted Friedman saying, "Paramount dictates when this film will be released. Cameron and myself have not yet finalized when Paramount will release this picture."

By now, the two studios were at each other's throats both in public and in private. Mechanic felt he was dealing with people who'd been selling widgets for many years, only to awaken one day and find themselves in the motion picture business. The film business was about gambling, and Paramount was risk averse. For them, it was about the money and not about getting things right. Even little things that weren't financially driven became a problem, such as when Cameron decided he wanted to hire James Horner to do the score. Horner's asking price was a bit more than the $500,000 line item allotment for "composer" so he wanted a slightly higher percentage of the soundtrack royalties. Friedman said no. Mechanic made several calls, working his way up to Jon Dolgen, chairman of Paramount's parent, Viacom Entertainment Group, who finally approved the deal.

And now they were about to blow their summer release date, and the press was salivating, ready to move in for the kill. Would they have had a better shot at making the date if Paramount had been more of an active partner? Yes. They would've stood a chance if somebody helped shoulder the burden, asking if there were things to be expedited. Should extra editors be added? Can we be doing something more? Getting things as ready as we could? That never happened. Their so-called "partner" had turned into that oh-so-annoying "friend" who always tagged along to dinner but never picked up the check. Publicly, the studios were barely able to maintain a modicum of civility. Barbs leveled by "unnamed sources" began appearing in the newspapers with great frequency.

When *Titanic* vacated the July 4 weekend, it created a wake that rocked every major release through the end of the year. Fox, sensing *Speed 2* might not live up to its original high expectations, moved the release up to June 27, when the only real competition was Paramount's *Face/Off.* Thus, Columbia's *Men In Black,* directed by Barry Sonnenfeld, had the field pretty much to itself, prompting the film's star, Will Smith to crow, "I own Fourth of July!" The actor had had extraordinary success with *Independence Day* on July 4, 1996.

The big question was where would *Titanic* dock? Everyone wanted to stay out of its path. When Harrison Ford, star of Paramount's Jack Ryan franchise, learned the studio was looking at July 25, he called Jon Dolgen to make sure his *Air Force One,* for Columbia, would steer clear of that date.

Mechanic liked August 1. Be the last one in and still have four weeks of summer playing time, then it's smooth sailing through fall. At that point, Paramount wasn't confident that Cameron would make any summer date. They started pushing for Thanksgiving, which was unacceptable to Fox, which had slotted two of its biggest films—*Anastasia* and *Alien Resurrection*—for that date.

"They were totally on this November thing and I thought it was idiotic," Mechanic ruminated. Typically, family films like *Mrs. Doubtfire* and *The Addams Family* had done well in November, opening on Thanksgiving and playing through to Christmas. But in the adult-themed entertainment category, where he placed *Titanic,* there were only two recent films that had done well there: *Ransom* and *Dances With Wolves,* which won nine Oscars. So, Mechanic thought, unless you thought your film was going to win nine Oscars, November didn't look too promising. Friedman persisted, spewing out an endless sea of computer reports that backed his case. The bickering continued.

Cameron, meanwhile, retreated to Malibu where he'd transformed his home into a post-production facility. The lush grounds consisted of several detached buildings arranged in compound configuration around a cascading fountain. The sound team had a building to themselves. A guest house held three editing bays. He set up two "V-Tel" video-conferencing links, one to Digital Domain and the other to Skywalker Sound.

Like every other shredded timeline *Titanic* encountered, the special effects schedule was a disaster. DD President and CEO Scott Ross argued, correctly, that they were unable to complete the bulk of their work before they received Cameron's cut sequences. But the director felt they could've been using their time better. Some of the model shots of the *Mir* subs on the ocean floor still weren't complete, and they could've worked on those any time. Cameron had already begun the process of farming out effects to other houses which caused some friction with DD. Fox had recently purchased a facility called VIFX, and they were in line for a sizable portion of what, after DD's 150 cherry-picked virtuoso shots, amounted to some of the showier work—notably the "breath" that eluded them in the post-sinking tank scenes, and the engine room sequence.

Steve Quale shot the latter as second unit, using an ingenious combination of miniatures and a real ship, the *Jeremiah O'Brien.* One of the few vessels afloat to boast the same triple expansion reciprocating steam engine technology as *Titanic,* the decommissioned WWII Liberty ship was berthed in San Francisco. Smaller than *Titanic,* and equipped with only one engine as opposed to *Titanic's* two, Quale was able to improvise, positioning one-third scale lights and catwalks throughout the interior to make the room look bigger.

Cameron's instructions to Quale: "Think of the dynamic, kinetic energy of *Das Boot.*" Quale complied with lively camera moves and lots of flailing crew members. VIFX digitally composited actors, shot against greenscreen, onto the catwalks. In order for VIFX to accomplish the work to Cameron's specification, it was necessary for DD to "loan" them some proprietary software, the home-brewed code that effects houses guard with jealous secrecy. Ross was not happy but Cameron insisted. Even though he was Chairman of DD, his allegiance was to the film.

When the dust settled, a total of seventeen effects firms contributed some 500 shots to the film. Idiots writing about the film would ask Cameron why he built so much of the ship when he could've done it all with visual effects. The answer was, because then the film would've cost three times as much.

Cameron patched into DD twice daily, previewing shots in progress. The V-Tel allowed DD to show him images for his comments. He could even mark them up with an electronic pen. Cameron had two V-Tel sessions a day, one at noon and one at 7:00 P.M. There were times when the 7 o'clock session ended at 11 o'clock at night, after they reviewed a hundred shots. The sessions were taped and a full-time employee did nothing but transcribe notes, typing twelve hours a day, on the farm-out effects.

Cameron had hired a young effects producer named Camille Cellucci. She started her career as an intern at Industrial Light and Magic and most recently worked at Sony Pictures Imageworks. She brought him film to review, which he watched on an editing machine called a KEM. Though it gave a more detailed picture than video, the KEM was still kind of dicey, so they worked out a system called FPP—Final Pending Projection. Once a week Cameron drove his Humvee down the Pacific Coast Highway to view film on a big screen at DD. Effects dailies unspooled with the jarring repetition of an endless loop. Cameron would edit all night. Packing it in at dawn, he'd sleep till noon and the V-Tel session would be his first meeting of the day.

The majority of Cameron's time was spent in the editing room. Dark and isolated, nothing could've been more removed from the frenetic activity of the Rosarito set. Blackout cloth covered the walls and windows. The Avid console combined the elegance of the executive desk with the techno-dazzle of a mission control board. There were lots of knobs and levers. A dozen tiny screens displayed freeze frames and waveform images. The main illumination came from two large monitors. Day after day, the pictures swam by, flickering electronically in fractured, non-linear time. Each scene had six, ten, twelve variations of emotion, some subtle, some extreme. The images were controlled by a computer keyboard that Cameron manipulated with the strokes of a concert pianist.

As with every other aspect of movie making, Cameron had always taken a very active role in the editing of his films. Unlike some directors, who are happy to hand off notes, Cameron sat side by side with his editors, guiding them through the process although the crank-and-cut technology that had been the industry norm until a few years ago limited his participation. When editing went digital in the 1990s and became as simple as word processing, Cameron decided to try it himself.

His first attempt was on *Strange Days.* Director Kathryn Bigelow was having trouble making some of the action sequences work and solicited his help. She had an Avid set up in one of the production suites on Lightstorm's second floor, just downstairs from Cameron's office. He rolled up his sleeves and dove in, enjoying the process enough to re-edit big chunks of the film. He made up his mind he'd edit his next film himself and joined the editors guild in the summer of 1996 so he would be eligible to receive a screen credit, something his non-union status prevented him from doing on *Strange Days.*

He caught on quickly. Working with an Avid technician hovering just within earshot, he was like a race car driver, with someone else to prep the gear, and could get around the track pretty fast. Cameron asked Fox for another editor to assist him and Harris, and after the usual economic handwringing they agreed. He brought on Conrad Buff, a veteran of *T2* and *True Lies.* Though they each worked on separate sequences, Cameron would eventually groom through the entire film.

On May 23 he'd been editing full time for two months and had thought about the release date long and hard. On the one hand, he felt a responsibility to deliver what the studio had reasonably been led to expect. On the other, he was compelled to follow his own instincts, protecting the asset with which he'd been entrusted. He spent a day "meditating with the movie," itemizing all he needed to do to lock the film.

Voice re-recording, a process known as "looping," would be time consuming. Though they always recorded "production sound" when filming, inevitably things needed to be fixed. Titanic initially had one hundred speaking parts and now, after some cuts, had ninety-two. It took roughly a half-day to loop an actor, and Cameron would need to spend five or six days with each of his two stars. He usually supervised all his own looping sessions, but now, in the interest of time, he hired a dialogue supervisor, Hugh Waddell.

The music was another major hurdle. A summer date meant Horner was under the gun. And then there was the final sound mix at Skywalker Sound and the color timing at the film lab. And even after all those elements were pulled together, he should probably watch the film a few times before determining if it was ready. How many times a day could he sit and watch a three hour movie? Twice? The math just didn't work.

In the preceding weeks they'd gone back and forth on the dates. To Cameron, *Titanic* never felt like it fit in with the typical *Die Hard-Batman-Jurassic Park*-type summer popcorn fare. But he'd never released a movie at Christmas, so he wasn't familiar with the market. His instincts told him Christmas was a time people were willing to have a more family-oriented, emotional experience with a film.

He picked up the phone and called Peter Chernin.

"We shouldn't do this," Cameron said. He didn't say we can't. "Rushing for summer will compromise this film. It will only be eighty-five percent there."

Chernin wasn't surprised by the call. He felt he was living in a parallel universe: the budget problems, the antagonistic press, the problems with Paramount. Then there was the movie itself. Starting with the scriptment, through the footage of the deep dive, and the dailies from Rosarito, Chernin had been receiving positive feedback. Now Cameron was showing him big chunks of assembled film. Earlier in the month Cameron had invited him to Malibu to see a rough edit of the last hour-and-a-half—the sinking sequence. Chernin was amazed. It was like nothing he'd ever seen before. Still, a delay to the fourth quarter would cost Fox $3–4 million more in carrying costs on *Titanic* production money. Cameron knew that. He was contrite. He offered fifty percent of the backend of his *next* movie, which he made clear would be no labor of love, but a surefire commercial pick.

"Okay," the executive said. "Give me a day to figure out how to play it."

On Tuesday, May 27, Paramount announced that *Titanic* would be released to theaters December 19, 1997.

Bill Mechanic was appalled at the thought of the public pillorying Fox would get as a result of the delayed date.

The press seemed determined to make Cameron out to be a bad guy, a director who abused his crew, who reached into the coffers of two studios, grabbing fistfuls of cash. Nobody seemed interested in whether it was a good movie. They were reviewing the budget, as if spending money was, in and of itself, a bad thing. On this film, the money went into the economy, into the pockets of working men and women rather than replenishing the bank accounts of the few. It wasn't as if the studios were going to take the cash and feed starving children or fund clean energy research. It was *Titanic* or two more Steven Segal movies and an Eddie Murphy movie. There were a few mentions that *War and Peace* or *Cleopatra,* in today's dollar terms, would cost more than $300 million each. If *Gone With the Wind* was made today, it would cost upwards of $400 million. Truthfully, if Cameron had known *Titanic* was going to cost $200 million, he would never have made it. No sane person would.

Throughout June, the spat between Digital Domain and Cameron became something of a sideshow. In an interview in the *L.A. Times,* Cameron cited special effects as the reason for the film's delay. Scott Ross couldn't believe it. The press smelled blood and pounced. Ross's business depended on meeting deadlines. And if DD couldn't deliver for its own boss, the chairman of the company, who could they deliver for? This was the kind of publicity that could kill them. The DD crew, struggling to impress Cameron, found the allegations demoralizing and fired back with their own innuendo. Cameron was ten weeks late with certain key scenes. On top of that, he was driving them mad with his perfectionism. He'd go crazy about the littlest things. "These aren't North Atlantic seagulls! North Atlantic seagulls have a four-foot wing span! These are the wrong seagulls. Redo them!"

It was the kind of story the media loved: Hollywood run amok. Upstairs, downstairs, drama at every level of the food chain. A death watch was on at Fox. Whose heads would roll? They were readying life support for Mechanic, first in line for the guillotine. As a highly visible number two, his firing would suffice if all Murdoch wanted to do was send a strong "signal" and let the shareholders know that News Corporation was not about to stand for wasted millions. Chernin was in slightly better shape. Few recalled that he had actually greenlit the picture. The spin just seemed to get worse and worse. But maybe there'd be an upside to the delayed release. The negative reporting would reach its zenith during the summer and by fall, when the picture released, all the horror stories would be old news. They'd be looking for something new to write about.

Fox spent the months between Christmas and summer wondering whether they'd lose $20 , $40, or $60 million on *Titanic.*

Speed 2 opened June 15 and tanked. The $125 million production opened to $16 million, and only went on to earn $102.4 million in U.S. theaters.

It was getting ever more tense in the Fox corridors.

Cameron came in for a meeting in the deep, dark hour of the drama and ran smack into Murdoch. Though he'd been expecting a strongly worded call, Rupert was playing it like a gentleman.

Cameron admired Murdoch and wanted the tycoon to like him. The media baron was doing something even he, at his most wildly ambitious, could never aspire to: changing the world. The public laughed when Murdoch launched a U.S. television network, and now ten years later the station was number two. James was impressed.

"I guess I'm not your favorite person," Cameron mumbled into his shoes at their meeting. "But the movie is going to be good," he offered hopefully.

"It had better be a bit better than good," Murdoch responded.

The movie didn't have to be as successful for Paramount to make money since their break-even was lower, which was kind of ironic. If *Titanic* was wildly successful, Fox stood to gain more; a little eleventh hour addendum they added when Paramount capped. Revenues would be split evenly until Paramount recouped its investment, at which point Fox would begin drawing sixty percent of the profits in perpetuity. But in order for Fox to see any upside, *Titanic* would have to be a monster, one of the top grossing films of all time.

No matter how good you felt going in, you couldn't count on that and, in this case, there wasn't much confidence going in.

Confidence, Cameron knew, implied certainty of the outcome but any film ever made is a game of chance. No one knows what market forces will be at work a year or two down the line when the film releases. Cameron realized he'd worked himself into a state, mentally, where he felt obligated to *guarantee* success, and that should never be the responsibility of any director. An artist should just do his best work with his particular talents; he'd remember that on the next film. Now, if he could only make it through this one.

Chapter Sixteen

I want to reach that state of condensation of sensations which constitutes a picture.

—Henri Matisse

THE ARRANGEMENTS for *Titanic*'s first editorial test screening on July 14 were made in utter secrecy by Tom Sherak. Peter Chernin and Bill Mechanic were ushered aboard a charter flight at Los Angeles International Airport with absolutely no idea where he was going. Cameron, Sanchini, and Landau joined the Fox executives on the flight.

Paramount was not invited.

Cameron was looking forward to the screening. He'd already been showing his Avid video cut of *Titanic* to small groups of people—his producers, a few friends that included Scott Ross, Stan Winston, and John Bruno.

But having a few showbiz friends over to your personal screening room was a far cry from watching it with the public in middle America. You never understand the film you *think* you've made until you see it with an audience of strangers.

The screening, arranged by the National Research Group, was set to take place in Minneapolis' Mall of America. Under the guidance of Joe Farrell, NRG enjoyed what amounted to a virtual monopoly on movie research. Prospective attendees were recruited from the streets. Selection was based largely on achieving the right demographic mix. Asked if they'd like free passes to see a new movie, the average American is usually thrilled.

Sometimes they're told what they're going to see, sometimes not. Breaking somewhat with convention, the Minneapolis audience was told they were going to see *Great Expectations,* another Fox release starring Gwyneth Paltrow and Ethan Hawke in a remake of the Dickens tale. Sherak was taking no chances. The executive wanted to get as far from Hollywood and the media maelstrom as he could for this first test screening. Reporters made sport of sneaking into such screenings. The film was still unfinished—with a temporary sound mix that Cameron himself cut in on the Avid and a number of rough-ins for visual effects—and in no condition to show the press. There was also some concern about the Internet. Bad Internet buzz had destroyed *Batman and Robin.* Guys point casting from Web sites were becoming the Siskel and Eberts of their generation.

Harry Knowles, for example, was an Austin, Texas-based computer geek who set his watch by CST—Cool Standard Time. Knowles' web site, www.aint-it-cool.com, was where Quentin Tarantino and Richard Linklater went slumming in cyberspace. Knowles, of all people, got wind of the *Titanic* screening through someone in his web of well-placed informants.

Knowles scanned the murky depths of Minneapolis for the lost liner with no less tenacity than Cameron himself had shown when manning the Mezotech on the ocean floor. Among the tech heads on the Internet, Cameron—with his toy-filled, science-fiction films—was a godhead of gadgetry, revered with an awe usually reserved for rock stars or computer software billionaires.

Knowles' entreaty went up at two P.M. the day of the supposedly secret screening, urging people in town to sneak in and send word his way. An hour later he had two hundred and fifty responses. That Knowles could mobilize that many spies from the streets of Minneapolis in less than twenty-four hours was an astonishing feat. "I unleashed the geek hordes upon the unsuspecting theaters of the Twin Cities!" Knowles cackled through the ether, recounting his coup with glee.

Sherak had chosen Minneapolis largely for its temperate summer clime, having learned his lesson on *The Abyss.* On the day they screened that film in Dallas it was 110 degrees in the shade and the air conditioning went out in their thousand-seat theater. Sherak wanted to halt the screening and give everyone tickets to another movie, but Cameron insisted they go on. Predictably, most of those who sweltered through the three-hour work print weren't wildly enthusiastic in their reviews.

When the Fox group deplaned it was ninety degrees, unseasonably warm for Minneapolis. Sherak was starting to get a little nervous.

Mike Ribble was an Edina teenager whose mother had a knack for picking up free movie passes at the local supermarket. Most of what she liked, Mike didn't want to see. *Great Expectations,* a remake of some old book, fell into that category, but he heard Gwyneth Paltrow took off her clothes in it, so he decided to go.

Ribble clearly remembers the evening. The lights went down in the theater and the Fox logo appeared. A giant ship filled the screen. Murmurs rippled through the theater. "Kickass!" he thought to himself. "I get to see the trailer for *Titanic!*" But then the title came up and he realized it wasn't the trailer—it was the real deal! James Cameron's *Titanic!* A roar filled the theater. It was like being at a Bruce Springsteen concert.

"What a rush," thought Sherak, "if I could bottle this feeling and live with it every day, I'd have the greatest life!"

At three hours and twenty-two minutes, the work print ran long but barely anyone stirred from their seats. Sherak looked at his watch, checking the pacing. An hour-and-a-half flew by. The audience laughed in all the right places, and not just polite titters. They cheered. Leonardo, in his Cinderella makeover, drew whoops and whistles when he appeared in his tuxedo.

The wild applause at the film's conclusion was music to Sherak's ears. Unlike the polite applause that made his skin crawl, this was the genuine article—the mother lode of emotion every filmmaker yearns to tap.

Cameron was in director's heaven.

Five hundred audience members turned in their research cards on their way out. Twenty people were selected at random to participate in a focus group at the back of the theater. To a one, they'd all heard of the film, and most were aware of its astronomical budget, but it hadn't biased them against the film. If anything, they wanted to see what $200 million looked like onscreen. One woman said the dialogue in the first-class dinner scene alone was worth $200 million.

Cameron felt giddy. The press might hate him, but real people liked his film. It made it all worthwhile.

By the time the Fox jet touched down in Los Angeles, the Internet was crackling with *Titanic* buzz. Twenty-five of Knowles' foot soldiers managed to get into the screening. Of those, twenty-three gave the film glowingly enthusiastic reviews. One pundit expressed surprise that *Titanic* wasn't the disaster movie he expected but a romantic historical drama with disaster elements. "I actually cared about the characters," he confessed.

"Makes everything else Cameron's ever done look half-assed!" backhanded another.

"Did you see Cameron? What was he wearing?" Knowles breathlessly debriefed one correspondent on-line.

"I saw him walk up the aisle," his spy reported. "He was wearing basic Cameron wear: long sleeve blue shirt—sleeves rolled up, of course—and blue jeans and his beard."

The July screening set a new course for *Titanic.* In the face of the grassroots Internet enthusiasm, the mainstream media—none of whom had seen the film—were forced to admit the possibility that the movie might actually work. The journalistic slant became less about predicting disaster and more about the colossal gamble the film represented.

It also marked a turning point for Fox. The studio had spent the past months bemoaning how much money they were about to lose. Now they wondered if they had less to worry about than they thought, although no one went so far as to suggest they might actually make any money.

Things began to change, too, at the review and research level. Test screenings would never be private again. NRG wasn't happy about that and neither were the studios. Sherak was appalled that the strictest secrecy tactics didn't keep the cyber spies away. This time it had worked in their favor but next time they might not be so lucky. The working press were at least governable to some extent because studio execs could always complain to someone's boss on the golf course, but the Internet guys wrote whatever the hell they pleased.

NRG took the cards and boiled them down to a statistical analysis for the research books. Cameron also took the five hundred cards home to read.

Audiences were asked to rate the stars on a scale of four—Excellent, Very Good, Good, Poor. Winslet and DiCaprio never rated below a Very Good—an eighty percent Excellent rating—which was virtually unprecedented. Bates and Stuart each earned sixty percent Excellent, which was considered outstanding. Zane achieved a forty percent approval rating, which was unheard of for an actor playing a villain.

The audience loved the scenes with Gloria Stuart and the denouement at the top of the stairs. They felt it was "unrealistic" that the musicians continue to play while the ship sank, even though that actually happened. The mystery involving the diamond showed up as both pluses and minuses but during the screening Cameron heard an audible gasp when Old Rose opens her hand to reveal the jewelry.

Most often mentioned as "Favorite Scenes" were the dinner, the sketching, the steerage party, lovemaking in the car, learning to spit, and the sinking. In that order. Card after card after card. Cameron was amazed. When he saw they were rating the sinking of the ship sixth, he knew he had a winner. Here he was, Mr. Action King, and he had them hanging on a combination of light-hearted frolic and drawing room drama. Action movies don't have three page scenes with people supping in tuxedos. (Though he did write a dinner scene into *True Lies,* it was notable more for what wasn't said—a lot of postmodern staring at plates.) *Titanic* had three meal scenes—a breakfast, a lunch, and a dinner—and each tested highly. As a writer, it was enormously gratifying because scenes like that were carried by the dialogue and acting alone. He'd written eight produced screenplays that generated more than 1.7 billion dollars in box office receipts yet he never received more than perfunctory notice for his writing. Even to him, it was just a means to an end. He liked to direct. He didn't like writing.

The studio had begged him to cut the spitting scene; so had his fellow producers. Everyone thought it was gross. The actors didn't respond well to the written scene and said they'd feel uncomfortable acting it. But he liked it. When he wrote, he did so with abandon, putting to paper what caught his fancy without thought to cost or "concept." Later, there'd be no shortage of people telling him what to take out. The spitting scene stayed, and when filming began, the actors actually enjoyed it. Now viewers were loving it. Critics don't know what audiences are going to like, and neither did studio executives, but these cards told the truth.

Cameron had never tested *The Terminator* or *Aliens.* He waltzed into the offices of the respective executives and said "Here are the cans!" *The Abyss* was the first film he tested, and though he never felt he really nailed the film he had in his head, he found the process valuable. When he heard laughter in the wrong places, he made notes. If he got a really strong pattern—half the people hated something—it would go, even if he loved it. His goal was to create the best possible entertainment for the greatest number of people who were, after all, just like him. He hadn't gone to film school, studied film noir or the screwball comedies of the 1930s and 1940s. He went to the drive-in and saw every piece of cheese ever made. He was that guy in the audience, that blue collar everyperson.

On July 26, 1997, post-production hummed along at chez Cameron and the director took a day off to marry Linda Hamilton. They had planned to get married when *Titanic* sailed, but that was supposed to have been July 4. The test screening had been like a ray of sun through the clouds. Why not do something for themselves? They had been dating on and off for seven years. It was her second marriage and his fourth. The Hawaiian-themed garden ceremony took place at Hamilton's Malibu home. The event was informal, with about forty family members and close friends. Their tousled, suntanned children—four-year-old Josephine, a beguiling blonde, and Dalton, Hamilton's seven-year-old son from her previous marriage—took part in the ceremony. Cameron cut a jaunty figure in a Hawaiian shirt and black tuxedo. Hamilton, still fit from *Terminator 2* bootcamp, went barefoot in a simple white slipdress. The wedding was covered in the tabloid paper the *Star*. Not surprisingly, their honeymoon was deferred pending completion of the film.

There were two more *Titanic* test screenings, one in Portland, Oregon, on August 12 and one five days later in Anaheim Hills, California. This time, there was no subterfuge. The audience was recruited using a list of ten films. Those who liked four of the ten—films like *Braveheart* and *Dances With Wolves*—were invited.

Cameron was particularly interested in gauging the audience's reaction to the film's length. The first test print ran three hours and twenty-two minutes. When asked if they felt the film was too long, eighteen out of the twenty people raised their hands. He still had work to do. Based on their preferences, he knew where to start. The opening scene of the *Mir* submarine deployment to the bowels of the wreck went on too long. He cut another six minutes. At the Portland focus group, seventeen of the twenty people put up their hands, but Cameron felt he was close.

The audience wasn't buying a watery chase through the grand dining room, where a gun-toting Lovejoy, the valet, goes after the lovers—and the diamond—as the ocean swirls up around them. Everyone seemed to feel the *Titanic* was sinking so rapidly that nobody in their right mind—even for great wealth—would think of anything but getting off the ship. The chase scene took the audience out of that greater jeopardy and tried to get them interested in a jeopardy they didn't care about. The scene had taken a week to shoot, went three days over schedule, and cost $1 million. Out it went. Interestingly, when Cameron had wrapped, he had a list of studio-suggested cuts the size of the Manhattan telephone directory. Not one of them suggested cutting the Lovejoy chase. Everyone, Cameron included, wanted to believe on some level that *Titanic* was an action movie and needed that type of element.

He cinched up a few other small details, including the sinking of the ship, for a total loss of one-and-a-half minutes. They tested it in Anaheim Hills. How many thought it was too long? Two. The moral of the story was clear to Cameron. "The perception of time is extremely elastic," he says, citing a topic that has fascinated philosophers from Aquinas to Einstein. "It's not a linear scale. If you're having a good experience—it's working, the experience is unfolding, rolling you forward in a gripping and organic manner—your feeling at the end of the movie is very different than if you had a moment of doubt, or something got in the way. The film probably only got about ten percent better, but it ignited a chain reaction. It was like a quantum step up to another level."

With the picture locked, Cameron turned his full attention to sound post-production. He had been meeting with composer James Horner every other day from April through August. Cameron rented a grand piano for his house which was starkly furnished in the Mission style; oriental rugs punctuated the spill of hardwood floors. Cameron was a man of simple but distinctive tastes. The dining room wall was decorated with dinosaur fossils. The piano stood before the wall of glass that ran along the southernmost side of his living room, framed within the greenery of the trees outside.

When Horner came by to play the piano, Cameron would sink into a chair, and Horner would perform from sheet music. A monitor and VCR sat nearby so Horner could synch to the video playback, like a silent picture era accompanist. Sometimes they would sit in the editing suite and watch the images unfold on the Avid, talking about the scenes. Creatively, it was a true collaboration in the best sense, but even so, there was some music that just didn't work for Cameron, even after those intense discussions. He asked Horner to rework several cues.

Sometimes Cameron suggested going very simple, with voice, with a subtle accompaniment. Sometimes Horner would disagree, but he tried to be flexible. A few times he dug in his heels. Cameron remembered one instance in particular: the scene where the two lovers are climbing over the railing to the pinnacle of the plummeting stern. Here was a primal moment, tinged with irony—three days ago Jack had pulled her over in the opposite direction. Now they were both fighting for their lives. Cameron thought it should be pure action scoring, a lot of percussion. Horner wanted to go thematic, to weave in their love theme.

Horner wound up drafting a few cues even though it was not how he felt comfortable working. But he complied in this instance. As Jack and Rose claw over the end of the ship the theme swells protectively, but is quickly overcome by a low, dark underscore. Cameron thought it brilliant; exactly the way it should be. By mid-August, Horner was still composing some important interludes, but he spent most of his time conducting a one-hundred-piece orchestra at Todd AO in Studio City. Located on a CBS annex lot where TV shows like "Seinfeld" and "Roseanne" taped, this was considered the premiere orchestral room in town. The more he and Cameron experimented and rerecorded, the more money they spent, and soon the score budget, like every other line item on the movie, was over the top.

On almost any film, music presented a financial dilemma. It was a time-honored producer's tradition, early on in preproduction, when the financial going got tough, to slash off the line item for scoring. What the hell. They wouldn't have to worry about it until post. When it did come time to scrape up the money for *Titanic*'s score, there was much wringing of hands, and some insistence of sticking with the lowball figure in the initial budget. Horner was earning considerably more than the going rate, but once Cameron set his mind on him, there was no going back. Fox was willing to be creative. Horner had a package deal, common for composers, which included a flat fee that had to cover the cost of the sessions, including musician pay. (This explains why many composers record out of the country, where musicians are paid less.) In a package situation, overages ate into the composer's own margin.

Horner would, at the end of the day, be delivering this score for zero salary, even after working on it twice as long as any other film.

For a long time, Cameron grappled with the idea of whether or not to put a song in his film. Though he didn't object to the *concept* of a song, he had serious misgivings about putting one to *Titanic.* "Would you put a song at the end of *Schindler's List?*" he asked himself. "I don't think so."

Horner, however, felt strongly that the film needed a song, especially at the end where the credits ran a substantive eight minutes. The composer believed that a song would help maintain the emotional state of the movie during the long credit roll and that a strong vocal would be the best way to end the film. He knew he'd never convince Cameron in concept because the decision was instinctual, but not necessarily logical.

Without approval from Cameron, Horner went ahead and asked Will Jennings to write the lyrics to his music. He then invited Celine Dion to sing.

A Canadian pop singer who seemed to usurp Whitney Houston as the studios' soundtrack goddess of choice, Dion was the perfect choice for the song. Horner knew her before she became "Queen Celine." She loved the song. They roughed out a deal and snuck off to New York to cut a demo in secrecy. It was a lot of work, but Horner felt the only way he'd have any chance at convincing Cameron was to present him with the finished song.

With the song in hand, Horner circled Cameron for weeks, waiting for the right moment to present his case. He was nervous and with just cause. He'd convinced Celine Dion to cut a demo, something she hadn't done in years. He was very clear with her that the work was purely speculative and James Cameron, the film's director, could always reject it. Even so, it would be embarrassing to have to tell her that they were not going to use the song. He believed in the song, and knew she did too. Also, it would be nice to have a shot at two Oscar statuettes, instead of one.

After a particularly sunny week, "a good long streak of positive vibes," Horner handed the director a DAT tape. "There's something I want you to hear," he said.

Cameron played the song several times, saying nothing. He recognized the theme, so he knew clearly that it had been written for his film, but how in the world did he get this recorded? Finally, after what seemed like a long time to Horner, Cameron turned to the composer and said, "This is great."

Not being up on his female pop vocalists, Cameron didn't recognize the voice of Celine Dion. Horner finally told him, all smiles.

Cameron liked the song, thought it was as good as, say, the theme from *The Bodyguard* or any of the best love songs of the past ten years. He agreed it might work to kick off the end credits though he still had some reservations and felt that using the song was a risk. Would he take heat for copping out and going commercial at the end of the movie? David Lean, whose collaboration with composers resulted in some of the finest film scores ever, never put a song at the end of a movie. Ditto Stanley Kubrick, Cameron's idol. He had to think about the song some more.

August 16 marked James Cameron's forty-third birthday. Though his beard was graying, he still had all his hair and looked fit, amazing, really, for what he had been through over the past three years.

He spent the night before his birthday, as he had endless evenings before, sequestered in his editing room, tapping at his keyboard in the blue glow of the monitors. The Avid technician sat quietly on his side of the blackout curtain and surfed the Internet as Cameron performed his final nip and tuck on the edit.

Long after dawn, Cameron emerged, blinking, from the editing room. By the time he was ready to head to his new home with Hamilton and the kids, the sun was up and his secretary was already loading a mountain of gifts into his car.

He decided he would include Horner's song. It seemed, on reflection, the correct way to finish the film, giving voice to the ideas and emotions of the film and putting them out there in the world, in the fabric of everyday life.

Also, it was bound to be a commercial success. Horner had just struck a lucrative deal with Sony Classics and Dion, who also recorded for Sony, had a new album coming out in the fall. Between the two of them, Cameron knew the song would get the big push. People would get hit by two or three bars of it, relive that emotion and, in a Pavlovian display of empathy, want to see the film again. At least that was a theory.

But hey, he'd never done anything like this before, and frankly, he'd be as amazed as anybody if any of this actually worked.

Chapter Seventeen

> Most filmmakers demand your work be really, really good. With Jim, his idea of really, really good is perfect.
>
> —Scott Ross

THE CELINE Dion song heightened the friction between Fox and Paramount. The song was going to cost money, and Paramount wasn't buying. Fox felt a Celine Dion song would be of greater value to the film's domestic distributor than to themselves and took a firm stand, on principle, that Paramount should pay for it. The only problem was, now Cameron really wanted the song. Cameron had his deal at Fox, and it was the studio's job to keep him happy, especially since a positive buzz on the film continued to build after the research screening. The media began speculating with reasonable certainty that Paramount, at least, would make some money from *Titanic.*

The Paramount team had been strategizing sales concepts since spring. Movie marketing is a legitimate if inexact demographic science with the same goal as most promotions: to draw a crowd and get your message in front of as many people as possible. This could be done via the generic route—wallpaper the planet—or by making a surgical strike to the target audience. The trick was to get it right the first time, because unlike colas, antiperspirant, or just about any other "product," a film's shelf life is limited and doesn't allow for a second chance. There is no cinematic correlation for the relaunch of Classic Coke.

With a movie, the idea was to get people into theaters that opening weekend—to "open." That way, the studio could still make a tidy haul off an awful piece of junk. An opening gross of $15 million was impressive, $20 million astounding. Given something to work with, any studio could pretty much buy its way to ten, hammering the airwaves with lots of TV spots. It wasn't hard to spend $12 to $20 million on advertising building up to opening weekend alone.

The marketing effort includes paid advertising, publicity and promotion. One of the early steps is designing "key art"—a galvanizing image for the print campaign of posters, billboards, and newspaper ads—as well as conceptualizing the theatrical trailer, a shortened version of which will usually form the basis of the television spots. The idea is to boil down the myriad elements into a succinct commercial "message" that will connect with audiences.

The campaign unfolds with a series of questions. What would women ages eighteen to twenty-four think? How about kids? With *Titanic,* the first question was: Is it a love story or an action film? Cameron had always felt the film was mainly a love story, though he chuckled the first time he read it described that way, in the production charts of *The Hollywood Reporter: Titanic.* Epic romance. Ha!

Paramount's teaser poster, unveiled in May, took a pretty hard line: a dramatic, six-foot vertical slice of hull, bristling with rivets and the command: "Collide With Destiny." It was catchy. But did it represent the film?

"How predictable," thought Mechanic when he saw it. James Cameron—Action Film. No brainer. But Mechanic felt they were already guaranteed every young male just *because* it was a James Cameron film. What about the other four billion people on the planet?

Paramount had a spectacular history of marketing success. *The Godfather, Saturday Night Fever,* and *Flashdance* were milestones, along with the transformation of several films into cultural phenomena—*Top Gun* and *Fatal Attraction* to name just two. Yet it was impossible to quantify the impact marketing had in selling these films. Who was to say that the film wasn't just *that* good? In this regard, Bob Zemeckis' *Forrest Gump* was the ultimate brainteaser. Conceptually elusive, not quite a comedy, not quite a drama, the film starred Tom Hanks, a comedy guy in a serious role. Based on a novel by Winston Groom, the movie became the top grossing film of 1994 and spawned cookbooks and a clothing line, a veritable gusher of licensed merchandise. The film was a boon of product placement for Nike, which got a serious image lift as Gump's sneaker of choice. *Forrest Gump* won six Academy Awards, reflecting well on Paramount's promotional efforts.

Marketing can, and has, saved many a mediocre effort from total embarrassment. Handled deftly, it can lend a patina of success. Take *Congo,* for instance. The film was a mess with some cool special effects. A studio generally knows well in advance of a film's release whether or not it has a bomb on its hands, a combination of research screenings and gut instinct. Paramount maximized its material by focusing their promotion on literary superstar Michael Crichton, who wrote the screenplay from his own novel. The posters, TV spots, and theatrical trailers all showcased Crichton's name. The film opened strongly but plummeted by weekend two. A sure sign of brilliant marketing. A great campaign can get them into theaters but quality, or lack thereof, catches up quickly.

Arthur Cohen was named head of marketing at Paramount in late 1989. Cohen was that rare bird, an out-of-industry hire. He'd spent the previous three years at the cosmetics firm Revlon. The slogan savvy marketer immediately put himself on the Hollywood map with his *Hunt For Red October* teaser campaign: "The Hunt Is On!" Cohen had that somewhat elusive skill: he could distill movies into concepts.

His marketing of the supernatural romance *Ghost* hinged on the invocation "Believe." Audiences did, to the tune of $218 million in North America and Cohen became the subject of admiring whispers at the best restaurants in town. *Indecent Proposal* was a big hit, for reasons that would hard to ascribe to anything *but* marketing. The print campaign, which looked like an ad for Calvin Klein underwear, officially earned Cohen the reputation of inspired genius.

For *Titanic,* Cohen and his number two, Nancy Goliger, came up with several key art images, but it essentially came down to an update on the "Collide with Destiny" teaser; that is, a romantic image that combined the lovers with the upturned ship's bow and the epithet "Nothing on Earth Could Come Between Them." Lansing and Friedman were pulling for the action imagery. Sanchini, who supervised marketing activities, found the softer sell more compelling and established a consensus with Cameron and Landau.

Fox marketing chief Bob Harper acted in an advisory capacity, but the studio would be picking up on the same key art for their international promotions, the only difference being that for some territories, DiCaprio's face—downturned in the domestic poster—was positioned more prominently in the foreign market.

Hard and soft versions of the theatrical trailer were tested with audiences, who rated both highly, but preferred the more story-driven piece, basically a tightened version of the ShoWest presentation. At five minutes, the *Titanic* trailer was still double the 2.5 minute limit allowed by the Motion Picture Association of America. Paramount had to obtain a special waiver for theater owners to run the piece, which was officially serviced in September. Theater owners reported that audiences were enthusiastically cheering the *Titanic* trailer, which, like *Independence Day* before it, became an event in itself.

On September 8, Cameron and company decamped to Skywalker Ranch, George Lucas' 2,600 acre spread in the hills of San Francisco's Marin County. Cameron was set to do six weeks of audio at Skywalker Sound. By now, the director had two new assistants. Lisa Dennis had been promoted to post-production supervisor and her second, Dan Boccoli, was assistant sound editor. Cameron's new helper, Nancy Hobson, checked in a few days early to make things comfortable for her boss' arrival. He was not traveling light. Cameron's baggage included an Avid, a KEM, and Dan Muscarella, a stoop-shouldered fifteen-year veteran from Consolidated Film Industries, CFI, who had been Cameron's colorist since 1991. The director would abduct him, "like a UFO," releasing him only when the negative was locked.

Skywalker Ranch is a little village of about a dozen buildings with its own fire department. Situated high in the San Raphael mountains, tucked amid rolling, gold hills, it is a post-production Shangri-La with a baseball field and a lake. Swans glide in the water, horses graze the fields. The main house, surrounded by a wrap-around porch, is an elaborate three-story Victorian manor built in the 1860s-style and home to the offices of Lucas' film production company, Lucasfilm Ltd. Large white doors with leaded glass welcome visitors. The entrance hall is dominated by a burgundy-carpeted staircase worthy of Scarlett O'Hara. To the left is a conference room that doubles as a dining room during less formal occasions. A doorway leads to a lushly planted solarium, all white wrought iron and glass, that serves as an overflow eating area for the nearby restaurant and cafeteria.

To the right, a small hallway is lined with display cases. Inside are a miscellany of treasures including a *Star Wars* Light Sabre, C3PO's hand, Indiana Jones' bullwhip, and a collection of Keystone Cops badges. On display also is Lucas' Irving Thalberg Award. The prestigious trophy, named for the fabled 1930s MGM producer, is bestowed by the Academy of Motion Picture Arts and Sciences on producers for their body of work and is the only Oscar Lucas has ever won.

Beyond the hallway yawns a living room, and then the music room, whose chief feature is a baby grand piano. A doorway opens off to a den-like media room. Another door leads to the library where 10,000 volumes line the walls. The staff includes four full-time librarians and researchers. When Paramount closed its library in 1987, Lucas bought the whole thing. He had so many books they didn't all fit in the library and he warehoused some in a building nearby. Lucas, who, like Cameron, is a writer, has collected the volumes as research resources for his scripts. They're mostly reference books. George Lucas loves history. So does James Cameron.

Cameron is working a few hundred feet from this Victorian manse in the Technical Building, or Tech Building, as it's informally known. The two-story structure, designed to look like an old winery, is lofty, with crossed-beam atrium ceilings. Outside, Chardonnays, Merlots, and Pinot Noirs ripen on the vine. The grapes are harvested and sent to Francis Coppola's Niebaum Coppola winemaker, where they are bottled under a private label.

An adjunct to the Tech Building, the 292-seat Stag Theater, is a state-of-the-art screening room that boasts the ultimate in THX—the movie theater sound presentation system developed by Lucas. Smaller, ancillary buildings, similarly rustic in style, dot the landscape, and house Lucas' corporate officers—heads of marketing, publicity, and business affairs. A complex of quaint country buildings serve as a bed and breakfast for Skywalker clients and Lucasfilm visitors. The rooms at the inn are all named for famous filmmakers. Cameron is staying in the private, detached residence known as the Coachhouse. Outside, two bicycles—one with a toddler seat attached—lean against a beam rail.

Landau is staying in the Orson Welles suite. The producer is in for the long haul, overseeing problems for his temperamental charge. When things were at their bleakest, Cameron said to him, "We're going to do this, and we're going to do it right, and I don't care if it kills me or you," and looking back, Landau felt there were times it nearly did. But now, there was hope. The film was incredible; all he'd imagined it could be when he gave up his cushy office job to follow a wild spirit to foreign soil. Of course, it was hard to be objective. He was so close. But the film seemed to transcend the motion picture experience. Cameron had done it. He put moviegoers on that ship and plunged them into the icy Atlantic. And he did it by combining the technical razzmatazz with beautifully realized characters. Jan de Bont put you in the middle of a twister, and it was fun, but when the dust settled, that was it.

It was the difference between a film that was merely a series of disconnected, dynamic visual elements, and one that had good old-fashioned storytelling. *Titanic* spoke right to the heart. Cameron's gift was to create a unique moviegoing experience, one audiences couldn't get from any other film. There had been so much attention to the budget, but look at what else was out there. *Batman and Robin, Speed 2, The Lost World*—these films each cost well in excess of $100 million, and all were sequels whose originals could be rented in the video stores. Among them, *Titanic* was the only original.

Yeah, *Titanic* had almost killed them, but they had made an incredible film and it was worth it. Dazed and exhausted, having spent the past two years swimming for their lives, it appeared they were finally being dragged into a lifeboat.

Mix A is the largest of eight sound editing suites at Skywalker. A cavernous, cerulean blue room, its distinguishing characteristics are a 23-by-16-foot movie screen and a 28-foot Neve Capricorn mixing console that looks like it could run the Starship *Enterprise.* There are usually three seats at the mixing board. On a James Cameron film there are four. Cameron takes the "sweet spot," in the center. Stationed to his left is Gary Rydstrom, lead mixer. To his right, are two sound rerecorders—Gary Summers, who specializes in music and effects, and Tom Johnson, who handles dialogue.

The sound setup was customized to Cameron's needs. Positioned behind them in the room were five computer workstations, which put every sound Cameron could possibly want at his finger tips. *Titanic* probably held the record for the instant accessibility of sounds—whether dialogue, music, or effects. That was in addition to the sounds that had been pre-recorded, or "pre-dubbed," for the final mix, which came in through the Neve.

The computer workstations were specially configured with silent fans. The three on the left controlled sound effects, "production sound" and automated dialogue replacement (ADR)—the dialogue recorded on the looping stage. They might have ten different versions of the same line and Cameron wanted to try them all. He enjoyed sound mixing because at this stage of the game, he could no longer adjust the lighting or the line readings, but he had an incredible palette of sounds with which to enhance his images.

"He was like a conductor of a huge symphony," says sound designer Chris Boyes. "Give me this over in dialogue, change this in music, and this in effects." Keeping their predub as a base, he had them add some things, a process known as "sweetening," or delete others. The sound effects terminal offered up last minute "fixes." When Cameron said, "I'd like a big metallic gong," or "Give me a subtle tinkle," Boyes could zip it over via digital network from his sound design studio down the hall. Nearby, another terminal controlled the archive of "production sound"—sound recorded live during filming. On the right side of the room were workstations for music and Cameron's temporary mix, which he used as the blueprint for the sound engineers. The film was actually presented to the test-screening audiences with Cameron's temporary mix.

Elevated slightly, at the back of the room was a more casual sitting space with leather lounging sofas, end tables, and a phone. The room was cushy in a techie sort of way with a slightly fishbowl feel, due to a large plate glass window that separated a seating area just outside.

An image of Kate Winslet in a lifeboat, staring mournfully at Jack as she is lowered away, fills the screen. The image cuts to rope, sliding on a davit pulley and creaking sounds permeate the room. Cut to Cal and Jack, bidding Rose adieu at the side of the ship as they chat amongst themselves.

JACK

There isn't any arrangement, is there?

CAL

Oh, there is. *(Pausing for effect)* Not that it will benefit you any. I always win Jack, one way or another.

Cameron wants the sound of the ropes just so. He wants it, for a split second, to be the dominant sound, lending a tactile feel to the images. The sound guys always wanted to pile it on. Cameron gets daring and has the dialogue track fade out entirely, swelling the music for a brief slow motion interlude. An hour later they were still on the same twelve feet of film. Filmmaking was, after all, a process of finely polishing a series of precious moments. An expensive process. Including post-production and marketing, *Titanic* cost $1 million per minute.

When Hobson breaks in to deliver a phone message, she approaches Cameron deferentially, on tiptoe, as one would a stranger's sleeping dog. He glances at the note, and, after a few more adjustments, excuses himself and leaves the room. Asked, in his absence, how it was to work with Cameron, the sound engineers look at each other conspiratorially, laugh, and roll their eyes as if to say, "Yeah, he's tough, in ways it would compromise our professionalism to discuss." But as the smiles fade, Gary Summers says earnestly, "He likes to teach. He's taught us everything there is to know about reciprocating steam engines, which is pretty cool."

In their way, they seem flattered that the director cares enough about what they do to spend the time in the trenches with them. Other directors didn't actually sit there at board with you, all day, every day. When they were mixing *The Lost World* they never saw Spielberg at Skywalker. They mixed the film, took it down to Amblin, and screened it with him there. Took notes. Sent him the adjusted print. Of course, everybody has their own style of working and Cameron's is very in-your-face. It could be a bit much but he speaks the language of the sound engineer, and like a member of a secret society, is afforded certain privileges.

Titanic was a longer mix than usual, both because of the three-hour length of the film and because the sound was complex and crucial to the story. The creaks and groans played a huge role in defining the splitting and sinking of the ship. At the other extreme, subtle shading was needed to heighten the audience's reaction to more delicate moments, like the tinkling of glass beads on Rose's evening dress as she steps, windswept, over the stern railing in her "suicide" scene.

As early as *The Terminator*, Cameron realized the importance of sound. Every sound got his complete attention. He had to feel that he owned it in some way. He was particularly intimate with *Titanic*'s sonic stylings, having mixed his own audio temp track on the Avid. He drew on a combination custom brew and Skywalker's stock library of 50,000 proprietary effects. It was largely through the efforts of Rydstrom that Skywalker Sound has one of the premiere effects libraries in the business. His isn't the only stuff, but it is the best stuff, or so the legend goes.

A fifteen-year company man, Rydstrom is one of those guys that is never without a microphone and DAT recorder. He'd even take it on vacation, driving his wife nuts as he hopped from his car to tape the sound of steel reverberating under a bridge, or rain hitting pavement. Sound engineers process this raw material through a synthesizer, mixing and melding for virtually infinite variation. Every big film has major sound moments that required custom-recording. The stock library provides the backdrop, the subtle shades and textures. Once a film wrapped, the raw sound material is indexed into the main collection and stored on hard-disk array.

Cameron considered the throb of the engine to be the heartbeat of the great ship. As sound designer, Chris Boyes was charged with breathing it to life. Cameron wanted the thunderous engine to sound like it was heating up in the "Let's stretch her legs!" scene, so they pieced it together from lots of individual sounds, big and small. Dah-dong! Dah-*dung!* Dah-dong! Dah-*dung!* Boyes wove together deep metallic hits culled from sliding pistons and machine cylinders with lighter sounds, including an "air brake" from a giant tug boat release.

The sound designer's job is to create the audio palette for the film. Sitting at the mixing console, the director and re-recording engineers paint in the colors. Boyes had been Rydstrom's assistant for the early part of Boyes's six year tenure at Skywalker, recently working his way up to peer status. When *Titanic*'s release date got pushed back, Chris was able to step up, because Gary was preoccupied with *The Lost World.* Boyes worked in a room the size of a small walk-in closet, stuffed with audio consoles the size of refrigerators.

Boyes had been working on *Titanic* since April. The big groans of the sinking and splitting ship were among the earliest effects he fashioned. Cameron actually got to spot the snapping, metallic sounds into his temp. Dozens of individual tones are interwoven for the final effect. Boyes harvested the sounds from a variety of sources. The most dramatic was a ship that was actually docked in the San Francisco bay, where it strained against its moorings in rough weather. He then "processed them heavily," ending up with something that sounds "almost like crying." The sounds were transmitted to Malibu via ISDN phone lines.

The whirring of the *Mir* submarines in reel one was an early undertaking that remained ongoing. Initially, word came back that Boyes nailed it, but Cameron must have changed his mind. Now it was September and Boyes was back to square one, experimenting, trying to come up with something new. *Titanic* had taxed him more than anything in his professional career.

"I want the water shaking the room!" Cameron instructs the Mix A team. Onscreen, water gushes through the steerage corridors where Jack and Rose beat a hasty retreat after she uncuffs him from his shipboard prison. "You haven't heard me say too loud yet. I want to use my mid-thorax as a hearing organ. The water should be shaking this room." The music and dialogue channels are cut. A gut-thumping whoosh and the anguished groan of twisting metal fills the room. Hearing it naked, it's amazing how much sound energy is coming out of the movie at this particular moment.

"I want a subwoofer groan in there that's just gonna *rock* the audience," Cameron tells Rydstrom. "This is the last place we're really going to be able to scare them with the sound of the ship."

Rydstrom adjusts some knobs.

Upon installation in May 1997, this was the largest all-digital film mixing console in the world, with 96 automated channels and 176 inputs, capable of mixing and matching 176 discrete sounds. With its built in memory, any adjustments made—EQ, sound equalization, panning (which sound comes from which speaker), level, digital signal processing (reverb and effects), and dynamics—were committed to memory.

Cameron leans forward on the console, expectantly, eyes locked on the screen.

Suddenly, the room goes silent. The Capricorn board has been crashing with alarming frequency. Skywalker Sound technical operations manager John Mardesich has flown in two codesmiths from Young Software in London to try and deal with the problem, but it's been two weeks and so far, they've done little more than lengthen, slightly, the duration between crashes. The board never acted up like this on *The Lost World.* There wasn't anything wrong with it, as far as anyone could tell, it was just that Cameron, with his five workstations jacked in and an insatiable desire to experiment, was demanding performance the console's designer never dreamed of, taking the console where no sound mixer had gone before.

The software specialists hurry in. After a brief appraisal, they proclaim the need to reboot, a process that takes approximately thirty minutes. Cameron bolts from the room. Taking the stairs two at a time, he heads down a long hall to his mobile color timing studio.

When he's not mixing or timing, he sits at the Avid in a room set up as his personal office. Aside from the Avid, a small desk, industrial table, and motel-quality sofa are the only furniture in the room. Though the picture is locked, he's still tweaking. Currently, he's changing some of the drawings Jack shows Rose during their big walk and talk. A series of nudes and a few portrait studies, Cameron drew them himself, from photographs of turn of the century impressionist art.

The KEM has been set up in what appears to be a storage room. In fact, it's a viewing room that looks down on the scoring stage. A heavy drape lines the glass wall. In the back of the room is a jumbled heap of mismatched furniture. The room is black except for the light emanating from the KEM, where Muscarella sits for hours at a stretch, pouring over the movie frame by frame. Color timing is the final adjustment in preparing the negative for its release printing.

Because scenes are shot over a long period of time, under many different lighting conditions, using different film stocks and incorporating effects, the edited negative more often than not sports jarring color discrepancies from cut to cut. Color timing provides balance and continuity, smoothing over the rough edges. Carpenter periodically drops in to see how things are coming along.

Though they are working on the KEM, the machine was actually not intended for color timing. The KEM is essentially an old-fashioned editing machine, advancing the film frame by frame. This machine was specially configured to allow simultaneous viewing on three two-foot screens, showing the work print, the rough timed print, and the color corrected print.

Most filmmakers color time in a film lab screening room, shouting out their comments to the technicians as the images flash by. Cameron was unhappy with that process. "See that shot? No, not that one, the one before it... well... it's several back now, but you know that scene where she comes in the door? It's too yellow." For his money, it was not a precise enough science, but most people liked it because it was quick.

CFI also developed a "proof print" timing system that breaks the reel down into shots, showing one to three frames per shot. This, too, was unacceptable to Cameron since the frames were picked at random. If the camera was panning in the shot, every frame could conceivably have a different color palette. He liked to look at the film in motion, getting an idea of the flow, tuning into averages.

After experiencing traditional color timing on *The Terminator,* Cameron said never again. He was going to do it shot by shot. For *Aliens,* he shocked the staff of Rank film labs in England with his KEM configuration. They said, "You can't color time on a KEM, that's ridiculous!" And Cameron's response was, "Yeah you can, if you take these optical printer filters and true-up the lamp houses and you read them with a Kelvin meter and you..."

Cameron's motivation was practical as well as aesthetic. He wanted to get it right on one or two tries. Normally, over the course of refining the color timing, a lab would run eight or twelve prints. The original *Titanic* negative was stored on twenty thousand-foot reels. Every time you pulled a print, that piece of negative was worth one twentieth of $200 million. A $10 million object the size of a dinner plate, and some $15 an hour lab technician was handling it. He could drop it, or it could be improperly loaded onto the printing machine or a power failure could occur and crunch the film. Disaster could strike at any moment.

While Muscarella toiled in the Skywalker vineyard, his color timing instructions were being modemed down to CFI in Hollywood where they were downloaded into a main server controlling the printing machine. Ironically, even with *Titanic's* delayed release, at this late stage they were still in a time crunch. Muscarella remembers several all nighters. Because of the scheduling pressure, while Muscarella color timed one reel, CFI would be printing another.

Titanic was complicated by its numerous dissolve shots as well as the three hundred "flops." Most films are printed from a single negative, known as A Roll, though some require two, known as A and B. On some reels, *Titanic* careened all the way to F.

The complicated exposure process was computer controlled, but whoever was threading those negatives had to remain alert. It was a tedious undertaking. Each negative was ultrasonically cleaned before each printing and the labs strive for a dust-free environment. Cameron had worked with CFI starting with *The Terminator,* and when they had one of his films inhouse he virtually owned the lab.

Sitting beside the lab man, Cameron hammered him with rapid-fire instructions for every frame. "Come up two points of red and add a yellow. Make it 33-37-30." Film color was calibrated to a red-green-blue scale. The film flashed by. Twenty-four Rembrandts a second, the director joked. He was in a good mood. Muscarella adored Cameron, overlooking his bouts of temper. Jim was tough, but all he wanted was someone who worked as hard as he did without making any mistakes. And if you did make a mistake, you couldn't BS him, because he was so smart. Muscarella considered him a genius, and like any genius, a bit mad. How else could you explain his total obsession with this movie?

Finishing the reel at hand, Cameron ambles down the hall and takes his seat at the Avid, reshuffling the drawings in Jack Dawson's sketch book. He is pensive. The release date, the cost of the film, its length—these are very important business aspects of a film, but they were getting more attention than the film itself. Ultimately, the only thing that is truly important is to do a good movie. Of course, if you can take care of business and deliver a great movie too, well, then you're a superstar. But if you can't, if you have limitations, or setbacks or whatever... He heaves a sigh, thinking to himself he'd never make another movie like *Titanic.* Fox had been more supportive than most, but they were tougher than they would have been if they thought it was a more commercial movie. Since summer they had been applying pressure to get him quickly on track with a bluechip blockbuster like *Terminator 3* or *Spiderman.*

Of course the film he *thought* he'd be doing next was *Avatar.* He'd written a 200-page scriptment for his original story of genetically altered life forms. The project was to have been telescoped into *Titanic.* A lot of the performance capture technology developed by Digital Domain to digitally populate the ship was directly applicable to *Avatar.* At one point he was prepared to embark on a one-year proof of concept film. It was that hard. He had to prove to himself he could do it. If he could, he had no doubt *Avatar* would be the coolest film ever made.

Effects supervisor Camille Cellucci pops her head in. She'd been making thrice weekly visits to the Ranch. There were still about five visual effects shots that hadn't been locked, and she was shuttling the reels for Cameron's approval. Did he have a second to screen shot 192? Landau follows her in. They're back up in Mix A. Cameron hoists himself out of his chair and heads for the hallway with the producer and effects supervisor pulled along on his momentum. He's a man who leaves a big wake.

Chapter Eighteen

Where is a height without depth?

—Carl Jung

FOX PULLED OFF an eleventh-hour coup. As Paramount attempted to whip the media into a frenzy for the film's December 19 domestic release, Fox stole its thunder by scheduling *Titanic*'s overseas premiere for November 1, at the Tokyo Film Festival. It was a gutsy move. If the film bombed in Tokyo, advance word could kill the film's stateside opening. But Mechanic was convinced the film would play well. Creatively, he was convinced this was as good a film as he was ever going to get in his professional life. From Fox's perspective as a corporation, they had moved from "What the fuck did we get ourselves into?" to "Maybe it was all worth it."

On a business level, who knew? While it didn't appear they'd get hurt badly—no *Waterworld*-sized writedowns of $60 million—there didn't seem to be much financial upside either. And that, after all, was the reason they were in business. Still, in twenty years, people wouldn't be judging whether it made or lost $10 million, they'd be watching the movie. If at any point in the future News Corporation decided to sell Fox, he could see someone buying it just to own *Titanic,* like Ted Turner who bought MGM for *Gone with the Wind.* Mechanic was convinced they had made, along with *Star Wars,* what would be one of the two most important films in the Fox library. And because he felt the buzz out of Tokyo would be good, he had Fox's international distribution division book the film there.

Paramount was not pleased. It was the Hollywood equivalent of checkmate.

Tokyo would kick off the first *Titanic* reviews. Once the date was announced, the trades frantically scrambled to formulate a review strategy. Either reviewers would be flown in, or a local correspondent recruited for the task. Both trade newspapers had reporters covering the festival, but neither had planned on sending a reviewer. They complained to Paramount about the expense and inconvenience. Paramount publicity topper Blaise Noto knew exactly how important these first reviews would be. A pot-luck Japanese correspondent could cause a disaster. The potential for disaster in the translation alone made you shudder. The *Hollywood Reporter* film critic Duane Byrge was a popcorn-munching movie lover who appreciated the Jim Cameron aesthetic and *Daily Variety*'s A-stringer Todd McCarthy was also worth chasing. Noto arranged an early screening for the local boys.

Orchestrating magazine publicity for *Titanic* was a tricky business for Noto and company. Leonardo DiCaprio had complicated things by promising an exclusive cover to *Vanity Fair,* a great favorite among stars who looked good but didn't have much to say. The glossy magazine was in the movie star business and believed in keeping the merchandise polished. Oh sure, they'd serve up the occasional sacrificial lamb—usually someone they felt was on their way out. DiCaprio's publicist delivered the word to Paramount: the actor would pose *only* for *VF* house photographer Annie Liebowitz, a celebrity in her own right.

Celebrities these days have turned into press prima donnas. They all have their own personal publicists and have publicity approval written into their contracts; the studio publicity machines are essentially at their mercy. Noto and every studio press czar longed for the days when movie stars were company men and women, working the film, pressing the flesh. As it was now, he had a mutiny on his hands from all the other magazines that wanted to cover *Titanic* in a big way. He couldn't deliver Leo for a cover shoot, and no one wanted just Kate. Not only that, but DiCaprio was refusing to do television, and Kate was shooting on location in Morocco—making a film called *Hideous Kinky,* no less—and would be mostly unavailable to promote *Titanic.*

This was bad. The biggest film of all time, and his hands were tied, publicity-wise. Finally, after much begging and cajoling, Paramount got DiCaprio to agree to pose for one additional cover shoot, and the studio decided it would be for *Newsweek.* The magazine had been aggressive in its coverage of the film all along, and its reporting had been friendlier toward *Titanic* than *Time*'s. *Newsweek,* the word went, was interested in juicing up its Hollywood correspondence, and they didn't want to cover *Titanic* like just another film.

A movie cover in a newsweekly was a fabulous achievement as they only did one or two a year. Marvin Levy, Steven Spielberg's personal publicity attaché, still got misty-eyed when talking about his 1977 *Newsweek* cover for *Close Encounters of the Third Kind.*

DiCaprio agreed to do the shoot only on the condition that Paramount hire the photographer and service the art to the magazine, so they could have some control over the process. Of course, *Newsweek* wouldn't promise the studio a cover; that would depend on a number of factors, including the story their writer turned in. But if all went well, there was no reason to expect they wouldn't get one.

Magazines like *Premiere, Movieline,* and *Entertainment Weekly* that were likely to want *Titanic* on their covers couldn't, because they had no interview and no shot. The only one doing active publicity on the film was Cameron, but magazines shunned anyone who was not instantly recognizable for a frontispiece. They just didn't move copies at the checkout counter. *Entertainment Weekly* wouldn't take no for an answer. The magazine was mightily offended by the *Newsweek* pact. Entertainment was *all* they did. They were there for the studios fifty-two weeks a year, and this was the thanks they got. Snubbed for *Newsweek.*

Word got out that the magazine would retaliate by breaking their story early. Once the movie screened in Tokyo, Paramount wouldn't be able to contain the story, and they weren't going to be caught sitting on their hands, waiting until *Newsweek* was good and ready to run their piece. *EW* began cobbling together whatever photography they could, using press kit stills and securing still images pulled from the trailer. That would surely earn someone a cease and desist letter, but hey, by that time they would have desisted already, so who cared? Paramount was frantic. They knew that getting scooped would sour *Newsweek* on the story. Not only that, they thought it would trigger a floodgate of early press, and they didn't want the publicity to peak too soon, more than a month before the film was in theaters.

It was a game of cat and mouse. Both publications were preparing their stories. Both wanted to be first, but neither wanted to come out the same week, which would convey a herd mentality editorial approach. By October 24, *EW* had a finished piece, and the word was *Newsweek*'s next cover story would be on infertility. Bingo.

James Cameron stared out the window of the United luxury jet en route to Tokyo from Los Angeles on Thursday, October 30. Hamilton and Hobson accompanied him on the flight. Before boarding the plane that morning, he was handed an advance copy of the *Entertainment Weekly* dated November 7 containing the article "Man Overboard" by Paula Parisi. It was the first major news break on the film. He perused the piece, and it made his blood pound. The bastards! He was appalled by what appeared to be a recapitulation of every negative thing that was ever written about the production, from the PCP poisoning to the injuries and the cost overruns and studio infighting. Their reporter had spent more time on the set than anyone else and this is what they print!

What's more, the writer opened the story with the "million dollar cut," the scissored Lovejoy chase. And it wasn't even couched as an attempt to improve the quality of the movie, which is how Cameron saw it. The piece just made him sound wasteful. Nobody was putting anything in context. The perception of this thing was so far off base from what they'd really done these past three years, it boggled the mind. Nothing he said seemed to change the notion that his film was a failure. But the test audiences had heard all those negative stories and they didn't care. They loved the film. Dealing with the cynical media was like trying to push back a glacier with your bare hands. It wasn't going to change until you set off a nuclear bomb in its path, and that's exactly what he intended to do with this film. He tried to put the article behind him and curled up to go to sleep.

He had more to worry about than any magazine article. There was a lot riding on this trip. Though the Tokyo Film Festival was not one of the more prestigious festivals in the world in terms of its juried prizes, it was well attended and had high visibility. Japan was the world capital of pop culture, and press from the four points of the globe were converging on the premiere of the biggest movie ever made. Things could turn around after this.

While Cameron slept, Landau and an engineering S.W.A.T. team were checking specs at Orchard Hall, a two thousand-seat concert hall in the trendy Shibuya district of Tokyo. Like every other aspect of filmmaking, Cameron was very particular about how his films were exhibited. Landau traveled with a Dolby sound specialist and a Hollywood projectionist. At the venue, they changed the audio baffling and increased the brightness of the projector bulbs. The largest of four venues in the Bunkamura Cultural Center, the Orchard was a concert hall converted to a cinema for opening and closing nights of the festival. In 1996 *Independence Day* made its Japanese debut here. But *ID* had already made $300 million in the U.S. by the time it played Japan and its fate was sealed. *Titanic*'s world premiere was far more consequential.

Throughout the morning, teenage girls were piled six deep on the street in front of Orchard Hall. Some had camped out for two nights to get a good spot to see Leonardo, the new demigod. Cameron and Hamilton were en route to the theater in one limousine, DiCaprio and his friends in another. Landau, waiting at the theater, was in radio contact with both. It was decided that Cameron would arrive at the main entrance, as planned, serving as a decoy for DiCaprio, who was rerouted to a back door for security purposes. "It was a complete mob scene," Landau recalls. "There were one hundred police scheduled for duty, and throughout the day officials called in a hundred more." Cameron and Hamilton hopped from their black stretch at sundown that Saturday night. The crowd surged forward, chanting "Leo! Leo!" Someone recognized Hamilton and a shriek went up. Of course everyone thought that meant DiCaprio had arrived and it was pure pandemonium. The director and his wife were almost crushed by the crowd as police dragged them into the theater.

Taking the stage to deliver welcoming remarks, Cameron and DiCaprio were greeted by cries of "We love you, Leo!" and "Romeo! Romeo!" One or two fans screamed "Cameron! Cameron!" To be sure, he had his own following of "otaku," or computer nerds, but the cries for him were probably just as much due to unfailing Japanese politeness. They didn't want him to feel left out.

Cameron's comments were brief. It was like being the opening act for the Beatles. He knew they didn't want to hear from him, but he tried to make it meaningful. "There are about twenty-two hundred people in this theater tonight, roughly the same number as were onboard the *Titanic*. If we were all on the *Titanic* now, and we hit that iceberg, three-quarters of us would be dead by the time the movie finished," he pointed out, dedicating the film to the fifteen hundred people who perished that fateful night.

DiCaprio called the Japanese fans "the best and most loyal in the world." He said making the film was "a long journey" and "the single most incredible movie experience of my life," adding, "it made a man out of me." As the lights went down and the movie unspooled, the director gradually relaxed. Japanese audiences were incredibly reserved, and about half those in attendance were media and industry types, the toughest crowd, but they were laughing in the right places, and by the time the lights came up, teary-eyed girls filled the aisles.

By Sunday morning, November 2, AP and Reuters had news reports on the wire. "The most expensive movie ever made, the disaster epic *Titanic,* made its maiden voyage with better results than the ill-fated ocean liner had," began the Associated Press piece optimistically. After quoting a few enthusiastic fans, who said they loved the special effects and were swooning with delight over the romance, the writer went on to quote a "media critic" who said he thought the excitement of the second half and the sinking of the ship would carry the film, but predicted the upside would be limited by the "slushy" love story which unfolded too slowly during the first part. "James Cameron wanted to write a romance, and I don't think he's very good in that genre," concluded the pundit.

The Reuters write-up was similar, juxtaposing audience enthusiasm with qualifying observations about the film itself. "Historical pundits will likely take some umbrage that the monumental disaster has mainly become a backdrop for a love story," the writer complained, going on to rib the director for having Winslet deliver "an obscene gesture using the middle finger, not a common action for women in 1912," and raising an eyebrow over the scene where Jack teaches Rose to spit. But ultimately, the writer concluded, "the film does pay respect to the enormity of the disaster." As consumer press coverage went, it wasn't bad.

But no one was prepared for the trade reviews that broke the next day, November 3. "Paramount should replace that white mountain in its logo with an iceberg for the next several months," advised *The Hollywood Reporter* critic Duane Byrge. "Not only will James Cameron's formidable cinematic vessel sail sensationally on domestic waters, but Twentieth Century-Fox, which has international rights, will find that *Titanic* will propel blockbuster results around the world," Byrge predicted, going on to note "*Titanic* plumbs personal and philosophical story depths not usually found in event-scale movies.

"It is a masterwork of big-canvas storytelling, broad enough to entrance and entertain yet precise and delicate enough to educate and illuminate. Undeniably, one could nitpick—critic types may snicker at some '60s era lines and easy-pop '90s vantage hindsights—but that's like dismissing a Mercedes on the grounds that its glove compartment interior is drab." Wow! This was the best review of Cameron's career to date.

Variety was similarly enthusiastic. "This *Titanic* arrives at its destination," began Todd McCarthy's review. "A spectacular demonstration of what modern technology can contribute to dramatic storytelling, James Cameron's romantic epic, which represents the biggest roll of the dice in cinematic history, will send viewers in search of synonyms for the title to describe the film's size and scope." McCarthy called the love story "as effective as it is corny" and called the three-hour-and-fourteen-minute film "fast paced." McCarthy, a "critic-type," did take issue with the dialogue being "peppered with vulgarities and colloquialisms that seem inappropriate to the period and place, but again seem aimed directly to the sensibilities of young American viewers."

Cameron was over the moon. Japan was nothing short of a triumph. A November 4 *New York Times* article characterized Paramount as "miffed" over their stolen premiere thunder, and said executives at the studio "fairly crowed over the muted reception" in Tokyo. "It didn't bother us because the Tokyo film festival is not a major event that is going to impact anything here in the States," said Friedman.

After a few days of officiating at the film festival, Cameron and Hamilton hopped a plane to Ireland for their deferred honeymoon.

At *Titanic*'s next stop, the Royal Premiere in London on November 18, the audience applauded three times during the film and thundered as the credits rolled. They were hooting and hollering when Jim and Leo stood up, which they never do in England, especially in the presence of Prince Charles, who attended with his two sons.

Also in attendance was another royal of sorts, the latest in a long line of chieftains of the Cameron Clan, the second oldest clan in Scotland, with a recorded history that goes as far back as 1200. Cameron's family traced its lineage to the band of notorious Highlander broad swordsmen, who hailed from Lochiel, an area of Lochaber. A clan contingent arrived on the shores of Nova Scotia in 1828, taking a "great circle route" almost identical to *Titanic*'s. The clan migrated to Toronto, and then to Caledon, near Alton. Cameron's particular branch wound up in Kapuskasing, where his parents grew up. The director was disappointed that the chief arrived in black tie, instead of his tartan kilt .

DiCaprio's *Vanity Fair* piece, which ran the week of the film's release, couldn't have been timed better. Liebowitz's cover portrayed the actor in stiff Edwardian-flavored formal wear. Inside, he wrapped himself in a swan and reclined in stovepipe jeans and snakeskin shoes for a look that was either rock 'n' roll or raunchy, depending on your perspective. The article breathlessly reported on "his lust for skydiving, bungee jumping and the like," delivering the news flash "he's still a regular guy." It was an article notably light on direct commentary by its subject, but the actor did confess that the *Titanic* experience was "*really* not my cup of tea—all respect to Jim and the actors who do that type of thing." DiCaprio was "very handsome, and has the smoothest skin I've ever seen on anyone over the age of four" rhapsodized the writer, who shed some light on his human side with Kate Winslet's insight: "to me, he's just smelly, farty Leo." In summary, *Romeo + Juliet* co-star Claire Dane mused she "still can't figure out whether he's really transparent or incredibly complex." Apparently, neither could *Vanity Fair.*

The traditional "cast and crew" screening of *Titanic* took place on Saturday, December 13, the night before the industry premiere. It was a way of thanking the worker bees, the grips and gaffers who didn't get invited to the swanky premiere, which in *Titanic's* case was scheduled for the following night. A more informal event, cast and crew screening took place at a multiplex theater in Century City. By now, virtually everyone was on to other projects. McLaglen was doing *X-Files: The Movie.* Carpenter and Muro were working together on an action film, *The Negotiator.* But almost everyone took the time to attend. They'd been through heaven and hell together, and with nine months separating them from *Titanic,* they were ready to reconvene, commiserate, and celebrate the accomplishment of the film itself. The crane operator, Larry Webber, flew in from Texas. Shelly Crawford was in from Vancouver, there were people in from Australia. This was a family reunion of sorts.

People arrived in all kinds of outfits, ranging from blue jeans and workboots to floor-length gowns on women who obviously thought they were attending a black tie premiere. Cameron played the gracious host, greeting people in the lobby beforehand. He thanked them for their hard work and dedication in an informal address before the film was shown. Afterwards, everyone streamed over to a party on a Fox soundstage next door, decorated circa 1970s with fake palm trees and mirror balls. Disco music blared from the speakers for the benefit of those who wanted to use the dance floor, which was empty for the first few hours but crowded by midnight.

Frances Fisher and Lewis Abernathy were the only principal cast members in attendance. Cameron took up a post near the door and kept up a steady stream of conversation with the many people who wanted to congratulate him and get his autograph. Fisher's driver hovered at his elbow for a half-hour, waiting for an autograph.

Movie premieres are ritualized events as unique to the denizens of Hollywood as the ceremonial acts of any tribe. Cameron described it as "the evening of long knives." All the people who had been so critical of him from behind their office desks, in their safe jobs, turned out in force to see the high wire act.

For the past year, Cameron felt like he'd been treading the high wire in a white leotard—with spangles on it. Now it was time for the triple somersault. If the movie tanks, it's the director who will take the heat. The dolly operator's going to work again, so are the gaffer and the DP. Of course, Cameron was lucky, having already established a successful track record in the sci-fi genre, to which he could always return. Fox was already talking about getting him involved with a remake of *Planet of the Apes*. They were having trouble with the script. At the very least, they wanted him to consider producing it.

Velvet ropes cordoned off a half mile stretch of Hollywood Boulevard. Limousines were cued up around the block waiting to deposit their glittering passengers. Red carpet lined the street in front of Grauman's Chinese Theater. Klieg lights sliced the sky. The veneer of glamour was undercut by "cocktail attire" dress. The event was a benefit for the Fulfillment Fund for disadvantaged students. Roughly three hundred tickets had been sold at $300 apiece. When people paid that much for tickets, they didn't want to be further inconvenienced by having to get all dressed up, on a Sunday evening yet, or so the thinking went.

It was a drizzly night, but that hadn't thwarted the long line of electronic press. A wall of TV cameras peered, insect-like, from the edge of the red ribbon. Gloria Stuart looked overwhelmed. Even at her heyday, the height of Hollywood's Golden Era, they didn't do it quite like this. Arnold Schwarzenegger, Mel Gibson, Celine Dion, Sylvester Stallone. The stars made the walk slowly. The executive guests and other attendees walked quickly by. Bill Mechanic was an exception. He was glued to Leonardo DiCaprio's side. The young actor had just come off two huge Fox films in a row, and Mechanic would be damned if he was going to have some Paramount executive wrapping an arm around the golden boy's shoulder in friendly camaraderie just when "Good Morning America" had its lens trained their way.

Winslet was a no-show. She'd planned to attend, but the death of a close friend prevented her. She'd missed the Royal Premiere in England and the junket there as well, having taken ill on the set in Morocco. There were whispers that it didn't look good. Cameron ran the gauntlet of cameras, carefully attentive to each interviewer's questions. Most of them were about *Titanic*'s budget.

Inside the theater, the Fox and Paramount executives were separated by an aisle. It was technically Paramount's party, but Fox had been allotted a block of tickets. James Cameron's parents were seated directly behind Peter Chernin, but didn't seem to know him. Viacom chief, Sumner Redstone, was there with his wife and grandchildren. Rupert Murdoch was not.

The lights went down with no warning, no formal remarks of any kind. A Hollywood industry crowd is the toughest in the world. Just ask anyone who's sat through a premiere of one of their films or performed at the Academy Awards.

Even so, the audience reaction to *Titanic* was unbelievable. They hooted and hollered in all the right places, laughing and bursting into spontaneous applause when Leo appeared in his tux, and when Kate grabbed the ax to break him loose.

The party was held in a heated tent erected over the parking lot out back. Cameron walked back to it in a daze. The relief he felt was not unlike waking up after a prolonged nightmare, to find it was only a dream. The early audiences liked his film. His Hollywood peers liked his film. Now the last and toughest test remained. The film would open on 2,674 screens on Friday. By Sunday night they'd have a pretty good idea whether it had all been worth it.

It was obvious that something extraordinary was happening when *Titanic* took the opening weekend with $29 million in ticket sales, besting *Tomorrow Never Dies,* which scored $25 million. *Titanic*'s three hour length meant it had fewer playtimes than the James Bond thriller. It was also on fewer screens—2,674 as opposed to 2,807. The best anyone had hoped for was a strong number two.

By week two, *Titanic* actually picked up steam for a haul of $35 million. An increase of 25 percent in the second weekend was practically unprecedented. The Bond film, meanwhile, experienced an

18 percent decline. *Titanic* reached the $100 million mark after only twelve days, prompting *Variety* to predict "the film now seems destined to reach $200 million domestically."

By February, *Titanic* broke a speed record, hitting the $300 million mark faster than any film in history. Arthur Cohen sent Rae Sanchini 300 white tulips—one for each million. "The three-hour plus epic drama continues to mock box office projections and shatter all previous models of film performance at the nation's theaters," wrote *The Hollywood Reporter* box office analyst.

Further confounding the experts, *Titanic*'s strongest showing was a month *after* it's initial release—Valentine's Day weekend—when it tallied $36 million.

The wake of Cameron's epic brought the box office to record highs, as moviegoers who couldn't get into *Titanic* went to other movies instead. Rupert Murdoch told Wall Street analysts that News Corporation would see a $100 million profit from *Titanic.* Fox had shed its image problem, and Cameron was suddenly being called "visionary" and "genius."

In Hollywood, the holidays extend through March in an endless string of celebratory galas collectively referred to as "Awards Season," which officially got underway with the announcement of the Golden Globe nominations. *Titanic* received a record eight. Accepting the Best Picture award at the January 19 ceremony, Cameron raised a few eyebrows when he took command of the stage, barking down the swell of music that should have been his cue to exit the stage.

The event marked the start of an extended run in the spotlight for Cameron, who took home trophies from the Director's Guild of America, the Producer's Guild of America, and the American Cinema Editors.

When the Oscar contenders were announced on February 10, *Titanic* received 14 nominations, tying the record set in 1950 for *All About Eve.*

Meanwhile, the film was topping the charts in France, Italy, Japan, Germany, and the U.K. By March 6, *Titanic* had become the first film to earn more than $1 billion in worldwide theatrical box office.

Cameron had to laugh. People were amazed by the numbers. The success of the film had far surpassed the outer edge of what even Cameron thought possible for a three-hour costume drama.

When he'd presented his case to Chernin three years ago, Cameron cited the performance of films such as *Gone With the Wind.* If you multiplied the number of tickets sold by the current tickets price, the Civil War epic would have grossed more than a billion dollars in North America alone. *Doctor Zhivago* would adjust to about $300 million. *Titanic* followed those themes, an intimate story told during a violent upheaval, but that type of success hadn't been repeated in more than thirty years. Hollywood had become a different world since then. Seven of the top grossing films of all time were in the science fiction/fantasy genre. None was a three-hour costume drama.

The odds of Cameron turning that formula into a commercial success were about as small as the chances of *Titanic* sinking—or landing a Harrier on top of a skyscraper. A million different pieces had to fall into place and failure of any one would have meant the difference between a hit and a miss.

Somewhere on the editing room floor lay a $200 million flop and a $400 million hit with breakeven potential. He managed to pare away everything that didn't constitute a billion-dollar-plus global phenomenon. The million dollar cut he'd taken heat for probably made them $100 million. At some point, a chain reaction was set off. The film went nuclear. Its audience appeal, its profit potential, soared.

Filmmaking is war, that's how Cameron saw it. War against the elements, war against entropy and disorganization. But ultimately the battle is between business and aesthetics. A movie's a product, but it's not a truckload of antiperspirant. It's a product that works on your emotions, on your mind. He had fought the war and won.

But even after all this success, it was hard for him to be completely happy. "A very expensive piece of crystal rolls off a table, and you catch it before it hits the floor. Most people think that that's the same thing as it not rolling off the table. But I'm just as mad catching it as if I didn't, because the situation occurred at all. It's not as big a solaceto me that this film has gone on to make so much money as it is to everybody else," Cameron mused in the eerie quiet of his living room, shortly before the Oscars. The grand piano was gone, as were the dozens of post-production personnel. Sunk deep into his chair, Cameron stared straight ahead through the plate-glass picture window as he spoke. "But," he sighs, "the only thing we could've really done wrong was to screw up the movie. And we didn't do that."

The 1998 Academy Awards ceremony took place on March 23, a year to the day since *Titanic* wrapped principal photography. Cameron sat in the Dorothy Chandler Pavilion with sweaty palms. As with anyone who tried to break into filmmaking's clubby ranks, the validation of his peers was, on some level, important to him. As the evening wore on, his team racked up trophy after trophy. Carpenter, Rydstrom, Legato, Horner, Chris Boyes, and costumer Deborah Scott all collected gold trophies, stopping on the way to the stage to hug Cameron, who had an aisle seat.

When it was time to announce the Best Director, he cringed, and when he heard his name called, he didn't even try to hide his jubilance, leaping up the stairs, tuxedo tails flapping like wings. On stage, he hoisted the trophy and whooped, "I'm the king of the world!," quoting his own script.

It would have been a high point in anyone's evening, but, as with a Cameron film, the climaxes kept building. There was still one more contest to go.

As Sean Connery read off the names in the Best Picture category, Cameron squirmed in his seat. *As Good As It Gets, The Full Monty, Good Will Hunting, L.A. Confidential, Titanic.* "And the winner is... *Titanic!*"

It was a more contemplative Cameron who went to the stage to accept his third Oscar. "In the midst of all this euphoria, it's hard to remember that this success is based on a real event that shocked the world in 1912," he told the glittering assemblage, first-class passengers all.

"The message of *Titanic* is the unthinkable can happen. The future is unknowable. The only thing we truly own is today. Life is precious." The director requested a moment of silence to memorialize the 1,500 lives lost, exhorting audience members to listen to the beating of their own hearts. His was pounding. Stillness filled the hall.

As he hung his head, at the microphone, in front of one billion TV viewers, Cameron thought back to that day, September 27, 1995, when the *Keldysh* weighed anchor at *Titanic*. They had a wreath-dropping ceremony to commemorate the dead. Hours earlier, the *Mirs* had been pulled from the ocean in bright sun. Now a thick blanket of fog enveloped the deck. A tract of sky showed through the clouds, and at its center was a white rainbow—a Glory.

Cameron wasn't superstitious and he wasn't particularly religious but this, he felt, was a manifestation of something. His memory of that moment informed every subsequent minute of his shoot. He had to do this right. So people would always remember *Titanic*.

Awards and Records

Titanic opened nationally December 19, 1997, after receiving a record 8 Golden Globe nominations a day earlier. On January 18, 1998, it went on to win four Golden Globe Awards, in the Best Picture (Drama), Best Director, Best Score, and Best Song categories. The Screen Actors Guild named Gloria Stuart the Best Supporting Actress of the Year (March 8, 1998).

James Cameron was honored by the National Board of Review for Outstanding Technical Achievement, and won both the Producers Guild of America Award of the Year and the prestigious Directors Guild of America Award.

On February 10, 1998, *Titanic* was nominated for 14 Academy Award nominations, tying the record set by *All About Eve* in 1950. The categories were: Best Picture, Best Director, Best Actress, Best Supporting Actress, Best Cinematography, Best Costume Design, Best Editing, Best Makeup, Best Art Direction, Best Score, Best Song, Best Sound, Best Sound Effects Editing, and Best Visual Effects.

At the Academy Award ceremony on March 23, 1998, it went on to win 11 Oscars, tying the record previously set by *Ben Hur;* Cameron's three Oscars tie him with Billy Wilder and James L. Brooks for most Academy Awards won in a single year.

By the time of the Oscars, *Titanic* had been number one at the box-office for fourteen weeks in a row.

Titanic beat all box-office records previously set. On February 24, 1998, a little over nine weeks after release, it became the highest-grossing film in history, surpassing *Jurassic Park*'s previous record, with combined and international grosses of $919.8 million. On March 1, it became the first film *ever* to gross $1 billion worldwide.

On March 14, 1998, *Titanic* surpassed *Star Wars*' $461 million record to become the highest-grossing film *ever* in the U.S., earning an unprecedented $471.4 million domestically in thirteen weeks.

By the Oscar ceremony, the *Titanic* soundtrack had remained number 1 on the Billboard Hot 200 albums chart for 10 consecutive weeks. It sold over 17 million copies worldwide in seventeen weeks, making it the bestselling soundtrack recording ever.

At the end of March 1998, as the box office receipts climbed past $1.2 billion, it was reported that James Cameron was offered between $50 million and $100 million by Fox to compensate for his giving up his backend deal on the film.

Filmography

The Terminator
(1984, 108 mins) Hemdale/Orion
Budget: $6.4 million
Domestic Box Office: $38.4 million
Foreign Box Office: $35 million
Executive Producers: John Daly, Derek Gibson; Producer: Gale Anne Hurd; Director: James Cameron; Screenplay: James Cameron, Gale Anne Hurd; DP: Adam Greenberg; Editor: Mark Goldblatt; Terminator Effects: Stan Winston; Music: Brad Fidel.
Cast: Arnold Schwarzenegger, Michael Biehn, Linda Hamilton, Paul Winfield, Lance Henriksen.

Aliens
(1986, 137 mins) 20th Century Fox
Budget: $18 million
Domestic Box Office: $85 million
Foreign Box Office: $72 million
Academy Award Nominations: 7 (actress, editing, production design, score, sound, sound effects editing, visual effects)
Academy Awards: 2 (visual effects, sound effects editing)
Executive Producers: Gordon Carroll, David Giler, Walter Hill; Producer: Gale Anne Hurd; Director: James Cameron; Screenplay: James Cameron; DP: Adrian Biddle; Editor: Ray Lovejoy; Alien Effects: Stan Winston; Production Designer: Peter Lamont; Conceptual Artists: Ron Cobb, Syd Mead; Music: James Horner.
Cast: Sigourney Weaver, Michael Biehn, Paul Reiser, Lance Henriksen, Carrie Henn, Bill Paxton, William Hope, Al Matthews, Ricco Ross.

The Abyss
(1989, 145 mins) 20th Century Fox
Budget: $40 million
Domestic Box Office: $85.2 million
Foreign Box Office: $46 million
Academy Award Nominations: 4 (visual effects, art direction, cinemtography, sound)
Academy Awards: 1 (visual effects)
Producer: Gale Anne Hurd; Director: James Cameron; Screenplay: James Cameron; Story By: James Cameron; DP: Mikael Salomon; Editor: Joel Goodman; Music: Alan Silvestri; Production Designer: Leslie Dilley.
Cast: Ed Harris, Mary Elizabeth Mastrantonio, Michael Biehn, Leo Burmester, Todd Graff.

TERMINATOR 2: JUDGMENT DAY
(1991, 136 mins) Carolco/TriStar Pictures
BUDGET: $90 million
DOMESTIC BOX OFFICE: $204.8 million
FOREIGN BOX OFFICE: $284 million
ACADEMY AWARD NOMINATIONS: 6 (sound, sound effects editing, visual effects, makeup, editing, cinematography)
ACADEMY AWARDS: 4 (sound, sound-effects editing, visual effects, makeup)
EXECUTIVE PRODUCERS: Gale Anne Hurd, Mario Kassar; PRODUCER-DIRECTOR: James Cameron; SCREENPLAY: James Cameron, William Wisher; DP: Adam Greenberg; EDITORS: Conrad Buff, Mark Goldblatt, Richard A. Harris; VISUAL EFFECTS SUPERVISOR: Dennis Muren; MUSIC: Brad Fiedel; PRODUCTION DESIGNER: Joseph Nemec III.
CAST: Arnold Schwarzenegger, Linda Hamilton, Edward Furlong, Robert Patrick, Earl Boen, Joe Morton.

POINT BREAK
(1991, 122 mins) Largo Entertainment/20th Century Fox
BUDGET: $24 million
DOMESTIC BOX OFFICE: $42 million
FOREIGN BOX OFFICE: $45 million
EXECUTIVE PRODUCER: James Cameron; PRODUCERS: Peter Abrams, Robert L. Levy; DIRECTOR: Kathryn Bigelow; SCREENWRITER: W. Peter Iliff; STORY: Rick King, W. Peter Iliff; DP: Donald Peterman; PRODUCTION DESIGNER: Peter Jamison; EDITOR: Howard Smith; MUSIC: Mark Isham.
CAST: Patrick Swayze, Keanu Reeves, Gary Busey, Lori Petty, John McGinley, James Le Gros, John Philbin.

TRUE LIES
(1994, 136 mins) Lightstorm Entertainment/20th Century Fox
BUDGET: $95 million
DOMESTIC BOX OFFICE: $146 million
FOREIGN BOX OFFICE: $218 million
ACADEMY AWARD NOMINATIONS: none
ACADEMY AWARDS: N/A
PRODUCERS: James Cameron, Stephanie Austin; DIRECTOR: James Cameron; SCREENWRITER: James Cameron; BASED ON A SCREENPLAY BY: Claude Zidi, Simon Michael, Didier Kaminka; EXECUTIVE PRODUCERS: Rae Sanchini, Robert Shriver, Lawrence Kasanoff; DP: Russell Carpenter; PRODUCTION DESIGNER: Peter Lamont; EDITORS: Conrad Buff, Mark Goldblatt, Richard A. Harris; DIGITAL DOMAIN VISUAL EFFECTS SUPERVISOR: John Bruno; MUSIC: Brad Fiedel.
CAST: Arnold Schwarzenegger, Jamie Lee Curtis, Bill Paxton, Tom Arnold, Art Malik, Tia Carrere, Eliza Dushku, Charlton Heston.

LOCATIONS: Los Angeles, Washington D.C., Miami, the Florida Keys, Rhode Island, Lake Tahoe.

STRANGE DAYS

(1995, 122 mins.) Lightstorm Entertainment/Twentieth Century Fox

BUDGET: $35 million

DOMESTIC BOX OFFICE: $7.9 million

FOREIGN BOX OFFICE: $12.5 million

EXECUTIVE PRODUCER: Rae Sanchini; PRODUCERS: James Cameron, Steven Charles Jaffe; DIRECTOR: Kathryn Bigelow; SCREENPLAY: James Cameron and Jay Cocks; BASED ON A STORY BY: James Cameron; DP: Matt Leonetti; EDITOR: Howard Smith; PRODUCTION DESIGNER: Lizzy Kilvert.

CAST: Ralph Fiennes, Angela Bassett, Juliette Lewis, Tom Sizemore, Vincent D'Onofrio, Michael Wincott, William Fitchner, Richard Edson, Glenn Plummer.

TITANIC

(1997, 187 mins) Lightstorm Entertainment/Twentieth Century Fox/ Paramount Pictures

BUDGET: $200 million

DOMESTIC BOX OFFICE: $515 million to date

FOREIGN BOX OFFICE: $756 million to date

ACADEMY AWARD NOMINATIONS: 14 (picture, director, actress, supporting actress, cinematography, film editing, art direction, visual effects, sound, sound effects editing, song, score, costume, makeup)

ACADEMY AWARDS: 11 (picture, director, cinematography, film editing, art direction, visual effects, sound, sound effects editing, song, score, costume)

EXECUTIVE PRODUCER: Rae Sanchini; PRODUCERS: James Cameron, Jon Landau; DIRECTOR: James Cameron; SCREENPLAY: James Cameron; DP: Russell Carpenter; EDITORS: Conrad Buff, James Cameron, Richard Harris; PRODUCTION DESIGNER: Peter Lamont.

CAST: Leonardo DiCaprio, Kate Winslet, Billy Zane, Kathy Bates, Frances Fisher, Gloria Stuart, Bill Paxton, Bernard Hill, David Warner, Victor Garber, Jonathan Hyde.

Author's Note and Acknowledgments

For those who care, I'd like to share how I came to write this book. I first met James Cameron in February 1991. I was covering technology for *The Hollywood Reporter,* and he was addressing the Society of Motion Picture and Television Engineers at the Los Angeles convention center. It was a few months before *Terminator 2* was released, and he previewed some of the elaborate digital effects from the film. I'd been following his career closely since 1989, with particular interest in his advancement of the art of computer generating imagery (CGI). The small taste he'd provided in *The Abyss* made apparent to me that digital tools would revolutionize filmmaking.

I was impressed with the clips he showed from *T2*—a molten, metallic villain, that could shape change, or "morph," to different identities. After his presentation, he joined me in a cement-floored lounge area and patiently answered an hour's worth of questions about this new science. I was surprised to find myself the only reporter in attendance. Technology, back then, at the onset of Hollywood's digital era, was primarily limited to things with wheels and sprockets and not yet sexy enough for the media.

T2 was released that summer, and was a smash hit, but it was the effects and Arnold Schwarzenegger that got the spotlight, not Jim. He remained a sort of low-key industry figure. Our paths would cross at public functions and I would interview him from time to time. In the winter of 1994 Cameron was selected to receive the ShoWest Producer of the Year award from the National Association of Theater Owners. He just come off the huge success of *True Lies* and had also produced the upcoming *Strange Days.*

As is traditional, *The Hollywood Reporter* publishes special editions celebrating the careers of the ShoWest honorees, and I chose to edit the Cameron issue. Working closely together on that project afforded me a bird's-eye view of his work and workstyle. I was fascinated not only by the images he put on the screen but by the lengths he went to do so. Wanting to capture the real James Cameron I wrote nearly all the editorial for the seventy-five-page section myself. With his encouragement, I also began crafting a proposal for a book documenting his adventurous career.

Of course, one question that came up repeatedly during my interviews for the ShoWest issue is "What's your next project?" He thought he had a handle on it, he said, but he wasn't ready to talk about it. When he was, I'd be the first person he called.

Then on September 30, 1995, I was sitting at my desk at the THR office, typing away, when my phone rang. This time, rather than letting it roll into voice mail, I actually picked it up, an infrequent indulgence. A tinny voice crackled through the line.

"Paula, this is Jim Cameron. I'm calling you from a satellite phone in the middle of the Atlantic."

Well, it sounded like a satellite phone. Okay. "What are you doing out there?"

"We're on a dive expedition, filming for my new movie, *Titanic*."

I don't know what was greater, my surprise that he'd honored his word and called me first to give me the news, or that the action auteur had selected for the subject of his next film such weighty matter as the greatest maritime disaster of the twentieth century.

We kept in touch during preproduction. It was apparent even then just how hugely ambitious the film would be. But the publishing community had zero interest in James Cameron. "James who?" was the most frequent rejoinder. Then, when you mentioned *Terminator* and *Terminator 2*, "Oh, yeah. Why would anyone want to read about him?" It continued on like that for months, throughout the production. Finally, when the negative press escalated Cameron and the film into the limelight, there were some nibbles, but nobody wanted the story I was pitching—an up-close look at a serious filmmaker, impassioned by his work and dedicated to his craft.

I did manage to get a feature assignment from *Entertainment Weekly* reporting on the making of the film, and between that and my writing for *The Hollywood Reporter* and *Wired* I wound up spending quite a bit of time on Cameron's set. I was impressed with the scale of the operation and even more so by how hard Cameron worked, putting so much of himself into this project. As the negative publicity mounted, I became perplexed. How could my experience of the making of *Titanic* be so at odds with that of my fellow journalists? Weren't we on the same set? Witnessing the making of the same film?

The man who did more than any other to revolutionize the look of film as we enter the new millennium deserved a fair shake, so I started to write this book, even without a publisher. I wanted a document to exist that accurately detailed what it was like to be James Cameron, making the biggest film in the history of cinema. I didn't know if *Titanic* would be a big commercial hit, but from what I'd seen of the raw footage, I felt it would be a great film, and that the publishers would eventually come around.

And they did, so my first thank you goes to Esther Margolis, president and publisher of Newmarket Press, for being brave enough to take a chance on me and on Jim when the conventional wisdom was still going against us.

To my own personal A-team, in alphabetical order: Robert J. Dowling, publisher and editor-in-chief of *The Hollywood Reporter*—a more intelligent and inspirational leader one could not wish to have; to one of the most talented editors I've had the privilege to work with, Katrina Heron, who turned many of my black nights dark blue; and to my husband, Michael Kochman, whose unfailing support made this project possible (and whose skepticism about it kept me rising to the occasion!).

This book would not have been possible without the assistance of James Cameron's friends, family and associates who were kind enough to sit through many hours of interviews. I thank them all, with particular notice to: Lewis Abernathy, Charlie Arneson, John Bruno, Mike Cameron, Shirley Cameron, Mali Finn, Tommy, Paula and Scott Fisher, Al Giddings, Jon Landau, Scott Ross, Ralph White. And a special tip o' the hat to *Titanic*'s official documentarians: Ed Marsh and Anders Falk, whose insights were invaluable to this book.

And in the executive suite, big thank yous to Bill Mechanic and Peter Chernin at Fox. A more artist-friendly pair of "suits" a director could never hope to find.

I reserve special thanks to the people who, in my zeal for information and materials, I particularly pestered, and at the head of that list would have to be Rae Sanchini, President of Lightstorm Entertainment. Over numerous lengthy lunches she captured my imagination with her fascinating tales of her boss's adventures and made me determined to document him.

Thanks to my editor on this book, Linda Sunshine, who lived up to her name. And to Keith Hollaman, executive editor at Newmarket, who made the hard parts easier to bear; to my agent Diana Finch at the Ellen Levine Literary Agency, who proved herself more than a business partner.

And I extend appreciation for the continued support of my friends and family at *The Hollywood Reporter:* Elizabeth Aaron, Ray Bennett, Alex Ben Block, Stephen Galloway, Noela Hueso, Lynne Segal—and last and most, Randall Tierney (and his wife Anne Marie).

For Nicole, who's too young to read this book now, but will hopefully get around to it someday.

And finally, thanks to James Cameron, a wise and kind man who is an inspiration to all who know him.

Index